**W9-AFS-627**

If you have a home computer with Internet access you may:
- request an item to be placed on hold.
- renew an item that is not overdue or on hold.
- view titles and due dates checked out on your card.
- view and/or pay your outstanding fines online ($1 & over).

To view your patron record from your home computer click on Patchogue-Medford Library's homepage: **www.pmlib.org**

Sonpri Gray

# kept

"*[Gray] is a unique, new voice.* kept *is a perfect storm of lust and excruciating pain... an almost unbearable peek into one woman's jailed life of chosen financial servitude.*"

*#1 New York Times Bestselling Author, Vince Flynn*

Brio Press
12 South Sixth Street #1250
Minneapolis, Minnesota 55402
www.briobooks.com

Manufactured in the United States of America

10 9 8 7 6 5 4 3 2 1

Edited: Victoria Miller
Book Design: Anthony Sclavi & Russell Boldt
Cover Illustration: Kelly Brown

ISBN 13: 978-1-937061-99-9
Library of Congress Control Number: 2011930661

Although inspired by a true story, this book is a work of
fiction. Names, characters, and incidents are the product of the
author's imagination or are created to be construed fictitiously.
Resemblances to actual events, locales, or persons, living or dead,
are not meant to be taken as true.

Dedication

To my Angel—I love you more.

*It is never too late to be what you might have been.*
—*George Eliot*

# Contents

# prologue

Ava, my curly-headed, three-year-old daughter, raced into my bedroom—wearing a bejeweled crown, lipstick, and nothing else—glad to see me awake during morning hours. I threw back the covers, but not to embrace her like she was probably expecting. Instead, I staggered quickly into the toilet to heave up the previous night's festivities, which included my portion of the thousand-dollar bottle of Opus One that our sommelier had chosen. It had been another evening of me disappointing myself, starting with how it had been the fifth straight night of abandoning my only child.

Last night had started out like so many others, with me, an hour before it was time to go, in heavy preparatory mode. I laid out my clothes and corresponding gems, then showered. As I went through my routine, I tried not to disturb Ava, who was in her room across the spacious three-bedroom apartment, watching *Bambi*.

While applying makeup to accompany my salon-fresh do, perfect French manicure, and conservative but sexy black Donna Karan suit from New York's Fashion Week, I realized how unhappy I was. Everything had to be perfect. Always. He required it.

I wasn't sure where and how things had gone so astray. At twenty-five-years-old, I had no idea where I had misplaced my once-defiant voice. Somehow, he had bludgeoned my confidence and purpose quietly into submission, and I had allowed it. I lost my control completely and a nasty, sinking feeling came over me. The person I had become was someone I did not want my daughter to know. I was nothing but a listless marionette.

I stared at the unrecognizable face in the mirror. My outside showed nothing of what I was. Not a bit of the real me. The form returning the glare was physically flawless, but, internally, it was in agonizing, tormenting pain and weighed down by deep regret. If my vulgar insides could be exposed, the reflected mirage would undoubtedly disappear.

There was no one in my life I could confide in or share these feelings with. I had to, and I would, suck it up. No problem, I had been doing it for years. But that night, something was different. I had been feeling especially anxious. I knew I was most likely in need of a professional evaluation because, although I desperately needed to stay home for my own sanity, I didn't. I was compelled to do what he expected of me.

I finished off my face with a few extra strokes of blush to accent my cheekbones. I was ready, on time.

Ava wandered into the bathroom. Her face contorted when she saw me dolled up. Her body slumped and she immediately began to whimper. She knew Mama was going out. Again.

Tremendous guilt overcame me; I could feel my temperature rise. I wanted to jump in the shower, scrub the MAC-aided façade off my face and curl up in bed with my baby to watch *Beauty and the Beast* for the 458th time, but I could not ruin the mission.

*Suck it up.*

*She will be fine*, I told myself. I reasoned that her pleas were because she wanted me to stay, not because she didn't want the babysitter to come—a huge difference.

I wasn't a bad mother. Or was I?

"Don't cry, Angel. Mama will be back." I wasn't sure if I said that to calm Ava or myself.

The doorbell rang. It was the sitter.

Quickly scooping up my devastated child, I answered it. Ava screamed and burrowed her head into my neck, causing Megan, my 100%-trusted, nineteen-year-old college student/godsend of a babysitter, to feel badly about having to be here once again.

I grabbed my purse as Megan gently pried my distraught

daughter from my body. I planted a customary kiss so that my lipstick would stain her forehead—tracks of mommy love.

Ava was tired, and her sobs were so emotionally rendered that I began to fear the long-term psychological damages that my nightly abandonment might cause. Maybe she too needed an evaluation. I made a mental note to talk in depth with her and to spend time doing the things that made her happy but I had to leave. He was waiting.

"I love you, Angel. Be good. I'll be back soon."

Again, who was I talking to?

Outside, the cool night air hit me. I needed the pick-me-up. Bogus pep was consciously added to my stride as I approached the car. My mind switched gears; it was time to perform.

He had been waiting for one whole minute, and the glances at his Omega timepiece told me he was slightly annoyed. I knew better than to be late.

Standing outside the car by the passenger-side door, Dr. Gunther Wydler was clad in his predictably boring attire: a shitty pea-green plaid sport coat, dark slacks, a white button-up, and his beloved Bally penny loafers that he would *never* change because of their comfort (except, of course, for a new pair of the exact same kind). He had that look on his face. It told me what I had to do.

I quickly apologized for my tardiness, blaming the sitter as I leaned in for a hug, but he dismissively shuffled me into the car. He hated public displays of affection no matter how small or appropriate.

His mostly grey hair was thin and scraggly. The only area where it covered his scalp completely was in the rear of his head; yet for some reason, he parted his hair near his left ear and brought about sixty strands over the dome to theoretically cover any signs of balding. I asked him once why he styled his hair like that and his defensiveness made me never inquire again.

The comb-over was not the single most irritating aspect

13

of his appearance. Others included his soft, girlish hands with perfectly manicured nails and the complete absence of skeletal muscle on his mushy body. But honestly, I couldn't care less if he was Quasimodo's first cousin, so long as he remained generous.

We arrived at the restaurant's valet. I pulled the pashmina tightly around my small frame as I waited patiently for Gunther to walk around and escort me from the passenger seat into the restaurant. All of the staff greeted us attentively, from the young, decathlon-bound valet to the overly amiable hostess who showed us to our table.

I hated the rituals that came when those with money dined out at horrendously expensive eateries: sprinting valet boys, coat checks, purse pillows, napkins laid in your lap, plastered-on smiles, teams of serving staff scurrying off to bring back a pre-dinner cocktail of top-shelf liquor or champagne —"Right away, sir!"

I hated this restaurant and all its pretentiousness. They were nowhere near three stars, yet the entire staff acted as if the restaurant review panel or the Michelin Guide folks were expected at any minute and damned if they wouldn't be ready. I even hated the ridiculous routine of wine selection as it related to my fucking entree.

*And why, Gunther, can't I order the Chilean sea bass and a cab just this once?*

Examining his putrid face, I realized that, most notably, I hated my date. I wanted to pop his eyes from their dusty, old sockets with my blunt butter knife. Instead, I smiled at him and asked about his day. Gunther needed to make himself seem important to his audience. So I kept his interest by pretending to be interested in him, his job, and his life. He rambled out all the details. Under the threat of murder, I could not have repeated a single word of what he was talking about. I had to snap out of it.

The penalty for not paying attention, for not catering to his ego by hanging on to his every word, would mean a terrible night for him, which would later be mentioned as all my fault; more important, he might withhold any pending cash bonuses. It would be seriously detrimental to risk his unhappiness and complete satisfaction, and I knew it.

*Pay attention!* I warned myself.

While he enlightened me on antioxidants being the next trend in science and marketing or since *we've* (being the nerdy, scientific type) figured out how to clone an eye, *we* would now be able to clone a human being—blah, blah, blah—my mind again drifted ever so slightly to more important thoughts, like how my daughter was doing without me or less important thoughts like, why the very old lady sitting at the table next to us had perfectly sculpted tits.

I survived my uncontrollable daydreaming by asking questions at just the right moments, questions that I knew he would answer thoroughly.

"So you can make people? From what?"

"Stem cells? I don't get it."

"After Hamburg, then where do you go?"

It was sort of fascinating to learn what was on the forefront of cutting-edge scientific breakthroughs, but my threshold for Gunther's verbal vomit had been met within the first two minutes of us sitting down. We were well into the second hour. I didn't know how much longer I could take the grating sound of his voice or looking at his pasty face. I was weary of the whole scene, torn between anger, disgust, self-loathing, and trying not to rock the financial boat that wobbled precariously beneath my feet. The reconciliation of these emotions did not come out in subtle or blatant mood swings; they just bounced around in my own head.

Tonight, I was not in the least bit interested in anything that came from Gunther's trap. If he had gotten the notion to ask me about my day, I might have come clean about plotting his demise or let him know that I believed I was a manic-depressive because of my dire life that he had so proudly created. The thought of asking about my day would never enter his one-track mind.

My life was far from calamitous by anyone else's standards, but to me, the word fit. I was so controlled that I had lost my voice in our relationship. I was too worried about pleasing and appeasing so that the rewards would remain intact that I no longer felt like myself; rather, I couldn't remember whom or what my former "self" was.

As we left the posh establishment, I could hear, barely audible above the bar patrons' chatter, the sultry voice of Billie Holiday crooning, "Good Morning, Heartache."

*How apropos. Good morning, fuckin' heartache.*

I faked a quick smile to the door handler as I slid into the driver's seat of Gunther's car. Gunther would rather me risk getting the DUI.

*Bastard.*

We ritually headed to his apartment, which was minutes away from my own, for our version of sex. For the lifestyle and money, it should have been no big deal—at least one would think. I had done much more, for far less (or nothing), but that night I vowed I wouldn't do any of it—no allowing the pallid old man to suck ferociously away at my tender nipples or go down on me, no faking the orgasm and then watching while he yanked on his puny dick, no simulated excitement to prompt a quick come. Nothing!

I was tired and had decided before dinner was on the table that I was going straight home to Ava. I would wake her from her sleep to cuddle in my bed. I would maybe serve up hot cocoa and put on *Beauty and the Beast*. We'd fall asleep peaceful and happy. Going home without giving him sexual pleasure would equate to a long overdue uprising of my strength.

*Nothing! I'm going home!*

I had found my voice.

*Good night, Gunther!*

As I walked him to his door, I was building the conversation in my mind of how I would deny him of my body. He must've sensed my hesitations.

His strategic mind knew that the next move would essentially seal his fate. He pulled out what looked like three thousand dollars.

"Spend some time with Ava tomorrow," he said. "We've been out every night. It must upset her."

*Damn it!*

As I palmed the money, stuffing it into my four thousand dollar Louis Vuitton handbag, he opened the door. I hushed my defiant voice and fell lustfully into his arms. The rebellion was tucked away for another day.

His armor of bravado kicked in because of his apparent intoxication and the thrill of buying his conquest. He was courageous and did as he pleased, aggressively tugging at my clothing. It was my cue to undress. He positioned me head down over the back of the couch so that my ass, highlighted by thigh high stockings that stopped short of covering the goods, was all that he could see.

He commanded the exercise with the skill of a high-ranking military officer. I was reduced to a new recruit, granting wishes and following orders.

"Spread your legs."

I did as I was told. I felt the fumbling fingers and wetness of his mouth as his clammy, baldhead pressed against my butt cheeks.

I screamed out in mock ecstasy as he delivered "oral rapture" from behind.

Then it was my turn. Thankfully, his manhood could only hold out for a short bit as I tussled it around in my moist palm.

It came to life under my touch. I watched the digital clock's bright red numbers go from thirty minutes past the hour to thirty-three minutes past the same hour and knew I was halfway home. I focused my efforts to make it so.

Exactly thirteen minutes later, I was walking through my front door. It was significantly less of a thrill than I had envisioned earlier. I paid Megan, half-assedly listened to the night's events, slurred out good-bye, and went directly to the bathroom where my night had begun to shower the repugnancy down the drain. I had disappointed myself again.

Trying to keep quiet didn't matter. Ava heard me. She wearily appeared with my lip print still visible on her fair-skinned forehead. It made me smile. Her petite arms wrapped around my naked legs. Then she said something that made me vomit up the lavish meal. I began to cry uncontrollably.

It was my turn to break down.

*Don't cry, Angel. Mama will be back* echoed over and over in my head, or out loud. I couldn't decipher which.

*Don't cry, Angel. Mama will be back.*

*Don't cry, Angel. Mama will be back.*

It was so loud. It was my only thought, drowning out all others. "Don't cry, Angel. Mama will be back," I mumbled.

I sat slumped over on the bathroom floor, dazed.

It was my daughter's panicked shriek that brought me back to coherence. I snapped out of my drunken, remorseful state. I must have seemed like a crazy woman. I couldn't go insane, not with her there. I had taught her to dial 9-1-1, and she was aching to use it.

I gave her a quick hug as I slowly pulled myself up from the toilet bowl rim and struggled with getting to the shower. I felt feverish and shivered with each step. My body, mind, and soul were in pain.

I robotically rinsed, leaving the door open so that Ava wouldn't worry and rush off to dial the emergency number. I made eye contact with her and smiled in an attempt to reassure her that her mother was okay.

"We'll go to Sea World tomorrow," I said, hoping for a grin. Nothing. She was clearly worried.

I hummed "Good Morning, Heartache." As depressing as the song was, my voice calmed Ava.

She sat curled up outside the shower door wrapped in a towel, exhausted, waiting for her mom to step out new and improved. Thankfully, she didn't witness the tears streaming into the warm water and disappearing down the drain, appropriately representing my life.

The mirror had shattered. The depression, contrived happiness, and painted face were no longer bearable. He could not be allowed to control my life.

Money had become a monopolizing and immobilizing force. I was morally and ethically wayward.

What was the cure for the life of a kept woman?

# one

My name is Savannah May Lovely.

My early childhood was fervent, full of laughter, fond memorable occasions, and huge family get-togethers, but it was also darkly laced with avoidable crap.

The early 70s were a time of peace, love, and bellbottoms. My parents were both striking. My mom was thin with long graceful limbs; my father was handsome and cool, like the Marlboro man. They were young hipsters, probably too young to have started a family. But my mom was raised to be a wife. Her expected duty of parenthood was inbred. Her path was laid out. My father, on the other hand, should have remained single until he could cope with the psychological residuals from the Vietnam War. Be that as it may, their family had started with and without their preparedness.

They juggled the responsibility of spouse-hood, stay-at-home motherhood and head of the household fatherhood with some carelessness. Many times, my older brother, Mikey, and I suffered because of it.

One winter evening, our parents were getting ready to go out. My father, who didn't speak much, kept asking, "Are you sure you want to go?" He tried reasoning. "It's below zero out there."

I was hoping he'd be more convincing, but my mother was persistent, probably sick of being cooped up in the house all week with a seven- and five-year-old and needing attention from her inattentive husband.

I was mortified when my mom said, "The sitter is on her way." That always meant there's no turning back. Marquetta, "the creepy lady," was our newfound babysitter; for my mother, she was a gem, but for me, well... not so much.

Instead of my usual hysterics when I knew Marquetta was

coming, I decided to try something new, hoping to ward off the invasion; I hid in the dirty clothes that were piled up in the basement. My parents didn't bother to look for me and snuck out without a good-bye, probably happy to forgo my foreseeable tantrum.

I heard Marquetta upstairs talking to my brother. She sounded cheerful. Mikey liked her.

I had rested on the fact that I would be buried in dirty underwear and stinky socks 'til dawn. The creepy lady would never find me. Just as I started to doze, Marquetta, with the assistance of my brother, pulled me out of my hiding place feet first.

Minutes later, Mikey was happily playing with his stupid army men, nestled comfortably under his covers, wielding the coveted flashlight acquired at the Shrine Circus, while I was being held hostage in my bedroom.

Her behavior was more aggressive than the other times when she just laid in my bed next to me, breathing heavy and watching.

My eyes were closed so tightly that my face hurt when I finally opened them. A scarf that Marquetta had thrown over the shade dimmed the Pooh Bear lamp. I took in mysterious shadows that seemed to scale the walls and ceiling, waiting to drag me into another world. My thoughts were shooting urgent messages. *Save me, save me.* I felt Marquetta move in the bed.

She jerked back the matching Pooh Bear bedspread, lifted my nightgown, and began licking my private area. I squeezed my eyelids tightly again, hoping a strong blink would magically make it all disappear. I whined, trying to wiggle from under her weight.

"Shut up, you brat. It feels good and you know it."

"No. Stop it." I tried to push her off of me.

She slapped my inner thigh, causing a sharp, stinging sensation that shut me up. Then she forced her exposed breast

22

near my closed mouth. She hit the top my head hard, but I wouldn't open up. She grabbed my fingers so firmly that I heard one knuckle crack, and then forced them in between her legs. I stopped struggling. I felt sick to my stomach, dizzy and light-headed.

The smell of old sweat and stale bread wafted up but was soon subdued by her breath that was heavily perfumed with Juicy Fruit gum. Her breathing escalated, then fell still. She abruptly left my room. I could finally exhale.

I quietly crept across the hall to sleep in my parents' room. Their door had a lock.

My parents returned, intoxicated. Although I could have told them what happened, I did not. I felt as though they would not have believed me. Marquetta was their trusted babysitter; I was just a little kid who, I admit, had somewhat of a reputation for stretching the truth a bit. So I kept quiet. I didn't even open the bedroom door when my mother tried to get in. I faked sleep. I kept them out for as long as I possibly could, protecting us all from a horrid truth.

Thankfully, Marquetta was never again "available" to babysit when my mother called her, but the damage had been done.

As the years passed, I forgot about her and that incident.


Mikey and I bonded, forming a great siblingship. He was my hero, protector, and really, my only friend. When our parents were too busy, we found ways in which to entertain ourselves.

Our brown house was situated in a poor neighborhood that was a mix of single-family homes and dingy government apartment complexes. We had an ugly brown car and an old, brown dog that had been around since before I was born. I guess it was only fitting to have a drab basement; half was laid with cold cement, the other half with brown shag carpeting.

The overly cluttered basement was packed with boxes of odd things accumulated from the past lives of both of my parents.

Despite how lackluster it was, we found it a fertile playground for adventurous, young explorers. Mikey and I "discovered" a hidden treasure, a crate of *Playboy* magazines. Jackpot!

Mikey flipped through the pages, sucking in general images and drooling, while I intently studied the pictures. The perfectly posed women smiling into the camera without clothes, and grown men with their legs spread, holding their penises so casually made me giggle. I viewed page after page of naked, happy people with flawless skin and flowing hair. I was only seven.

I had a habit of praying to Jesus Christ in soft whispers.

"Jesus Christ, please give me boops…" That was what I thought they were called. "…smooth skin and hair down there, so boys will pay a whole buck to look at me. Thank you, Jesus Christ. Goodbye."

Mikey, more excited than I had ever seen him, wanted to rip out the pictures, stuff them into his pockets, and hit the streets. I stopped him, promised his day in the spotlight, and then I begged for a few moments to devise a plan. His hooligan friends would have to pay a dollar to see the boops.

Mikey was the lookout. I paged through the magazine until I found a picture that was small enough to fold and roll into a Pez dispenser. I had been collecting them forever and had found the perfect usage.

Then I noticed Mikey pacing the basement stairs. If our mom came down, he'd bolt to the laundry room where I had set up operations, and in his *we're-so-busted* shrill voice, scream, "Here she comes!" forcing her into an all-out sprint.

I slammed the magazine shut, slid it under a pile of dirty clothes, and went to instruct my older, but not wiser, brother on the art of espionage.

I pulled him over to the couch.

"Just watch TV. We can hear her on that first stair. It creaks. All you have to say is, 'Mom, don't come down. We're playing hide-and-go-seek. Do you want to play?' She'll turn around. That'll buy us ten to fifteen minutes. Time enough for me to wrap things up. Got it?"

"Got it," he confirmed.

I rolled ten Pez-turned-porn dispensers. I rid the area of evidence and hoped that by using the earlier issues in the bottom of the crate, no one would notice.

I said a prayer, that time to God, because it was very important. "God, if anybody finds out about the missing pictures, let it be Daddy and not Mama. Amen."

If my dad noticed, one, he would under no circumstances inform his wife (who didn't want "that filth" in the house in the first place), and two, he would beam with pride at his freaky protégé of a son, not suspecting that I had anything to do with it.

Mom, on the other hand, would take one look and guess by the neatly extracted photos that it was I, Savannah May Lovely, who was the perverted freak without a doubt peddling pornography to the neighborhood boys. She'd have been right on both accounts.

I made fifty of the cleverly concealed novelties before the pictures were all but gone from the pages. Mikey was the man.

That was just one of many conniving ventures that unfolded during my childhood. I became pretty well known for my brazen schematics. Family get-togethers weren't complete without three or four recounts of past or recent Savannah-isms. Aunts and uncles would take turns reminiscing about how I charged the neighborhood kids to play in our yard, created a contest for everything doable, sold Mrs. Iverson's flowers from her own garden back to her for a dollar and how I, a waifish kindergarten brawler, fought Bradford the bully for my brother by kicking him where the sun didn't shine, then forced him to pay me restitution for his crimes.

If the adults running my life had groomed the gift of gab or were at least were minimally supportive of the entrepreneurial spirit of their magnate child, I may have been able to formulate a precise plan to catapult us into the top economic percentile, forgoing years of doing without.

From ages seven to nine, life was relatively stable. No major highlights or catastrophes, but as it went, things took a turn. I had grown up in the bottom half of middle-class, then at nine my mismatched parents finally separated and we took a drastic plunge, ending up well below poverty level.

I was traumatized for many reasons around this time: the lack of money meant we couldn't afford anything and the dog that I had known my whole life was attacked and eventually died from the wounds as there was no room in the budget for a vet. I switched to a public school, abandoning all my parochial childhood friends: again, no money. However, the worst wasn't because of lack of funds. It came one seemingly perfect spring day. I was witness to a deception that mortified me.

Driven by the sound of curiously bizarre noises, I opened my brother's bedroom door only to see my father mounted by Sarah, my mom's best friend, their naked bodies merged into each other. My father suddenly stopped fornicating. He had seen me too. I slammed the door shut and went to watch the idealistic depiction of life on the popular television show *The Brady Bunch*.

*I bet none of those kids walked in on Mr. Brady being humped by Alice.*

I never said one word to Sarah, not even to answer a question; she ceased to exist. I'd look in her direction hoping that she would say something for me to vehemently ignore. It got so that, for a while, I stopped putting an h at the end of my name, so as not to be reminded that that whore and I had even had that in common. It was bad enough her named started with an S.

The hardened look of disappointment I gave my father kept him from making direct eye contact with me for months. I carried around the burden of information like a hundred pound weight, wanting so badly to tell someone who would erase my recollection or explain it all away.

My father was a low-life cheater and too embarrassed to talk to me or even apologize. He just left me to the horrendous secret that he knew I would keep. When the announcement of divorce came, I was unfazed, even a bit thankful. My dear mother deserved better and could now forge forward, a strong and independent woman without the burden of her man.

That was not how she apparently felt. I don't think it was her love or contempt for my father, an attempt to gain attention, depression, or the inability to handle life; I believed that my mother truly believed that she had failed her family and God. This God-fearing woman suddenly had a need to visit heaven and sort out her differences, face-to-face with the big guy.

Mikey and I were home. It was the first day of our bout with chicken pox. I was happy to miss school, mainly because I didn't have cool, trendy clothes—a concern I did not have when I attended private school; a concern I had from being poor.

It was a glorious spring day, too nice to be indoors even as new, itchy clusters formed under my pits. Mikey and I were intent on igniting a small pile of dried leaves, hoping to get a camp fire going so we could roast marshmallows that I had pushed onto a stick. My birthday was just three weeks away. I was going into double digits.

"Well, what do you want for your birthday?" Mikey asked me.

Mikey was the kind of big brother that every girl should have. I adored him and he me.

"I don't know," I lied.

The truth was I did know. I had been fantasizing about a huge surprise birthday thrown by all my favorite friends and

27

family equipped with a three tier cake, a table dedicated to holding wrapped gifts, pink and yellow balloons, and decorations filling the grand ballroom of a huge mansion, because I surely didn't want my party in our small, dank, rodent-infested home.

The leaves were a bit damp and wouldn't catch fire. I was about to run to the house for newspaper when we heard whimpering coming from our mother's slightly opened bedroom window. Mikey, who had been assuming the role of "man of the house" because of the pending divorce, bounded into action. I trailed after him, a bit more apprehensively.

We arrived at our mother's bedroom door and knocked. The house had become eerily quiet; even the outside traffic noises seemed hushed. Mikey instinctively knew to be worried; our mama never cried. Mikey knocked again.

"Mama? Mama, open the door," he added as he jiggled the locked door handle. "Go call 911."

*Go call 911? What for?*

I couldn't register his request because I just didn't understand the emergency.

"Go call 911!" he yelled with tears in his eyes.

I dropped the matches I'd brought with me and darted to the kitchen phone.

After I blurted out a dozen terror laden answers to the emergency line attendant in the cadence of panicked hammering, I rushed back down the hall to help Mikey try to break in. We pounded and yelled until our fists were bruised and bloodied. We left dents and splintered slits down the unyielding door. Mikey hurt his shoulder and then used his heel; it was all in vain, as it did nothing to rouse our mother.

The room was located on the first floor and the outside window required a ladder, something we did not own. I ran to our neighbors' houses. No one was home. I returned to find Mikey sobbing and still violently kicking at the bedroom door.

Only thirteen minutes passed before the ambulance and police arrived, but when rendered helpless in an emergency, thirteen minutes is an eternity.

The cops and EMT scurried into our home, busted down her door with an ax, and began resuscitation procedures. Mikey and I were holed up in the bathroom across the hall, unable to fully grasp what was happening. The reality hit hard when we heard our mother cough and gag, sucking in air and the policeman said, "Overdose."

*Were those sounds of life?*

"Attempted suicide," he casually added.

*A life she wanted to end?*

The whole scene felt like a movie. Mikey and I were mere spectators, uninvolved and just watching the events play out in sequence, the details of which I would never completely recall. I was in shock.

Tears streamed down our small, distraught Calamine dotted faces. I tried to hug my brother for some confirmation that something I loved was near and well, but his arm was dislocated from its socket. It was an injury that had been put on the back burner, trumped by our mother's kismet. I was never hugged.

The ambulance was driving away with my mother.

"Come back, Mama."

It hit me. They were taking my mom away!

I ran after the stupid white truck, trying to rescue myself from her abandonment.

"Please don't leave me!"

My dad, who had just arrived, jumped from his car and chased me as I moved carelessly into the middle of the busy street. When he caught up to me, I swung wildly, crying and yelling.

"It's all your fault! Don't touch me!"

I pushed his arms away, denying his hug. I kicked his

shin with all my might and walked back home, breathless and sobbing hysterically.

*Why did she want to leave me?*

The following days were quiet. Both Mikey and I were wallowing in pity. Our father was to be our primary caretaker until my mother returned.

Not only was my father a workaholic and a chain smoker, he was an alcoholic too. Dear ol' Dad, except for providing the financing, was incapable of the daily maintenance of his family, and even he was aware of this shortcoming.

Mikey's and my fever pitched and the pustules of our chicken pox became frightening and nearly impossible to not scratch. Sad, sick, and missing our mother, we found solace in one another. Since my brother's arm was in a sling that he proudly wore like a badge of honor, and which was probably unnecessary but very essential to his healing process regarding our mother's ordeal, I helped him by rubbing the Calamine lotion on his bumpy back. I also stopped him from fussing with his much-worse outbreak of the nasty disease.

Our father did little to ease our discomfort. He'd mutter an occasional rhetorical, "How ya doing?" at best. The reality was that we were both messed up. No adult took our mental state into any type of consideration. We had to deal the best way we could: suck it up and pretend that it didn't happen.

We never asked our father the whereabouts of our mother or when she might return. Our father was quiet and wouldn't think of divulging any particulars, even if we had asked. We were kids and were not involved in grown folks' business; this had been instilled since birth. My dad mostly ignored us and avoided any conversations by telling us to go clean something, or he'd simply turn up the soulful 70s music, a sign that he did not want to be bothered. We did know that our mom was getting better; the reports from her parents and other concerned friends and family members placated our worries. The best thing we could do was to survive our father and not burn down the house.

Our father left to go to work for the local newspaper. I didn't have the slightest idea what his job entailed. I was just happy he was gone. He was a mysterious figurehead, silent, stoic and devoid of emotion. Mikey and I were better left alone. We wondered why he was even there, since the family stopped by to drop off food, usually a casserole, and to bring more Calamine lotion or whatever dessert we requested. Nonetheless, he was our dad and it was his obligation to look after us; I'm sure that's how it was situated in his mind.

Even though we filled our days basking in the joy of being unattended by letting our imaginations run amok and by igniting dried flower arrangements, an old rag doll, and a roll of toilet paper, we missed the love and structure that could only be gotten from our mother.

After the fourth day of mom's absence, our dad called in Sarah to "help out," which spawned a deep feeling I can only describe as revulsion. Sarah flailed around my mama's house like a fish out of water, trying to make him and us happy.

Thoughts of premeditated murder should not have crossed a youngster's mind…but still…

*That biddy better not climb up in my mama's bed. I swear I will stab her through her huge, bouncy boobies and leave Sarah the Slut gurgling on her own blood.*

Sarah was my father's "secret" to everyone but me. Had he forgotten that I knew? It was blatantly disrespectful of him to have Mama's best friend, his mistress, play caretaker.

*What an asshole.*

By the start of week two and after we were rendered non-infectious, my father had had enough of single parenthood and shipped us off to my aunt's house. I'm sure she offered and I'm even more sure we were all packed and put in the car before she could hang up the phone.

When we arrived, the strange feeling came over me again—abandonment. Mikey bolted from the back seat and disappeared, off to find the boy cousins. I just sat with my heart racing and a need to curl up and cry.

"C'mon here."

My dad was always bad at reading the situation and had no clue of what he should say or do. He just stood by the open car door with our bags in his hands, ignoring my frightened face.

"Daddy, will Mama come for us?"

It was the first conversation that I had initiated in months.

"Yep. Now, c'mon here."

He said it without even looking at me. I forced myself to swallow the lump that had been pressing on my throat. I took my bag from my father and walked with my head held high, praying to God that he was telling the truth.

My mom's sister birthed nine, nearly stair-step children. It was a chaotic household, full of action and communication, far from the quiet sultriness of home.

My cousins were peculiar; rather, they were repressed, sheltered, and part of a cult-like, tyrannically run family. Their peculiarity was not their fault. Their father, Uncle Ove—the name when said fast conjured a really sweet fellow—was a self-proclaimed minister. He consulted with God for the better part of each day. I was both repelled and excited by the whole aura, especially when Uncle Ove got the Holy Ghost and his fast-talking prayers reverberated through his domain. We'd all frightfully scurry to hide at the furthest point of the house, the basement, all the while sniggering.

My cousins were forbidden from playing board games with dice or cards. They could not dance or even listen to the Devil's music (anything non-gospel). They couldn't watch TV programs other than the news or go to the movie theatre. Pretty much everything fun was prohibited. Any broken rules were punishable by severe beatings, extra chores, and hours of prayer.

It was confusing for me because I loved my cousins, but I hated their home. Still, it beat watching the obvious and disgusting relationship develop between Sarah and my father.

The first day of my arrival, my favorite cousin, Joy, and I took a walk through the woods that were adjacent to a nearby cemetery. I never liked the woods and almost always refused to go into them for fear of being stolen by zombies, lost or forgotten, injured, or tormented by my cousins because they thought it was fun to scare the shit out of me.

But the woods were different with Joy. She held my hand and pointed out things that she thought might be of interest, like a strangely shaped wild mushroom or bright green moss growing on a log. She loved the woods; this time, she took me to her favorite spot along a thin stream. We sat on the rocks watching the water for ten minutes before she spoke.

"Don't worry about your mom. Life has plans for her."

She had opened the door to a conversation. I stepped in, telling her all about the day my mom tried to leave us. I divulged my secret about Sarah and my dad, relieving myself of its weight. I told her about every negative thing that was impeding my life.

"Well Savannah, bad things happen," Joy said simply.

She directed her attention towards the trickling water, mesmerized by where it was going. Her intensity made me look too. We sat quietly contemplating this seemingly profound idea: "Bad things happen."

"Let's race back!" Joy cried as she suddenly jumped up.

The explanation of *why* the bad things happened to me was summed up in three words—bad things happen. It wasn't made complicated. I loved Joy.

As I raced through the woods trailing my favorite cousin, trampling the leaf and dirt covered path, leaping over fallen branches and pushing twigs away from my face, hope swept through me. Joy had forced hope upon me like a much needed cool breeze, making me smile.

The first week at my aunt's went off without a hitch, but then, it was the thirteenth of April, the day I was born ten years prior. I kept the event to myself. My cousins weren't allowed to celebrate birthdays anyway. Plus, any dreams for a surprise party were squashed when my mother left, strapped to the gurney, loaded into the back of an ambulance, and rushed away. My new birthday wish was for the damned ambulance to drop her back off.

All eleven of us kids had spent the morning doing the mandatory chores but even a full-time cleaning crew could not slow the inevitable, ever-flowing return of mess. Finally calling it quits, three of the six sisters and I headed to our favorite place—the foot of Joy's bed.

Joy forbade us from actually touching her bed but she laid out a large pallet on the floor for us to comfortably gather around. She started her story where she had left off the previous night:

"I said, 'Wait, mister. I got to look at it first.' He was trying to put it where things normally only come out."

My other cousins got it and in chorus chimed, "Ugh!" I went along but had no clue what Joy was talking about. Often, when things went over my head, I would ask for an explanation; Joy would also sometimes see my quizzical expression and explain, or I would act as if I got it and hoped that things would be cleared up. The latter was what I decided to do.

"He moaned, irritated by my request, but rolled his fat ass off of me and reached for the floral, peach and green lamp's on-switch. His wife must have decorated before she wound up missing."

I got excited. I was putting the pieces of the story together. My cousins were too. We smiled at one another.

"I sized up his penis and immediately said, 'Mister, that big ol' thang is gonna cost you extra.' I had to think quick 'cause he said, 'How much?' —Now, I could blurt out a small amount. He might get disappointed and accuse me of scammin', or I could give an amount that was too high, which could turn him off and I might miss out on some extra cash. And Johnny Ray don't like me missin' out on no money."

We all said that line with her.

"Johnny Ray don't like me missin' out on no money."

Johnny Ray was the character's pimp. Joy told stories all the time about Johnny Ray. We sometimes liked him, like when he tracked down Tricksy's killer and cut his poker off and then shot him in the stomach. Tricksy was one of his favorite girls. Other times, we prayed for him to die, like the time he made Beauty suck off fifty men at a bachelor party and swallow their cum, or the time he beat Nella so badly that she couldn't move for a week, let alone turn a trick (which he made her do because she shorted him fifty dollars). He didn't even let her go to the hospital! She could have died. He hurt her so badly!

"I guess I settled on the right number, 'cause he turned off the light, spit on his little penis…" We all laughed. "… And shoved the thang right into my—" Joy suddenly stopped.

A loud baritone voice boomed from the other side of the door. "Joy?"

He was the reason I disliked being there.

With the fear of God haunting us all, Joy simply pulled the (cover-up) Bible from her drawer and threw it on the edge of her bed, in the event he should have opened the closed door.

"Yes, Daddy?" she squeaked out.

His first words didn't carry an edge.

"What are you girls doing?" he asked.

Whew! Her life was spared. He hadn't heard the Johnny Ray fables! He just came calling for whatever reason—we didn't care; she would not face death, not today!

35

Smiles crept across our faces. We were seconds away from a full-on silent celebration. Then he said, a bit too calmly and coldly …

"Please come here."

We all froze at the sound of his voice.

My uncle sauntered off. That time, he purposefully made us aware of his dominating presence.

We looked empathetically at our narrator. Pure pity consumed our faces. If he had heard any of what she had just said, she would probably be killed.

Joy sucked in what would be her last hopeful breath and exited the room.

I wanted to cry. My bottom lip trembled and tears began to well up in my eyes. We all sat silently wondering what to do. Eventually, curiosity got the best of us. I had no choice; they elected me. I was the least likely to get in trouble because I always had to pee.

"Savannah, go to the bathroom," they instructed, which meant: listen at the closed master's door.

I reluctantly but inquisitively crept down the long hallway. It was dark. I could see a sliver of light escaping from under his door. As I turned into the adjoining bathroom, I could hear whispers and then sounds. The noises frightened me. They were similar to the sounds that emanated from the basement during prayer meetings.

If only I could hear Joy's voice, I'd be able to report back that she was okay. But I only heard Uncle Ove doing what they referred to as "speaking in tongues."

The enactment behind the doors seemed too intense, since there was no prayer meeting in session.

*What is he doing to her?*

Then I heard them: slight, high-pitched whimpers. My heart pounded loudly enough to expose my covert operation. I so badly wanted to rush in and pull her away from her crazed father. Then he bellowed, and it seemed as if the house rumbled.

I sprinted back toward the safety of my cousins and buried myself in the pallet. They tried to get information, but I didn't know what to tell them. They heard the deafening roar. What did it all mean? Was Joy okay? Did he find out about Johnny Ray? I didn't know. I only knew that I was traumatized and worried about my favorite cousin. The tears and snot headed south, joining up on my quivering lips. I wiped it all away with one swipe of my sleeve.

Moments later, Joy entered the room. She was forever changed. Her appearance stunned us. She was ragged; her face was moist and red. She looked as if she had gone through a huge dryer.

We knew things were serious when she asked to be left alone, a request that was extremely rare in a household that large. We were grateful to honor it, probably for fear of learning what had happened, otherwise known as preservation instinct. It was better not to know.

We tore out of Joy's room. The girl cousins met up with the boys and instant pandemonium broke out; everyone was sharing their own versions of what happened at once.

Mikey pulled me aside. We carefully sat on the rickety front porch, fearing splinters. I wanted to tell him everything. Tears started to fill the rims of my eyes again. He handed me a small box wrapped in the funny pages from the newspaper.

"What? Did you think I forgot?"

The tears immediately fell. My eyes begged for the one thing that the moment was missing.

*Please hug me, Mikey.*

He was a boy.

"Don't be a baby. It's not that big-a-deal."

Just like that, my brother was gone, back to the camaraderie of the boys. I wiped away the tears that again joined up with snot and opened the box. It was his baby ring, a 14k gold band that our mother kept for him. It fit my boney finger perfectly.

*Happy birthday, dear Savannah. Happy birthday to me.*

Our next-ranked cousin herded us girls into the laundry closet that was piled high with over-filled boxes and trash bags of garments for both sexes of all ages. Nothing was ever discarded in this house, just recycled. The room held decades of clothes, which made for a wonderful hideout. This cousin attempted to finish Joy's story, but none of us paid attention to her boring rendition. I toyed with my new gold ring. Our minds were reeling from the day's events. Johnny Ray and his gang dissipated and were never heard from again.

In the end, I didn't know where the trick had stuck his penis or how the woman disappeared—the irony.

Although I didn't understand everything in Joy's stories, they seemed beyond forbidden and my senses told me that they definitely were. It was not just that the subject matter was heinous, but it was also Joy's key role in corrupting our minds and, more important, our souls. If merely dancing in that house entitled you to a beating, what punishment other than a slow death would suffice for the detrimental, purposefully rendered tales of pimp Johnny Ray and his band of whores?

Over the next few months, Joy lost touch with all reality. I noticed her downward turn from one moment to the next. She wasn't interested in listening to Michael Jackson or playing slutty dress up even if I enticed her with "pilfered" makeup from our grandma's drawer. Nothing. She preferred to be alone. Her once impeccable oral hygiene was abandoned; soon after, she stopped bathing or even combing her hair.

Uncle Ove called her to his lair more often to "pray over her"—pray, spelled with an *a* not an *e*, but *prey* was probably more accurate. She obliged. He used her as an example of God's wrath or the Devil's doing. Although I couldn't prove it, I believed her own father was molesting her regularly behind those closed doors.

Joy deteriorated before our eyes, but we did and said nothing. The person we knew completely disappeared, and what was left was a skinny, babbling, crazy girl who threw fits and could not care for herself; her beautiful name no longer fit.

That magnificently chaotic playhouse became filled with solemn teens, self-confined to their rooms. Her fate affected us all.

Joy's insight was unusual therapy for a scarred little girl. She made light of sex and clarified terminology like *69*, *rape*, and *orgy*. She explained human nature and the intricacies of less-than-normal relationships. She gave me a view on matters that were very different from what was taught or learned from conservative society. I took what she said and ate it up with the same casual flair with which she dished it out. The ideas and experiences, in all their nastiness that she so vividly described, were a part of real life, and I learned that any "Cinderella" stories should be viewed with skepticism.

My reality changed. I could accept the death of a dog, divorce, mental breakdowns, and less than perfect parenting. I healed from the shocking naked *Playboy* pictures of cock and pussy, from the pedophile babysitter, and from seeing my daddy screwing a trusted family friend.

Joy's stories made life understandable. She exposed the fallacies and explained to me that bad things happened—period. There was no denying, no excusing, no Biblical reasoning.

Bad things simply happen.

But just like that, Joy became vulnerable, as I grew strong.

Our mother returned. She, nor we, ever spoke about what happened that frightful day and our lives returned to our new normalcy, without a patriarch.

That two months at my aunt's house altered my views on life

and left me with beleaguering thoughts: How could a person so strong and sure of life be so fragile? What made people want to kill themselves? How could I escape becoming life's casualty?

# two

I spent the ninth grade in complete seclusion at a remote mountain location only accessible from our Midwest town, in our case, by a train trip across the country, a Greyhound bus from Seattle to Spokane, a cab ride from Spokane to Chelan, a two-hour ferryboat trip up-lake, and a grueling hour-long, switch-backing bus ride up eleven miles.

My most prevalent thought was: *There is no escape.*

My mother took us to a remote Lutheran-founded mountain village. The Catholic religion had failed her in her time of need. Life had dwindled to working hard to pay Paul because some guy robbed Peter, or that was what she constantly told us. And the newly drug-infused inner-city collided with a mom working full-time with two fatherless children and it seemed like a losing battle. She had to get away for her own peace of mind and her children. She needed a new lease on life. My life, however, was snatched from under me. Mainly, I missed my best friend since the third grade, Mary.

Mary and I connected out of necessity—kids needed friends. She became my best friend out of the habit of being around each other over time. Our friendship was fairly shallow; our conversations remained predictably at first on dolls, then as we got older on fashion, and as we wrote back and forth in my absence, the transpiring theme was whether or not I needed a bra yet and everything regarding boys. Even so, she was my best friend and I missed her.

After the initial shock of being uprooted and re-planted, Holden turned out to be astounding.

The chores were shared amongst the staff. It was a welcome break from having too much responsibility. Our sense of time altered because of the lack of modern technology. It was neither welcome nor possible in such a faraway place. There were no TVs, radios (except for emergencies), phones, computers, cars, markets, arcades, dry cleaners, or any other modern conveniences.

There were twenty chalet-style buildings, each within spitting distance of its neighbor, which contained families; craft and wood shops; a hike hut for hikers, fishermen, and campers; and a huge game center with bowling and pool tables. There was a community dining room that served breakfast, lunch, snacks, and dinner; a place of worship; and there were also daily group sessions on a wide variety of subject matters, such as theology, current affairs, and human rights.

The village matured me beyond my years. The staff and visitors prompted healthy discussions, which would force me to analyze, debate, express my opinion, and rationalize. The atmosphere was one of deep thinkers and people championing important causes. I had never heard of many of the people, places, or things with which they seemed so familiar. My mind was a super-absorbent chamois, expanding under the wealth of knowledge.

I learned the significance of the term "all-inclusive," meaning no one should be excluded when it came to a person's color, sex, or sexual preferences from written content, religion, rights, or justice. Prejudiced behaviors, intolerance of all things discriminatory, and what it truly meant to love thy neighbor were subjects that were echoed throughout the year I spent at Holden.

We wrote expressive letters to Congress regarding our contempt of the atrocities in South Africa due to the Apartheid system. We sent comments on the importance of gay rights to editorial columns and wrote essays on inexcusable social injustices, political havoc, worldwide inhumane suffering, and the role that our beloved country played in all of it. We were environmentalists and minimalists, gasping at consumerism and wasteful inbred behaviors.

I learned to juggle, became quite the avid reader, learned to survive for seven days in the forest with very few provisions, ate healthy organic foods, and rappelled from cliffs. Moreover, being alone with my thoughts and appreciating bountiful, beautiful surroundings became second nature.

It was truly a place of respite and discovery on many levels. Thanks to that quiet mountain retreat center that my mother dragged us to kicking and screaming, I was blessed to have an experience that would leave marks on my intellectual development and parts of my character forever. I was thankful for the life-changing event, however...

By the end of our yearlong commitment, mountain fever had set in, and I was sure I'd never return to that atrocious place ever again. A high school with only four kids sucked, especially when one student was my older brother, one was named Savanna (without an h), and the other ninth-grader, and the last hope, was also a girl. For an adolescent, heterosexual teen, that was no bueno.

After my return to civilization, I became obsessed with boys and music, not the hymns and corny folk stuff—Joni Mitchell, Bob Dylan, and Pete Seeger—that we were subjected to in the Cascades, but with the soulful explosion of hip-hop, R & B, and pop music.

A theme that I was obviously attracted to became my favorite: powerful women controlling their destinies. I listened to Shelia E's hit, "Glamorous Life"; "What's Love Got to Do with It" by Tina Turner; "Rich Girl," "Sara Smile," "She's Gone," and "Maneater" by Hall & Oates; "Easy Lover" by Phil Collins and Philip Bailey; "She Works Hard for the Money" by Donna Summer, and so many other songs that had to do with the lives that women had chosen for themselves.

Those messages resonated with me. I yearned to be like those females who sang the lyrics or who were the subjects of the songs: powerful, strong, gorgeous, wealthy, in-control ladies who possessed the ability to make men melt with desire.

My sophomore and junior years were spent at an inner-city magnet school. I became popular because of my athletic skills in basketball and track and field; athletics aside, I was just your average female geek, far away from melting the hearts of men.

Art and English were the subjects in which I clearly excelled, but I enjoyed photography and steel drums as well. I was one of a few students asked to join the steel drum traveling band.

The things I took pleasure in, I mastered. I actually loved school. My love of learning was combined with normal teen yearning, resulting in my becoming a genius flirter.

Our band was immensely popular as we pounded out favorite tunes on our pans, and in turn, our twenty members became well known. The band was heavily populated with boys, which was one of the main reasons I joined. I was boy crazy and every male specimen in the band was subjected to my advances. My hormones were ablaze, and all I needed was a single taker. One fellow (finally) was interested and returned my flirtation.

*Gee whiz, what does a lass have to do to get a lad to take notice of her raging hormones?*

Like I said, I was obsessed with boys and music. Eye blinking, stares, bashful smiles, and jokes were all that the relationship amounted to, but I got a taste of what it was like to be the object of infatuation and adored by a male teen. I was hooked on romance.

My friends and I had crushes on every cute and/or funny young man in a fifty-mile radius, but I never attracted *boy*friends. My build, thin and athletic rather than voluptuous and curvaceous, was the main culprit. However, Antonio Macon saw my potential.

Antonio and I met at a cheesy neighborhood gym dance. He asked me to the basketball court turned dance floor during a slow song. My heart skipped a beat. I almost fell when I stood up; my legs were weak, plus, I wasn't used to the two inch heels I was wearing. I took my time walking down the wooden bleachers. The last thing I wanted to do was to fall on my face. He found a spot in the middle of dozens of coupled, sweating bodies. I melted into his arms. We swayed back and forth for two whole songs.

*He must like me.*

I was elated for the chance to dance with him. I didn't expect much more. When he asked for my phone number, I almost died.

*This cute boy wants my contact info?*

I said the seven digits slowly but with memorable intonation.

Throughout the night, he would occasionally find me and recite my number. It made me giddy. At 11:00 PM, the gym lights came on. I saw how the aggressive florescent voltages highlighted every flaw in the faces of my peers, made their eyes squint and sweat glisten. I spotted my man at the far end of the gym. I could not let my love interest see me under such a magnifying glass. I thought he would lose all interest, or get instant amnesia. I hit the floor running, hoping to make it across the gym and out the front door into the protective guise of darkness, ensuring his call.

I slipped a few times, pushed my way through the slow moving crowd, and made it.

That night I slept in the living room to be near the kitchen phone. At 1:15 AM, it rang. I knew it was Antonio.

At five foot six inches tall, with a long, wet Jheri curl, a car, a cool name, and being a student at the University of Minnesota, Antonio was a catch. He wore polo shirts with the collar up because he was from the cool part of town, Minneapolis. For us St. Paulites, that was considered hot shit.

Shortly after meeting Antonio, I quit everything so I could spend that valuable time with a boy who saw me as someone worth spending his time with. Sports, band, track, and trivial hobbies couldn't compare to my newfound obsession. Even school, if it hadn't been a requirement, might have taken a back seat to gazing into his eyes.

We met every day after I got out of my last class and before he had to be home for dinner. His mother cooked every night and expected her family to be at the table whether they were hungry or not. Mikey and I were lucky to even have food in the house and wouldn't appreciate our mother's efforts if she had made them. We were grown teens. Caring for ourselves had started long ago. Still, I envied the unity of Antonio's structured home, the only thing I missed following the divorce of my parents.

One glorious day, sitting on my front porch stairs teaching me the paradiddle, Antonio abruptly stopped.

He turned to me and said, "Will you be my girlfriend?"

"Yes!"

I was elated. My world was perfect. I, Savannah May Lovely, had a boyfriend.

The girls in my circle were extremely jealous. No one could figure out why on earth Antonio Macon, with all his attributes, would be interested in a skeletal, four-eyed, tomboy eleventh-grader like me. Mary, although she didn't admit it, was perplexed as well. I thought he saw the beauty underneath the glasses and thin frame but really, it was because I had learned to kiss. By practicing on my fist and watching the kiss scenes in movies very closely, I had somehow become skilled.

We dated for nine months, seeing each other nearly every day. I felt lucky. So did he. To celebrate the monumental occasion, Antonio took me to a fine dining establishment, Red Lobster. It was delicious! And it was the most expensive culinary delight I had ever had.

After dinner, Antonio and I headed back to my house to make out. My mother was out of town, and I was supposed to be at Mary's house for the weekend. Mikey was never home.

I took a bubble bath and changed into comfy pajamas. Antonio poured my first alcoholic beverage of Seagram's Strawberry wine cooler into our sophisticated, long-stem plastic champagne flutes. We toasted to our nine-month anniversary with promises of making the relationship last a lifetime.

We started out like usual, on the couch, with me (this time in a nightgown) on my back and Antonio fully clothed with his hand squeezing my tits. I moved his hand from on top of my nightgown, up through the bottom opening, over my flat stomach to the soft flesh of my small breasts. He moved the whole nightshirt up so that it bunched around my neck and then sucked away at my nipples. He dry humped me, forcing his solid penis into my pubic bone for twenty minutes while alternating his mouth between lips and nipples.

For those nine months, every time we made out, he would try to take things a bit further and, every time, I would stop him after he unzipped my pants and just before his fingers ventured underneath the top of my panties, causing major unsaid frustrations. This time, when his fingertips slid under my panties, I didn't stop him. He stopped himself out of anticipation of me putting the kibosh on his plan. I lay there hoping he'd attempt to go further, but he didn't.

I kissed him more passionately, moving in sync with his body and thrusting my mid-section upwards. My breathing picked up and my moans surprised even me. I was ready to be de-virginized and Antonio just kept the usual routine in play. I was now the one frustrated, but I could not make the first move. It would be totally unladylike.

*What else can I do?*

I had never touched his man part before and thought that that didn't qualify as a suggestive first move. I unzipped his pants and realized my mistake. Within seconds, Antonio was naked on top of me trying to get his penis inside me. He abandoned the kissing and devoted his full attention to that one task: insertion.

It took some time but we both wanted it. With tears in my eyes, I cringed from the initial pain; I was seventeen. I made love for the very first time, to my very first boyfriend, under the relaxing effects of alcohol.

"I love you."

"I love you too, Savannah."

I assumed that we were going to be bonded by that experience and would remain faithfully together forever. But then something happened. Tonio (that was what I called him after we consummated our relationship) had an older brother, Cori, who was flamboyantly gay. He had attended cosmetology school and was responsible for my first makeover.

Cori's first line of order was to perm my hair so that I could abandon thick ponytails and French braids for sexy tresses. He told me about the small miracles called contacts. My eyes, for the first time since kindergarten, weren't hidden under thick glass and awkward frames. He took time to show me how to properly apply makeup. The red Revlon eye pencil that required a flame in order to produce enough black liner to give me the Morris Day, Apollonia, and Prince eyes, which was all the rage, got tossed as less was more and my eyes were truly beautiful, almond-shaped windows to my contemptible soul.

When I emerged as a "knockout," I started becoming familiar with the word "promiscuous," as if the two ideas were somehow linked. My newfound looks and teen adolescence came together recklessly. What had Cori created? Maybe he had simply uncovered what had been slinking around the whole time.

Why did I so easily fall prey to the superficiality of my good looks and what impact these looks had on my male counterparts?

Why was society so much more receptive and friendly to me? The obsession with beauty amongst my peers and people in general was insane. I was happy to have escaped the years of self-consciousness.

*What happens to a young girl's ego and self-esteem if a makeover doesn't do the trick?*

When I attempted a conversation with Mary regarding this subject, she was in the middle of applying lip gloss for the third time that hour. She put her gloss in her fanny pack and zipped it shut.

"Do you think I'd look cute with an asymmetrical bob hair cut?" she asked with all seriousness.

I could only shake my head and reply.

"Yes, you would."

Tonio was happy to be having sex, governed by it even, and he was proud of the way I looked, thus, he was oblivious to the man-monger that I had become. I was accustomed to him treating me well. He was a church boy to the core, reared to hold doors and, at all times, to remain respectful to elders and women. Tonio's securely grounded attention only made me rebel. He was "home base," but my natural people skills, recent transformation, and rotten inherited cheater genes led me astray. Plus, Mary's response proved that looks just simply mattered, and damn it, you couldn't stop the grown and sexy. I began sneaking around, playing the field, cheating…just like dad.

*Thomas*

My first man-on-the-side was Tonio's antonym. It was popular to be a drug dealer at that time. The dope boys in my hood were the ones with the fly cars and the confidence. And it was confidence that wooed me when Thomas handed me his number.

He had done it while walking cuddled up with a girl. Perhaps it was his ballsy arrogance that made me want to respond to his sneaky overture.

On our first date, Thomas picked me up in a tricked-out, black-on-black Cadillac with gold rims and the music nearing ungodly decibel levels. The pounding bass could be heard and felt from blocks away. He wore his naturally curly hair in a neat ponytail and was sporting a purple velour jogging suit with no intentions of jogging, as shown by the gold and diamonds dripping from his ears, neck, and wrists.

Thomas got out of the car to talk on a transportable cellular phone that was a sign of his ostentatious wealth. My mother was appalled by, of all things, the fact that he honked for me. I could not simply just leave the house, I had to wait until he came to the front door. My mother and I sat looking at one another and waiting. After twenty minutes, she said, "Go." She never met Thomas.

On our next few dates, I met him at the park around the corner from my house so my mom wouldn't get so freaked out.

Thomas and I spent a lot of time simply driving around in his car. Sometimes we met up at the lake with other dope boys in tricked out cars blasting the latest rap tunes while their pretty girlfriends sat shotgun.

Even though I had heard through Joy's stories about uninhibited sex, I still had yet to experience it and wasn't sure if I ever would. In my mind, only fast, slutty girls did the nasty things, like oral and anal sex, or unconventional positions. Still, there was a chance that I was wrong.

Sex with Thomas was the polar opposite from what I had known with Tonio. Firstly, Thomas could take it or leave it. His indifference turned me on and made me surprisingly anxious to give it to him. Secondly, Thomas didn't spend time kissing or romancing. He simply felt between my legs, making sure I was wet, pulled out his substantial tool, and stuck it into me while I lay face down. A new position. I loved it and I didn't consider myself a slut by any means.

Juggling two guys became frightfully easy. A personal code of conduct was of no consequence. Lies rolled off my tongue just as effortlessly as truths. And yet, I had the nerve to be critically judgmental of Thomas.

One Sunday, my family was to have dinner at my grandmother's. I spontaneously invited Thomas. I undraped him from his trappings and still found it difficult to clean him up enough to present him to my relatives.

I couldn't help eyeballing his six foot two inch frame suspiciously.

"Is everything aw–iight?" he asked.

He was a drug dealer and looked the part. Even without the gold trinkets, his domineering street swagger remained. And, unless he sat silent all night, his vernacular would be a dead giveaway.

"No," I replied.

I respected my elderly grandma and her thoughts of my decision-making. So he couldn't come in. Plus, I had to remember that he was the other man. I shouldn't even be with him out in public, let alone in the presence of family who adored churchgoing Tonio. Lesson learned from my father's grave mistakes.

I gave Thomas a kiss and told him to wait in the car or call me later. He couldn't believe that I would desert him at the doorstep of a feast in progress. He sped off, music loud enough to wake the dead.

The next day, maybe out of a desire to let me into his world since he would not be allowed in mine, Thomas took me with him to deliver crack.

The middle-aged woman recipient was in a bad way.

Everything about her was heartbreaking—her unkempt hair; faraway, glassed-over, bulging-eyed stare at Thomas's hands; her filthy surroundings; the rotten stench; and especially the framed family pictures suggesting happier times. Hopelessness was all I saw when we entered her dismal apartment. Tears filled my eyes when she said she didn't have any money and Thomas removed the microwave from her already barren home. Why did I go inside with him?

*Savannah, why are you with someone who finds this acceptable? Normal even?*

In the car on the way home, Thomas told me that she'd be calling in an hour for another fix. He thought it was funny and couldn't understand why I was so shaken up. I finally blinked and the tears fell heavily into my lap.

"What will you take then?" I asked, with an obvious attitude.

"The lamps," he replied without hesitation.

I knew then that Thomas was not for me.

When he told me that he did go back later and removed the lamps in lieu of payment, I wasn't as upset. I started to wonder: who was right and who was wrong? This woman had chosen drugs. She chose to trade everything she owned for a hit. Was he a bad person to oblige her and profit from her stupidity?

Oh, well. She was better off milling around in darkness anyways. It would be a constant reminder of how low she'd sunk—void of light, like her hopeless life.

After that event, I dumped Thomas. I couldn't reconcile what I had witnessed with what I knew to be right, even though the woman on crack was the victim of her own demise. I classified him as a lowlife drug dealer who didn't have a moral fiber in his body.

Yet, I still cheated on Tonio.

With each boy, I became more experienced.

Although I was less than an ideal girlfriend, I still loved

Tonio and thought that if we spent more time together, a love journey of sorts, that I might stay closer to the path of righteousness.

*Yes!*

I needed a break from all of the handsome temptation in the Twin Cities! Perhaps a voyage would keep our love aflame, burning for fifty-plus years like both of our grandparents'.

It was Tonio's brother, Cori, who encouraged us to attend college at the University of The Virgin Islands on the island of St. Thomas. After his vacation to the island, he showed us photos mainly of himself lying in skimpy swimwear on white, sandy shores of blue-green waters. Why would I think of attending school anywhere else?

Tonio and I made our plans to take off to the faraway and relatively unknown—at least to my family and me—island, as most of them hadn't been further than Chicago. My relatives loved and trusted Tonio. He was my protector and friend. They trusted him to take care of their prized possession. Tonio was an angel whose pleasure it was to oblige and cater to the love of his life. He was infatuated with my mind, body, and spirit. We were one, like soul mates.

They believed that I was an exuberant eighteen-year-old, a rebel, an adventurous maverick paving the way for future exploits. My entire family—grandparents, aunts and uncles, cousins, parents, including my dad—showed up to see me off. Everyone cried. No child in the history of our family had ever voluntarily left the continent. I was the first.

I studied the faces of Mikey, my mom, and best friend Mary, as if it were the final goodbye. My loved ones waited at the gate until my plane became a dot in the sky.

# three

Beautiful Isla was what I called St. Thomas. It was just
as tranquil and picturesque as the up-close and personal
snowcapped Cascade Mountains of eastern Washington State.
The palm trees were amazing as they leaned towards the sun.
The flowers bloomed like they were vying for attention from
every onlooker. The sea and sky melded into one bright shade
of turquoise, making the horizon indecipherable. The place was
remarkable.

Month one as Tonio's girlfriend in Beautiful Isla was
limiting. He and I were always together. Our classmates slurred,
"Savannahantonio," as if it were one word or one person. We
were completely without means—broke—and thus, confined to
campus. On rare occasions, we explored the downtown area. We
were regulars at the ritual beach scene on Sundays at Megan's
Bay. All of the hip students cluttered the white sand in their
beach best. That was the extent of our island experience.

The extinguishing of the love flame between myself and
Tonio occurred in month two. I found letters from "the other
woman." He had been dating her for over a year.

After reading every last lust-filled letter, I decided I'd try
to never speak to him again. He was invisible. My ears deleted
the sound of his voice. I heard not one word that came from his
cheating trap. Anger swirled inside my heart so vehemently that
I had to mentally force myself to calm down every time I saw
him. I had crafted the art of the cut off with my dad's girlfriend,
Sarah, years ago and it came in handy.

I realized that Tonio and I were no different. I too had been
a cheater. My love letters from Brian, "the other man," were
nestled safely inside my roommate Dawn's lingerie drawer.

Tonio and I were one and the same, but the laws of

committed relationships were different for others than they were for me. If I would have professed my guilt, asked for forgiveness, and forgiven Tonio, my life might have taken a completely different path. I did not; it simply wasn't in me. I was the poster girl for hypocrisy and accepted my role graciously.

After the initial anger subsided, the feeling of physical and emotional detachment from my first true love seemed the only thing that remained. Twice, I almost went running back to Tonio, but I was stopped by pride and a single question: How could he do this to me? I cried into my pillow every night for weeks to ease my pain. I had lost my soul mate.

Dawn slept through my sniveling, consoled me, and encouraged me to get out and socialize. My heart ached for a while but with each day and each expelled tear, it hurt a little less.

Life after month two, as a single, self-identifying woman, was the catalyst to the start of an eventful rebellion. I was healed and ready to move on. I emerged with a fresh outlook. The way I saw it—whew!—I could enjoy all that the rock had to offer.

"C'mon, Dawn!"

Dawn and I knew the docking schedule of the Navy ships that came to port. One was due in. We put on our skimpy beachwear and hit the main road leading into town. Walking alongside the cars that were zipping by, we turned around to face the oncoming traffic and stuck out our pointer fingers, then aimed them toward the ground—two moves that turned our stroll into hitchhiking.

A topless jeep with a bronzed, blonde, beach-bum type swerved off the road, kicking up dust. We rushed over and hopped in. I learned he was a scuba diving instructor and took his card when he dropped us off in the middle of Front Street turned sailor boy town.

"There is *nice* new meat, just off the boat." Dawn was scanning the sea of white uniforms, practically drooling.

"Jesus, look at *them*." I raised my whole arm to point out the two strapping, nice-looking young men, hoping they'd catch on that we were scouting and that they were our first choice.

"Right or left?"

"Your turn to choose," I said as the smiles that engrossed their handsome faces led them in our direction.

"Left," Dawn blurted out before I made up my mind.

We casually moved around each other while talking and laughing. When they got near us, things were all sorted out. I had Mr. Right.

"Hi," we chimed.

"Hi. Are you guys gonna show us around?" my guy asked with a smile that flashed perfectly straight and white teeth.

Dawn and I looked at each other; we had planned on doing much more than showing them around.

"Dating" sailors got old, even after getting quite creative, like making up horrendously tall tales about ourselves—like we were trust fund babies, orphans, or fugitives. On one occasion we pretended she was deaf. I was the only one who could interpret her sign language.

"My friend said nice cock, although she's sure the white trousers aren't doing it any justice," I screamed the verbal translation above the loud reggae music blasting from one speaker.

"Tell her she looks great," the sailor said.

I flashed a series of hand movements relaying his sentiment. We spent the whole night dancing, drinking, and communicating via signs with our hopeful new sailors.

"How can she stay on beat so well, if she can't hear the music?"

"She can feel the vibrations," I replied.

"Ohhhh!!!"

Dawn eventually cracked up at some stupid joke and the cat was out of the bag.

"How did she know what you said?"

He was right. I hadn't signed it. I chuckled. What could I say?

"I'm sorry," Dawn said through her guttural laughter.

They were so upset and we were bent over in our chairs with long bouts of uncontrollable laughter. They walked out, stiffing us with the bill. We even laughed at that.

But the fun had worn off. I was bored of reckless and senseless dating.

*Play time is over. It's time to get the party started!*

First things first, this wild cat needed to get her paws on some money. I applied to and received, on the spot, a job at an Arby's. It was situated on the waterfront, prime territory for the cruise ship tourists.

A hostess seated the guests, and if they were lucky, they got me as their waitress. I was a skilled server who believed in service with a smile, compliments, and heavy flirting—all for the love of tips.

Money could be made on campus even though everyone was pressed for cash. You just had to be savvy. There were three important facts about students: they were broke, they were hungry, and they were obsessed with looking good. So being a confident capitalist, I struck a deal with the head Arby's chef de cuisine. It was simple. I'd give him one dollar for every sandwich he gave me. Transporting the yummy novelties back to campus and selling them for three dollars—first come, first served—worked wonders.

Most nights, I barely got to my dorm before being bombarded. I always sold out. Sometimes, if there were still hungry mobsters, I'd order several large pizzas from my hookup at Pizza Hut and charge three dollars per slice, again securing a profit.

The girls, many of whom were away from home for the first

time, took their looks more seriously than their classes. I was among them. So, I setup Salon Savannah. Those in desperate need of hair relaxers could come to me, rather than go to an overpriced professional. A forty-dollar tub of perm could be applied to eight people at twenty dollars a pop, yielding a profit of $120.

The tips from my Arby's job and the income from my side hustles allowed me to go into the loan-sharking business. I'd loan $100 and expect $145 by the end of thirty days. If I had to wait, they'd have to give me something of value to hold, and ten percent interest compounded was added each additional month. Most students settled when they got their student loan checks.

I loved working and Arby's was marvelous. Aside from the money, the other benefits of working there came in many forms. It was centrally located and drew a mix of islanders, merchants, and visitors. The visitors came from all over the world. It was where I met the who's who of the island's political arena—its doctors, lawyers, businessmen, and its drug dealers and addicts.

Shortly after I started working, I met the chief of police. He was off-duty and had come to grab a bite to go when he heard an argument brewing between my boss and me regarding whether or not to serve a customer.

The customer in question was my friend, a seven foot two inch Rastafarian named Raz, who hunched so badly that he appeared to be only six feet three inches. He had a rare disease that would make him grow until an inevitable early death. He lived in nature (some would say he was homeless) and smoked medicine (again, an alternate name was dope or ganja) nonstop.

Raz was my protector and buddy. He walked me to the bus stop after work and visited Arby's just to say hi. On some occasions, I'd tell him to come have lunch or dinner on me. My boss forbade it, which was why we were at odds. The chief stepped in and fervidly agreed with me. My boss turned red, pissed off for sure.

Raz got his food to go. The chief waited for a thank you from me.

"You owe me big time for butting in and, because of your machismo, my boss is sure to dislike me," I said in lieu of appreciative words.

The chief laughed.

"I promise I'll make good on a favor," he said.

My social skills were honed and my Rolodex expanded. I practiced and perfected extorting tips, all while becoming a mild alcoholic.

Back on campus, it became increasingly difficult to maintain my grades or focus. Work and a healthy social life were overshadowing the reason I was there: higher education. My grades were slipping from the dismal C's to the dirty D's.

I contemplated dropping out of school, but Dawn and random classmates were amped about me competing in the Miss UBI pageant. No one said a word about the importance of education.

Nope. I had character and natural beauty. My grades improved ever so slightly, and I signed up. My sole motivation was the cash prize and a year of tuition.

The exploitive pageantry experience was quite rewarding. Sex sells. The whole event was based on that fact. Only the beautiful girls applied; only the fit girls would dare take on the swimsuit competition; only people looking to see who was the sexiest would attend. Of course, we had to answer a question intelligently and perform a "talent," but mostly, the whole ordeal boiled down to which person could best represent the college and attract attention.

If all the girls had been morbidly obese, hairy, or butt-face ugly, no matter how talented or intelligent, the show would have been cancelled. No advertisers would risk degrading their product on an ugly chick, and people would not be inspired to attend. The universal thinking on beauty still disturbed me, but it also motivated me to misuse the system.


*Dr. Wilson*

Part of our pageant duties included soliciting businesses for sponsorship and prizes. That was how I met J. Wilson, a doctor of internal medicine, and not a moment too soon. I had to maintain a C average, so between schoolwork and the rigorous schedule that the pageant staff made us adhere to, I was working fewer hours, which meant less income. Dr. Wilson wasn't interested in contributing to the pageant. He was interested in me.

Dr. Wilson was stout, with an enormous head supported by shoulders that went from the base of his neck toward the ground, giving the illusion of having no shoulders at all. This misshapen man also had hips and wide thighs that sucked in the crotch area of his slacks when he walked. His face was old and pinched, and his eyes were unusually bulgy. However, his money and generosity were well-known and discussed amongst the islanders. So with some effort, I managed to squeeze dining with Dr. Wilson into my schedule. He went from just liking me to being completely enamored overnight. And I found a reason to actually enjoy being a pageant contestant—my very own personal sponsor.

By costly date number four, I asked Dr. Wilson if he could put my mom, who had come to visit, in a hotel, rent a car for me, and take me shopping for my big night, the beauty competition. He did all of that happily.

Under the influence, I crashed his rental car. I told them to bill Dr. Wilson for the damages. The good doctor was upset, gave me a lecture, and then proceeded to invite me to dinner to discuss the matter. I showed up to the expensive restaurant with my mother who was his age. He was livid at my audacity and probably embarrassed by the fact that he was fixated on a child.

*What does he honestly expect, dealing with an eighteen-year-old? Maturity?*

He graciously suffered through dinner and excused himself after paying the ridiculously high tab, claiming a medical emergency. I could tell by the callous good-bye that hoping to hear from him again was wishful thinking.

I was wrong. He invited me to his house. He was looking for repayment for the hotel, car, numerous dinners, and the shopping spree by way of sex. So I showed up two and a half hours late, just about the time he told me his son was due home. A lot of forethought went into avoiding sex with Dr. Wilson. He made me want to puke, but his son made me want to drop my panties on the living room floor. Surely, this beautiful boy was adopted or took after his mother. I looked at him like his father looked at me, lustfully. I very badly wanted to make J. Junior fall hopelessly in love, but I thought that would propel Dr. Wilson over the edge. There was little to gain, so I left it alone.

During the weeks leading up to the pageant, I became infatuated with my steel drum instructor, Michale. Michale had dreadlocks down to his perfect butt. He was striking. His body, style, sense of humor, and sex appeal were only a few of his attributes. Unfortunately, his repulsive smell will forever be etched in my memory. I held my breath, flirted, and teased, but I could never bring myself to have intercourse with him out of fear that his penis would leave my vagina rancid forever.

Every now and again, a song comes along that just fits who you are at a given moment. Janet Jackson's "Pleasure Principle" was me. *Baby, you can't hold me down!* Michale was a musical genius, a Mozart of sorts. With all the beautiful Calypso music he knew, he didn't understand why I wanted to play that particular song, but he taught me anyhow.

The Miss UBI title didn't go to me. I did receive a standing ovation for my steel drum and dance performance, equipped with stolen Janet moves including the infamous chair maneuver, and I received a fancy-schmancy, satiny Miss Congeniality sash and gads of meal coupons to Kentucky Fried Chicken that I eventually sold.

My drinking subsided while I was a contestant, but the pageant ended, my supportive mother returned home, and the semester broke for the holidays. I had an exorbitant amount of time on my hands. Alcohol was a friendly companion. Under the influence, I inevitably made bad choices.


*Xander*


Xander Babis was one of the most notorious of the local, young drug runners that docked in front of Arby's and whistled at the pretty girls and big asses. He'd look, but he was more reserved, too cool to chase women so bullishly. His broad smile made his eyes squint, causing him to look half-Asian. He was fine. But something about the sly, extremely confident, well-dressed thug with his gold chains and precious stones reminded me of Thomas, so I deflected his subtle advances. Plus, everyone knew that he had a reckless girlfriend.

As selfishness and stupidity collided, I woke up one late afternoon and decided that the remainder of the beautiful day needed to be spent on the ocean, not the beach. Fine-ass Xander and his boat came to mind. Staying away was made a moot point.

*Sorry, Xander's girlfriend.*

Unannounced, Xander showed up on campus looking for

me. The island was only fourteen by four miles, a small rock surrounded by water. People were always (literally) just around the corner. To pop in on someone was quid pro quo. Xander found me. I knew the seductive message I had left him earlier would make him drop whatever he was doing and come running.

Xander and I spent many days together. He was a good lover, very passionate. We did everything on his boat, which was always loaded with the necessities, namely alcohol. I wasn't a pill popper or coke sniffer, but there were plenty of those party favors as well.

Typically, after a day of cruising the island, Xander and his cohorts would hit the nightlife with me in tow. That was how I met Joe.


## Joe

Joe managed the hottest and most popular club on the island: Club Hitz. He was beyond fine and fully aware of the verity of that opinion, as was evident by the number of clamoring females always surrounding him.

One evening, Joe pulled me aside. He claimed he loved my style and told me that I was the sexiest girl he ever knew, yadda, yadda. He was laying it on for a reason.

*Two can play this game, buddy.*

I turned up the charm by slowly running my finger over his broad chest.

"Does that qualify me for a career at your club?" I finally said.

"Absolutely," he said as he seductively bit his bottom lip. "When can you start?"

I began the following evening with no training and no paperwork, just a white shirt, black miniskirt, a tie, a cummerbund, and heels that made me five feet nine inches tall.

My aggressive and personable ways made me the most

requested waitress. The job was easy, and it was a blast! I was dubbed "the chick who bought shots," so the partiers in my section had a blast, too. I loved my bartenders and tipped them accordingly, overly tipping out Joe, as he was the only one who truly needed schmoozing.

I didn't realize it entirely, but innately, I knew how to manipulate situations for my benefit. I had done it my whole life quite naturally. Total awareness of my behaviors was right around the corner.

Joe watched me work. In no time, he was setting up my section for the "guests with money." It probably helped that we began our highly anticipated inner-office affair without the knowledge of our coworkers, his plethora of girlfriends, or Xander.

Xander was unsurprising. I no longer thought it thrilling to screw on a boat or in his car. Joe's pad was modern and very clean. It was the first time I had ever seen a Bang & Olufsen stereo.

I wasn't the only one sleeping over. Joe was a womanizer. He had perfected romance, kissing, and oral sex, mainly because his man-part wasn't a big pleaser. No one had it all. It wouldn't last anyways. He was far too pretty to be bogged down with any one person. I thought the same of myself.

Friday and Saturday were my nights to shine at Club Hitz, even when the next semester began. I went from being called a slut to being cool to being placed on an iceberg pedestal. My dorm-mates were in awe. I hooked them up, solidifying my status.

The club gave each employee a five-person free-entry guest list. Being a smooth operator, I discounted the door price by five dollars and sold each (actually free) entrance for fifteen dollars, creating a seventy-five-dollar tip for myself each time I worked—sometimes more, if the other two waitresses weren't going to need their guest list privileges.

The club couldn't find out about the loophole or they would not have allowed it. My college pals were happy because they still had five dollars left for a drink. They ordered from me, and of course, I took their fives and got the round from my favorite bartender for free. I threw in a shot later in the evening. I made between three hundred and fifty and six hundred dollars in tips each night. For my unremitting infatuation with money, I worked at Arby's and Club Hitz up until spring break.

Spring break was huge on St. Thomas. The students returned to their respective homelands, hopped islands unknown with friends, or ventured Stateside, leaving the campus like a ghost town. Arby's was full of spring breakers from other places, but the weather wasn't cooperating with their plans. As I was scurrying around attending to too many tables to keep a professional pace, I kept getting questioned.

"When is the sun going to come out?" they asked.

"Is it going to rain like this all week?"

The questions mixed with being overworked finally took their toll. I was placing a nice, older couple's basket of food on their table when the woman began to speak.

*Lord, let it be about anything besides the rain.*

"Is tomorrow going to be sunny?" she asked with a soft smile to accompany her frail voice.

"How the hell should I know? Does this uniform read 'Weather girl'?" I replied with venom.

It is a fact that tips decrease when the weather sucks, especially when the server is pissed off and walks around with a really bad attitude. The dreary gray ocean and monetary pittance made me start asking myself the dumb question: *When is this shit going to stop?*

My birthday was fast approaching and I had nary a plan.

*Badi*

Badi Liyanage from Sri Lanka worked as head chef on a yacht

65

owned by a prince of some Middle Eastern country. They came frequently to the island. And whenever they docked, Badi came to Arby's, stared at me, ordered a Coke, and left a twenty-dollar tip. Three days into my spring break, Badi worked up the nerve to inquire about my vacation length. I told him. A smile engulfed his whole face. What he said next made me realize the power of positive thinking.

"Would you like to go to Puerto Rico?"

That was the moment I understood how life worked. Certain opportunities presented themselves to people who were open to accepting them. The answer to my yearning for sunny weather and a birthday plan manifested through Badi's vacation proposal.

I made it happen. I willed it into focus.

I had been making things happen my entire life. The sudden realization of how powerful thoughts and deep wishes could manifest astonished me. I truly believed that, at that moment, I was in charge of my destiny. My decision and desires were what guided me every step of the way, ending me up in the exact place I found myself.

We are not simply victims of circumstance. We have choices. We have the ability to create our own world. If we could conceptualize what it was that we desired and then with every fiber worked toward the goal, it would be realized. I was ready to craft my world!

"Hell yes!"

Of course I would go to Puerto Rico! I would have gone even if I had to quit working or if school was in session. I was ready to take life by its reigns and ride off into some unknown sunset, even if it was with a man who I had just met. Fearful, I was not! Excited and enchanted by the proposed fully-paid vacation, I was. If the sunshine wouldn't come to me, then damn it, I would go to it. I left the miserable island aura and went on the extravagant vacation, eager to discover new places.

When we arrived in San Juan, the clouds were even more daunting. So, we hightailed it to Miami where the prideful sun blazed relentlessly. It was the most exciting place that I had ever been. Everyone I knew watched and loved *Miami Vice* for the picturesque scenery and flamboyant lifestyles (and Tubbs and Crockett). The Miami beaches were a mecca for stunningly beautiful people. Young, carefree crowds infested the nightclubs and hot spots, which were known money magnets.

Mysterious Miami whispered my name repeatedly until I succumbed and fell victim to its dazzling glitz. I knew that it wasn't the last I'd see of Miami. I put that wish out into the universe. It would be so.

The night before our trip back to the island, I hit the town for one last hurrah. I celebrated my nineteenth birthday bouncing from club to club with complete strangers. Badi was too exhausted to join me, mainly from running around all day looking for gold bars. Strange but true, I regret to say, I learned nothing about buying gold bars, nor did I steal his.

I didn't show up back at the hotel until two hours before our plane was due to take off. Badi was upset, and the only way I could tell, because he was way too sweet to curse me out, was by his hand propped on his hip. The bags were packed and at the door. I stripped down naked and jumped into the shower.

Badi could not believe it. He wanted to be on time and I was messing it up. He stopped his silent tantrum when I put his hand on my wet thighs. I lured him to the bed. With my fingers and perky tits, I teased him. He came within five minutes and we made the flight.

Badi and I kept in touch for a while after that, but like most past flings, he faded into memory. He would never know that his invitation had precipitated a major change in me.

Although Tonio was a great first boyfriend, setting the chivalry bar high, and Dr. Wilson was the first older man I hustled, I credited Badi with opening my eyes to a give-and-take relationship, not based on love or an old man's blinded lust for a young girl, but a mutual understanding of what one could do to satisfy the other.

Our trip set in motion the thought that I didn't have to actually even like someone to receive wonderful things; they could justify giving me wonderful things with the understanding that I, in exchange, would share my time. The details of the things and what was done with the time were subjective and inevitably left up to me. It was a fascinating discovery, an exchange where both parties could be mutually satisfied with the resulting outcome.

After my return from Miami, I learned that I had been fired from Arby's. It was for the best. I had already grown bored and would have eventually quit.

My grades were in deep despair. I went to classes so I did not fail completely but studying was only an afterthought for me. I did very little homework and barely passed my exams. Most of my time was spent off-campus.

Studying, manipulating, and controlling people around me was my hobby, a game I played. I toyed with the general population just to see what my power could accomplish. My thoughtlessness sometimes caused casualties, but I did not care. It was all very informative.

My savings amounted to eight thousand dollars. I was nearly debt free and sent money home to repay my grandparents and help my struggling mother. I was proud of myself even if, scholastically speaking, my freshman year was a disaster.

When the school year ended and everyone prepared to leave campus, Tonio, who had brought me to that fantastic place just ten short months earlier, wanted to say good-bye. I obliged.

I stepped from the shiny red sports car that I had been driving for the past week as its owner was, probably, up to no good. I spoke via our mutual friend, Dawn, who was standing between us.

"Tell him, 'Bye.'"

Tonio expressed his concern about my psyche. He said he felt responsible for bringing me here. He had some legitimate worries, I admitted to myself. It was the first time in nine months that I had spoken to him directly.

"What worries you, Antonio?"

"Whose car is that?"

"Paco's. Why does that matter?"

"Puerto Rican Paco, Paco?"

I didn't answer. I looked at my watch.

"Paco is like, thirty, and he has a bad rep."

"Is this about Paco? Because I don't have time. Anyways, it's a little late to be jealous."

"I just think that you never really got a chance to mourn."

"Mourn what?"

"Me...our breakup."

Loudly, without caution, regret, or care, I told him how I truly felt. I spared nary a swear word. I berated him for five long minutes; he fell silent and walked back to his car. My last words as I drove off were curt.

"Dawn, please tell Antonio... 'There, I fucking mourned.'"

The reality was that I had mourned in a superficial "woe is me" kind of way, a way that was acceptable. There were even tears; he was just not a witness. I concealed my emotions and sucked it up. I suspected he was just looking for an opportunity to express his feelings. I denied him and by doing that, I probably did myself a huge disservice. Accepting apologies and granting forgiveness were moral cleansers that I hadn't yet learned. Bad things simply happened and life had continued.

My classmates and I exchanged our obligatory farewells. I hugged and kissed Dawn. I bid good riddance to the awful food and the suck-ass art instructor who had given me a D.

The next semester would not see the likes of me. The school

was better for it. I defiantly bucked their system. My path on that island would take a different turn.

## Paco

I asked Paco if I could crash on his couch until I found a feasible living situation. He said yes. A bad feeling came over me.

Unlike the other men that I milked, Paco had to be handled with white kid gloves. I was wise enough to sense his fragility and behaved accordingly. Paco was a good friend, but there were always ulterior motives behind his kindness; his eyes gave him away. They spoke a different language than his actions. I was well versed in both—kindheartedness and cruelty.

Paco helped me with the move into his one-bedroom, roach- and mouse-infested project apartment. In the following weeks, I made sure to make myself scarce around Paco and the loitering pests.

I picked up a day job at a restaurant called Palm Tree Way on a narrow passageway that connected a back street to the main street, capturing the foot traffic of shoppers as they scuttled about buying stupid, cheap souvenirs at ungodly prices. The restaurant was situated ideally. They served lunch and happy-hour hot wings that were so good and so spicy that you had to curse after each delicious bite. They were known for the "free" wings but were chastised because of their extortive methods of turning a profit. They only sold fourteen-dollar, blended drink specials at happy hour—no soda, no juice, no water, just costly drinks. It was ingenious, as there was no possibility of eating the things without quenching support, solidifying the fact that nothing in life is free.

Paco and I rarely crossed paths. If we did, I was on pins and needles, tiptoeing around his frayed feelings. His aggressive and fluctuating mood was probably due to his cocaine habit. I tried to offset his disposition by purposefully being overly nice, offering to help with chores or to pay some bills, even the rent. No matter how sweet I was to him, he found something to complain about.

True. I was using Paco for shelter. But, I asked to stay with him and he had said yes. I did not feel obligated to pay him with my time or body. I had to find a new place quickly. He wanted something that I would not give.

It was a Friday. I had finished at Palm Tree Way and headed to Club Hitz. Joe called the entire staff in to prepare for the weekend. I came bearing the scorching wings. The bartender poured our favorite cocktails and many glasses of water.

Apparently, the club's owner was in town. Joe explained the reasoning behind why we had to be on our best behavior and why the club had to look immaculate and run smoothly. He passed out new ties and cummerbunds. Joe secretly gave me a pair of stiletto heels that would surely put me at five feet ten inches.

Night came. I had a decent section, and the club was hopping. Dr. Wilson, who had somewhat forgiven me after our non-tryst, frequented the club. He wasn't seated in my area but requested me. That made the other waitress angry. She didn't want me tending to her tables. To keep the cattiness to a minimum, the doctor and his party were moved so that I could accommodate the request. The men with him would undoubtedly be impressed by my presence. The façade was going to cost him.

He ordered Dom Perignon (the champagne of choice back then). I tacked fifty dollars onto the price and poured generously; they ordered another bottle—fifty dollars more. Soon, they were tipsy. Three cute girls milled around the club aimlessly. I spotted the trio and honed in. I took far too long mincing words about Dr. Wilson and his friends. They were down with whatever.

Why had I wasted time on explanation when the only word that registered or mattered was "money"?

The scantily dressed girls adjusted themselves as I introduced them to the drooling Neanderthals. I informed the Doc, loudly, that the ladies would like champagne. Dr. Wilson instructed me to bring another bottle. I said, "Should I just bring two, Doctor?" The girls, wide-eyed, snuggled into the booth with their newfound friends. Dr. Wilson not to be undone, replied, "Make it three."

Glasses were on the table before he finished his sentence.

"Three more it is. Drink up, ladies," I said.

Then I whispered in the doctor's ear, "I expect to be generously compensated for what just occurred, and I'm not talking hundreds."

His wink was his handshake, but I didn't trust him, so I stole his wallet from his jacket, which he had left strewn over a chair while the entire party hightailed it to grind with each other on the dance floor to "Push It," the ultimate dirty dance song. For a moment, I felt I'd done something wrong, but it quickly passed.

I got six hundred dollars from his tab, two hundred from each of his cronies, and fifteen hundred from his wallet. It was a financially victorious night (for me), and he was too wasted or too embarrassed to bring up any losses from his wallet, or he didn't care because he was focused on getting punany.

I arrived at Paco's at six in the morning and changed into a T-shirt and shorts. I needed at least three hours of sleep before getting ready for Palm Tree Way, which opened at eleven. I could make a killing because the ships docked and the tourists would be in town, spending hard-earned vacation dollars on overpriced food.

My thoughts were interrupted by the morning sex that was occurring in the next room. I quietly tucked my wad of cash into one of my four hiding places. That time, it was the lining of my suitcase. I took my place on the couch, skipping my bathroom routine so as not to disturb their pleasure. I was too exhausted to clear the couch of roaches and hoped for the best as I fell immediately into a deep slumber.

Prodding rudely awakened me.

"You have to go," said Paco harshly.

"Okay. Can I just get some sleep first?" I responded, barely coherent.

"No, I don't want you here anymore," he spit through his teeth.

I felt the rage before I even looked in his direction. I started to get up. I wanted to leave without incident, but my heartbeat sped up; it was a warning.

"Fine. Can I pick my stuff up later?" I asked.

"Just get out!" Paco grabbed my shoulders and lifted me from the couch. "Now!"

Scared and mad, I kicked him in his privates. He buckled to his knees.

"I'm sorry but don't ever put your hands—" I couldn't even finish the sentence.

He was all over me. His lady friend came rushing from the bedroom. Paco had me by my throat. I guess he had forgotten what had just happened, because he left his family jewels unprotected again. I became a foot pugilist, kicking ferociously, and that time, I was not sorry. He fell. My heart was beating so loudly that I couldn't hear anything else.

I grabbed my purse and ran toward the door.

Paco, with one hand holding his crotch, snatched me by my hair, pulling me back onto the couch. His girlfriend, not liking what she was witnessing, came to my rescue just after he landed his first punch. I was able to get out of the apartment.

I ran down the disgusting stairwell barefoot. I felt excruciating, thudding pain under my eye and along my cheekbone. I made it to a pay phone and called my old friend, the chief of police.

The morning was a mess. I was exhausted and angry. The purchase of uniforms was a priority, if I was going to make it through the day. The first thing I needed to buy was a pair of shoes.

I waited around until the shops opened, with a paper towel stuffed with ice given to me by one of the Rasta men who sold fresh coconut milk. I was trying not to appear destitute. I used the time plotting my revenge on Paco.

The chief met me in a waterfront park. In full cop gear, he was intimidating. He was respected on the island because he was cool with everybody, even the do-bad types. He believed that everyone had a heart and could be a good person, if shown the way. I told him about Paco. He was fuming. His theory didn't apply to men who hit women. I was hopeful when he agreed to accompany me to retrieve my belongings first thing Monday morning. He also guaranteed that everywhere Paco went, he would be subtly harassed by way of moving violations and parking tickets. I laughed, for the first time in a long time. It felt good.

The two days of preparation for Club Hitz's owner's arrival paid off. The club looked and smelled spectacular. The carpets were cleaned. Everything from the candles to the table linen was replaced. The place was scrubbed, dusted, polished, and made new again. The club and I were so fresh and so clean (right down to our skivvies). We were all ready for a hot Saturday night. Even my fresh black eye added to the mystery that the evening was about to unleash.

The bartenders, feeling the spirit, concocted pre-Saturday night shots as Rick Astley's song "Never Gonna Give You Up" set the tone. They lined them neatly on the bar and we rejoiced. Joe disappeared to smoke his customary joint. I had dabbled in marijuana but didn't find it comforting. The paranoia, giddiness, and hunger pangs were too much. No, just like my father, I preferred the mood-altering qualities of alcohol. So, after throwing back two shots, I set off to find Joe. He usually sat in his car. He wasn't there. Around the back of the club was where I found him, lounging on an outdoor bench. He wasn't much of a talker, but I had to extract some information and find out if I could crash at his place as I was officially without shelter. I opened with asking about Xander.

"Locked up," Joe said very matter-of-factly.

Xander was always in and out of jail. His family owned a nice chunk of property that included a waterfront shopping area. The entire penal system was a conglomerate of relatives. So he'd be out soon, unscathed and unchanged. I switched subjects.

"Hey, why the fuss over the owner's arrival? Bathroom attendants? C'mon!"

"Do you know who owns the place?" he asked as he took a drag on his huge joint.

*Uhhh?*

I had always been too embarrassed to ask. It seemed like everyone knew and I didn't want to look like the fool who didn't. And there I was. What's the saying? A dumb question is one that wasn't asked?

My look of ignorance gave me away and he continued as he was holding in his smoke laden breath, "This place is Mafia owned. The cat's straight outta Sicily." A cloud was forced out of his mouth on the last word.

We talked a bit more about nothing in particular. Joe was always good for tidbits of info.

As I was walking back to the club's entrance, coming up

the grand staircase was an entourage of ten extraordinarily dressed men and women. Their attire captivated me. Islanders were fairly casual. I'd put the group in Monte Carlo or New York. Then it hit me.

*The* Alberto Mannino had arrived.

I trailed them into the building and then scooted off to the restroom to touch up my shiner while they checked in for their dinner reservations. I used the bathroom attendant's fragranced lotion and tipped her two dollars.

The party of ten had decided to sit on the patio. While the servers were rearranging the tables and guests who were already seated to accommodate them, they opted for drinks in the bar area. They had just sat down when I returned.

I was more fascinated than nervous, unlike my two fumbling co-workers. The women in the group were polished and stately; the men were confident and equally as groomed. They spoke to one another in the beautiful language of Italian, but I could tell I was the subject at least twice. I knew immediately which one was Mr. Mannino. The men turned their attention toward the small man with his chest puffed out. His head was held high. That was not something he did on purpose. He was a very powerful man and his stance was proof.

Grasping his frail hand was a beautiful young girl, seventeen at best. I approached the group, greeted them warmly, and asked if they wanted beverages. I caught a glimpse of his intense glare but wouldn't give him the pleasure of catching my eye for more than that millisecond. For reasons beyond my control, I found myself instantly and deeply involved in a game of cat and mouse. I was not going to be the damned mouse. The women ordered frozen fruity drinks. Now, with the men, I took their orders while sensually eye fucking them one by one.

I still hadn't made visual contact with Alberto Mannino. I

had planned a nice little treat especially for him. The boss was ready for his turn. Like a preschooler waiting for the recess bell, he stood at attention, excited, anticipating.

"What would you like?" My focus remained on the tablet upon which I was writing. I gave him no energy. Crushed, he ordered a pricy Cabernet.

Nonchalantly, I went about delivering their orders, never looking directly at the boss. When they were finished, I cleaned off the tables, all the while still ignoring Mr. Mannino. I kept the charade going until his party left the bar and headed into the restaurant.

He trailed behind his guests, desperate for my recognition, but his one last glance toward the bar, toward me, would be his final affirmation. (Men of power needed constant confirmation of their strength and importance. Their egos are demolished without it.) So I decided to reward the little mousy with a returned stare, cat eyes blowtorching his soul. He had asked for it.

The club filled up quickly. The line outside was already pretty long, and it was only eleven. By midnight, it would be packed. By 1:00 AM, they'd stop admitting guests and no one else would be allowed to enter unless someone exited. The club closed at five in the morning.

As poor ol' jailed, drug-running Xander sat behind bars, his main squeeze made it past security and decided to act up. I guess she had found out about her man and me. Her cranberry and vodka, glass and all, came hurling toward me.

*Who gave that known alcoholic her meds?*

All I could do was smile and shake my head. I couldn't blame the bartenders. I was as wrong as two left feet. I deserved that, and probably even if it were followed by a slap and a thorough ass-kicking, it wouldn't have halfway paid me back for the number of times I did her man on his boat, not to mention in his car.

Security was not so gentle, mainly because she was in fight mode. I hoped Xander got out soon so they could lick each other's wounds.

One of the other two waitresses gave me a black opaque body suit to replace the stained button-up. Thankfully, I had gone with black undergarments on my shopping spree. The cat suit fit in with the night's theme. It was amazing with the miniskirt and sky-high heels. Joe suggested that it be the new uniform. We all agreed. I had Xander's girlfriend to thank for this turn of events in my favor.

My section was marked with fancy gold-plated "reserved' placards. Joe did it to create the illusion that an important guest/ celebrity might be in attendance. My frustration showed.

"Looks like a no-show for Michael Jackson. You can go ahead and seat my tables now," I told him acidly.

Joe had his tactics and normally looked out for me. Club Hitz's VIP section was definitely more for locals who had some champagne bottle buying money to throw around, and no one thought otherwise. Holding out on such a busy night was just mean.

Left with an empty section, I busied myself with picking up glasses and cleaning tables in other parts of the club, hoping to let the boss get a glimpse of his hardworking employee. While my co-workers were raking in the dough, I was broke, not to mention homeless. The crowd thickened. Joe passed by with couples that looked ready to spend money, but they were not seated in my section. They'd slide him twenties thanking him for the tables, while I was doing nothing and getting nothing. Joe winked at me.

*Is he messing with me? Power trippin'? What?*

When a well-known, big tipper was seated outside of my section, I was about to quit. That just damaged my ego.

*Maybe Joe's punishing me for the Xander's girlfriend incident or my sarcasm, or maybe because he's shown me too much favoritism.*

Finally, Joe seated my section.

"You owe me," he quickly said before disappearing to retrieve champagne to accompany the club's new crystal ware.

Alberto Mannino had returned.

My smile, which was too big to conceal, made the others jealous. Joe had set me up, and everyone knew it.

As Joe and I served the group, I couldn't help but notice Mr. Mannino and Joe conversing. When I got back to the wait station, Joe approached me. Instead of spilling juicy gossip, he asked, "What is it with you?"

*Whatever do you mean? Oh, that? My sexy, sweet innocence mixed with cunning, sensuality, and the rare ability to make men melt?*

"The boss asked if you could dance," he continued without an answer.

"What did you tell him?" I asked.

"I told him you dance like a white girl."

"Ha, ha."

Joe's voice dropped to a whisper. He asked again hoping for an answer.

"What the fuck is it about you?"

*I don't know, man. I don't know.*

"Can I go dance?"

"Shit, he's my boss. You tell me."

Under the strobe, timed with the pulsating music, Mr. Mannino and I danced an unforgettable dance… for two hours, without a word.

We held hands, moved in sync, shook our booties, swayed our hips, and slow danced when the music wasn't slow. His unusual gyrations made me smile and mimic him. He laughed, and we twirled and twisted until I couldn't take it anymore, meaning my feet hurt like hell.

At three in the morning, his party called it quits, too. It felt like family when we said our good-byes—kisses on both cheeks.

I treated everyone with the same benevolence, even my dance partner.

"Good night. Thanks for the dance. Do come again."

And just like that, they were gone. *Hmmm...* I wondered if my dancing the night away and subtle flirtations sealed with a candid good-bye had worked. Questions plagued my thoughts: *Did I make an impression? Why do I want to see him again? Will I see him again?*

I cleared the table, smiling at my strength. I knew the answer.

A bunch of drunken nobodies sat down at my VIP table. They commenced to shout their drink orders.

"You can all have beers on me. Deal?" I said to them.

I was tired and concerned where I was going to lay my head that night, as I still hadn't asked Joe for refuge. I dropped off the beers. They managed to scrape up a ten-dollar tip.

Just then, I realized that that was the only money I had made all night.

"Damn it," I blurted out to no one in particular.

I had spent all my available cash on clothes earlier, and credit was not yet a part of my life. A hotel room was out of the question. My earlier jubilation turned to stress.

When I returned to the drink station, Mr. Mannino was there waiting for me. The corners of my mouth rose just a bit. I wanted to pray out loud but instead thought, *Dear God, please let it be that he remembered that we are in the United States where tipping is customary and it is considered quite rude if you don't do it (especially when your wait staff performed an exemplary service, such as dancing all night in new high heels). Amen.*

"Savannah, will you join me for lunch tomorrow?" he yelled above yet another Rick Astley song ("Together Forever") as it faded into a Debbie Gibson tune.

Who needed tips or shelter?

I leaned in and faintly replied, "Lunch would be lovely."

# four

It was Sunday, and most stores were closed. Again, I found myself inappropriately dressed. I had the choice of wrinkled khakis and an equally wrinkled uniform shirt, or my smoke-reeking outfit from the night before. How tacky. Wrinkles it was.

Joe, with whom I ended up staying, dropped me off on Pizza Hut's front steps. Joe was a churchgoer, an on-time, early-morning churchgoer. I was going down a very different road; church was laughably out of the question.

So instead, I sat outside and waited two hours for the restaurant to open. I was famished by eleven o'clock. Mr. Mannino was due to pick me up at noon. I could eat my fill of pizza now and then have a salad on our lunch date, but the pizza chef took too long.

Mr. Mannino pulled up at exactly noon. When he got out of his newly washed Land Rover, I noticed his silk button-up shirt neatly tucked into his faded blue jeans, a black leather belt, and black loafers. He was casual. *Thank goodness, my attire may fly.*

Luckily, I hadn't yet embroidered Palm Tree Way onto my shirt. He entered as I was polishing off my first piece. He smiled, sat down, and grabbed a slice. At least he wasn't an uppity food prude.

His first question floored me. Again, my instincts were correct. He was the one! I knew it even if he didn't; he was the one. His question was simple, but oh so complex.

"What can I do for you?"

I was reeling from my answer and subsequent conversation. I spilled my guts. I cried, trembled, and sought solace in his frail arms. He stroked my swollen, discolored eye, and I felt his pity. That motivated me to drench his silk shirt with salty tears and mucus. Boy, I was good—really good. I now had a place to reside.

As we drove to my new home, I realized that I hadn't even known that his part of the island existed. Tucked away neatly, there were hundreds of acres of plush, natural forest owned by him and his family.

Suddenly, I remembered that his last name was Mannino.

What the hell was I doing? How many bodies were buried out there? Who would come to my rescue if this feeble yet powerful, infamous man suddenly decided to attack me? Maybe he was a psychopath and I had read him all wrong?

I held on tight to a pen that was floating around the bottom of my purse. Thank God for the tools of the trade. I was prepared to gouge out an eye or puncture that bulging blue vein in his seventy-year-old, craggy neck.

The tires on the crunchy gravel road made the scene more eerie. We came to a slow rolling stop outside of a small house. There was nothing else in sight. In the distance, I could hear the ocean, but as we were coming up the winding waterfront property, I occasionally saw that the coastline was rough, rocky, and steep; the cliffs plunged a thousand feet into bitter cold waters.

The little white cabin looked forlorn, left unaided to survive alone in the haunted forest. Would it be my protector and friend, or was the house the actual enemy? Rusted hinges secured old wooden doors, and the two porch stairs creaked. When Alberto opened the door, it was actually very nice, quaint, and clean inside. There were no bloodstained mattresses or hanging farm tools. The house contained everything I would need, even toiletries. But in the coming hours of darkness, the questions would be answered.

We spent the day walking on the property. The cliffs weren't so bad. The ocean view was breathtaking, and by the time night came, I was pretty sure no harm would befall lil ol' me.

I expressed my gratitude.

"Thank you so much. Not sure where I was going to end up."

I gave Mr. Mannino a hug but held on a few extra seconds to make sure he didn't feel the urge to come back and murder me.

*Keep your enemies close.*

Even though the house and forest were relatively quiet and not at all creepy, I couldn't sleep. It is always the idiot who relaxes and falls into a deep slumber that gets beheaded or carved into a million pieces.

Outside my box, there was absolute darkness. It was as if someone had dropped my tiny abode into a tar pit. I knew I couldn't stay another night. Even Paco's abusive antics beat that little house of horrors.

When the Range pulled up in the morning, I was packed and ready. Mr. Mannino was surprised to see me awake.

"Savannah, you're up."

*I was up all night! Can we get the hell outta here?*

"Alberto, I appreciate you letting me stay the night, but this won't work. Can you drop me off in town?" I asked.

"No. You will stay with me," he said with authority.

End of discussion. We drove off in silence.

Bye-bye, bitty house; hello, oceanfront mansion. Before we went "home," there was one teeny thing I had to take care of, seeing as it was Monday morning and I was due to meet the chief to pop in on ol' Paco.

Paco probably didn't expect me to come back at all, and surely not toting weight like the chief of police. He was probably petrified. Yet, still he faked like he wasn't home. If he only knew Alberto Mannino was patiently waiting for me.

I checked for his key, which he kept above the door on the frame ledge. No key. I pounded.

The chief shouted, "Open up! It's the police." It was a cliché, but it was true.

Nothing.

I yelled at the top of my lungs, "I will scratch every surface of your car, slice open your tires, and bust out the windows if I have to walk down those horrid stairs without my stuff."

"And I won't stop her," the chief added.

The door opened.

Paco threw out my two suitcases and slammed the door. They had obviously been ransacked. Thankfully, my hiding place hadn't been discovered, so my money was still there. I pounded again.

"Where's my radio?"

*I can't live without my radio!*

"I sold it," he said.

*Wrong answer.*

I loved that radio. I had one tape in it, Al B Sure. And I was damned if I would part with either.

"Then consider your car trashed!"

The chief and I turned to walk away. We had a car to destroy.

The pawned radio appeared out of thin air equipped with wet dream Mr. Sure.

Mr. Mannino wasn't privy to the humorous reclamation of my humble belongings, as he had opted to wait for me in his truck with the windows up and doors securely locked. I don't think he had ever seen, let alone lingered in, the ghetto on this island or anywhere else in the world.

He focused on his surroundings, never letting anyone out of his sight even as I approached the car with my luggage and the chief. The shirtless Rastafarians smoking reefer under a palm tree, the large number of teen boys milling around a few big booty girls, and the barbecue pit that was located in the middle of the parking lot were not unusual to me, but I could see where it was quite the scene for a novice ghetto dweller. Even for a notorious mobster, hoods were intimidating.

The chief instructed Mr. Mannino to take good care of me. He left without a good-bye. It was actually the last time I would see the chief. We were even. But I wasn't finished with Paco.

I had trouble deciding which payback to use; would I put raw popcorn shrimp in every vent, crack, and crevice of his home so that in a matter of days, it would stink to high heaven? Or should I cut out circles in the nipple part of all his beloved silk shirts? Or would I hide gay pornography in places that I thought his girlfriend might snoop, ruining his ladies' man image? Hmm…

Weeks later, I let myself into his place, quickly bagged up all of his right foot shoes, and disposed of them in a dumpster across town. It was my way of saying, "Your ass ain't right."

Back in the truck, Mr. Mannino proceeded to the far eastern side of the island; it was a gorgeous place. The moment we arrived, I was besieged by emotions—nervousness, elation, hopefulness, hesitation, anxiety, and vindication.

My life situation was still precarious at best. I was torn between doing what was best and riding an unusual roller coaster to its end. Something told me to sit tight and strap up.

Above all, I was intrigued.


*Alberto*


All my previous petty schemes seemed so trivial. I went from neophyte to specialist, just like that.

The sprawling oceanfront place was something torn from the pages of a dream home magazine with every amenity imaginable. It was magnificent. The four upstairs bedrooms were decorated like nothing I had ever seen. Luxurious richness had obviously been the theme. White marble flooring was laid throughout the house; even the spacious maid's quarters were exceptional. It felt like I had hit the lottery and was home sweet home!

"I love it, Mr. Mannino. How long can I stay?"

He was impressed with my enthusiasm and turned on by my gullibility.

"You can stay as long as you want. This is your home. But you must call me Alberto."

"Alberto it is," I said mimicking his Italian accent.

The maid rounded the corner. I was sure she had heard his candid invite. He instructed her to leave the guest room alone and informed her that I would be moving into it. Maid's quarters turned guest room just for me. I wondered if his command meant that I didn't get a servant.

I smiled and made an attempt at an introduction, but the middle-aged black woman turned and walked away.

*Eff you too, Aunt Jemima. I ain't hardly worried 'bout you.*

"It was nice meeting you," I bellowed after her.

Alberto seemed oblivious to her apparent rudeness, but I sensed that there was more to why she was upset by my presence.

The days that followed were nothing short of amazing. Alberto and I spent time becoming friends. He introduced me to his visiting children: the beautiful young girl from the club and a handsome son. They came every summer from Sicily to bake in the soothing island sun.

They were one year on either side of my age, but they were light-years ahead of me. They were worldly and confident. They possessed power and commanded attention, not unlike their old man; it probably had something to do with bearing the last name Mannino. In addition to that, they both spoke six languages fluently. I was in awe.

I wanted to go to parties and hang out on yachts, but Alberto had me on lockdown, confined to where he could keep a close eye on me. It was nearly impossible to get away. Running off to party with my peers was out of the question. He barely allowed me to continue working. I was clearly not going to be his children's friend. I was solely his.

One week, I had worked back-to-back doubles. After the third double, I came home to a house that felt barren. Something had changed. Alberto informed me that his kids were visiting family in New York. We were alone.

He had become increasingly possessive, and I knew his children were getting in the way of him getting his way. I felt the tension.

Alberto Mannino was a feared man. His piercing eyes were beady and dead, but they danced a jig whenever he looked at me. I knew the power that I held over him, but like with Paco, I had to be careful, very careful. The shift from thoughtfulness to selfishness could occur at any time; indeed, things had already begun to change. Even though Alberto and I spent lots of time together, it wasn't enough. He wanted all of my time and my working two jobs conflicted with his needs. His subtle, ever-present pressure, such as waiting to take me home when my shift ended, even when it was five o'clock in the morning, was growing wearisome. We were out of sync.

Alberto and I were not an official couple, but people assumed we were. I became highly respected by default. The people at my job were less friendly and more standoffish. I hadn't so much as kissed Alberto, and here Joe had accused me of being... *what?* His mistress? He was married? Joe explained that he was married to the Sicilian mother of his children whom he would never grant a divorce, even if she had the courage to ask, which she apparently didn't.

I had cheated and was fairly comfortable with the concept, but cheating with a married man seemed sinful and perhaps reminiscent of my father's broken sanctity.

I struggled with understanding my hurt feelings. Did I care? It was then I realized that in order to play games, you couldn't fall prey to believing your own lies. Both sides had to play to get what they wanted. You had to keep it real with yourself, or you'd lose track of your goals and that was a terrible thing.

But at nineteen, what were my goals? What was it that I was searching for from this situation? I truly didn't know. I was content working and saving money, living an interesting life, and exploring my powers. My goals would eventually develop. But at the time, I was curiously aware of those emotions. Maybe it wasn't hurt that I felt; maybe it was anger, perhaps because I had read him wrong, or because he had lied, or because he really only considered me a concubine when I thought I was so much more. Things are what they are, no more for sure, and maybe they are less.

Still, I had this mix of anger and feeling insulted guiding my sensibility, which Alberto astutely sensed. It could have been the sneers when he came around my job to take me home, or maybe when I purposefully said, "Go home! I can get a ride from Joe," knowing that he was the only man in the place who could stir a small attack of jealously in Alberto. Or maybe it was when I said, "You're a liar." In any event, Alberto was determined to correct whatever might be ailing me and that was exactly what I wanted to happen.

The next morning, breakfast was prepared as usual. Typically, I just slept through that part of the day. But I was excited to see what Alberto had in store for his reparation, so I met him on the terrace. I had quickly moved on to the resolve to forget the problem. I didn't really care. I'd have to let him express his feelings, explain his circumstances, blah, blah, blah. I knew the story, but I had to be patient and let it unfold. That was the only way to instill guilt and get the upper hand. How I played it would determine how badly he felt. How badly he felt would then determine what I would gain. The problem was I had to know what it was I wanted. I simply wanted him to feel terrible.

What a waste that was. I could have gotten so much more.

We sat on the patio facing the ocean. It was a perfect day. I took in the scenery with all of my senses. I could even taste the salt in the air from the ocean's spray. I half paid attention to Alberto's droning. My mind and soul were at peace, but my face showed disappointment, and I had pre-selected the words on my tongue that were just waiting to roll out. No matter what he said, I was prepared.

"Savannah, what is the problem, Savannah?"

I loved it when he said my name twice. It meant he was begging.

"How could you? I thought you cared about me," I whined.

Before he trapped himself in a series of defensive escape phrases, I blurted out the question. "Alberto, are you married?"

He tactfully avoided the question of marriage and explained that Gizel was his girlfriend. A wife and a girlfriend? I was momentarily flabbergasted. What the hell was I doing? I could have chosen to walk away from breaking the commandment against adultery, but I did not.

"Savannah, if you are not the lead dog, the view is always the same." He stared at me, "Are you my beautiful leader?"

I knew where he was going with this manipulative game... So, the only questions that remained were: who was this Gizel? And would she easily fall three paces behind me, the new emerging leader of his pack?

"Yes," I answered with a little more assertion than the moment called for.

Who was I becoming?

Alberto went on to explain that Gizel was in South America and was due to return at summer's end. My living situation would be comprised. I had to act quickly solidifying any long-term arrangements. So I acted. But in my mind she and I were competing for the same place and one of us would win.

"What do you mean? I've been living here, 'dating' you, and thinking you actually cared about me, and at the end of the summer, you're kicking me out? What a fool I've been to actually start falling for you." Then came the tears... Oh my God, the tears.

Alberto was at a loss for words, momentarily, as I wept uncontrollably.

"Savannah, I said you could stay here for as long as you like. I meant it, Savannah," he pleaded.

Alberto explained that Gizel would welcome me. She would not protest my presence.

*What?*

It finally struck me that I was to become an additional live-in "girlfriend." If I wanted to stay his lead dog, I would have to accept the fact that both of his "other women" would have to reside under the same roof.

What I later found out from Joe was that Gizel had gotten caught by someone that Alberto sent to "keep an eye on her" traipsing around Brazil with a lover boy, and that Alberto was purposefully replacing her or taunting her with a possible replacement, namely, me. Which episode of the Twilight Zone was I in?

It took my brain a moment to analyze the situation and my options.

1. *Savannah May Lovely, get the hell out! Keep your dignity intact. You are way too good for this madness.*

2. *Stay and play the new role as good friend, but not lover. Hmm, that has some benefits, without going "there" or...*

3. *Stay and be everything that Gizel is not, starting with faithful. You could be the one learning languages and vacationing in foreign destinations; you could be pampered*

*and retired from strenuous labor. You could be his main
squeeze.*

*But, oh no! Stop the presses…*
*You will eventually have to learn to kiss his seventy-year-old
wrinkly, paper-thin, crusty lips and possibly other wrinkly, paper-thin,
crusty parts!*

Alberto must have sensed my apprehension. Me
contemplating my situation was not what he wanted.

"Come! We'll go shopping!" he fervently announced.

I was hesitant, but he insisted. I, like a simple teen girl,
switched from deep concentration on my current predicament to
mentally matching up outfits of cool bathing suits, sundresses, and
sexy sandals.

On our way, we stopped at a specialty grocery store. Surely
that would be just the first of many places we'd go. Everything I
saw in the aisles was new to me; there were hundreds of different
pastas, as well as seafood and meats that I had never seen or
even heard of before. I could have spent hours just examining
everything. I was astonished. Alberto was thrilled as he spoke
about all the various items. In the end, we bought food to feed a
small country.

"We will have guests tonight," he said with too much
excitement.

Back home, he began instructing me on how to prepare
authentic Italian dishes. I was a willing student and totally forgot
about beachwear and the Gizel conversation. Caprese, prosciutto,
pancetta, calamari—I was enthralled with Italian cuisine.

For the moment, I was staying. After seeing his guest list,
you'd think I would have bolted, but instead my fascination
doubled. I had heard and ignored the rumors of Alberto being a
mobster. He was just Alberto, with an ill-fated last name. There
were no mysterious hit men making attempts on his life, no secret

meetings behind closed doors, and not even other Italians or a Jewish accountant milling around. He was a normal cat. Then I saw the guest list; there was nothing normal about it.

Leonardo Peccati? C'mon, did I go from the *Twilight Zone* to *The Godfather* just that quickly?

We finished the dinner preparations, and Alberto presented me with a beautiful dress and shoes to wear for the occasion. It was too elaborate for my taste, but I put it on to please him. I felt special, made-up, and out of place all at once. When his guests arrived, the look on their faces said it all.

*Wow! You really outdid yourself this time, Alberto!*

I was not as comfortable amidst such legendary figures as my attire suggested. I was extremely nervous. I hadn't been around class at this level and was skeptical of how I should perform seemingly simple tasks, like using a decanter or correctly pronouncing 'Perrier' water (Pair-ee-ay not Pee-air) and all the Italian food items. Still they drank red wine that I helped choose and dined on bruschetta that I pieced together, and I was proud of that.

My youthful innocence captivated Don Peccati's attention and caused a small rift. Our dancing was the catalyst to a Mafioso war that had been impending between the families—just kidding. Leonardo seemed nice enough, a bit frisky, but otherwise not suspicious.

There was a huge man whose first name escapes me (something that ended in -ie or -y), probably with a middle name of "the" and the last name of something from the animal or tool category, like bull, tiger, saw, or hammer. I could definitely see him strangling a "dirty rat" with a clothes hanger.

When the evening ended, together Alberto and I cleaned up enough to make the maid not curse us.

"Thank you, Savannah. You were a prince among frogs," Alberto said with a wide grin.

I wasn't familiar with that saying, but I accepted the odd compliment and gave Alberto a genuine hug.

Alberto and I spent many of the following days exploring islands on his custom-made speedboat. I was a great captain and once took the water rocket out solo. I didn't go far as I was scared the media would find my bloated body washed up on some uninhabited island and spin my life as a Mafia mistress and drug smuggler who had been murdered while attempting to flee her tyrannical captor.

The thought of Alberto killing me, and the morbid murder making it to national headlines, crept into my mind often. I really didn't know why, but even so, that summer was one of the best of my life. But by its end, Alberto had started to become domineering. He practically forced me to quit my day job and, eventually, Club Hitz. The club friendships had turned sour anyhow. Even Joe claimed that I thought that I was special.

I was special, and I did think that, but I had thought that since I was a few days old! I didn't treat them differently because of my new beau. They were the ones tiptoeing on broken glass, scared and mad at the world. I still talked about the club and the ridiculousness of things, like any job. However, I used my relationship with the boss to make changes that worked in everyone's favor. I was upset that our once cohesive team viewed me as a hated outsider.

Alberto asked me to quit, claiming he worried too much about my safety. I was not exactly sure what he meant. But I did quit, leaving Joe and the club to carry on without me, and opening up my schedule for Alberto to carry on with me.

The weather on St. Thomas that summer was unbelievable. Just when I thought I had seen the most perfect day ever, the next day came, beating it out ever so slightly.

Alberto and I would get up, have breakfast, and dress for the day. He'd pack drinks and snacks for the boat. We'd hop into the truck and head to the marina located just down the hill. Our plan was no plan. We just sped off and stopped wherever we felt like snorkeling, swimming, eating, or just relaxing on the massaging waves.

After such a day, Alberto and I returned home. He unloaded the truck and I went down to my room to shower. I came back up prepared to invite him to a lovely fresh seafood dinner at a local hole-in-the-wall place that I loved and one that he had never been to. I had just entered the living room when Alberto came flying from his bedroom, naked. I thought he was fleeing an intruder. My eyes darted behind him, trying to locate the threat. Suddenly, Alberto grabbed me. I was stunned. Still thinking he was saving me from some unknown masked man, I didn't react at first. Then he threw me onto the couch. My back hit the decorative pillows, and my bare legs bounced off of the seat cushions. Before I realized what was happening, Alberto's fingers were inside of me.

I was blown away by this turn of events. I tried to fight, but that seemed to fuel him. He was operating on adrenaline and I, fright; it was an uneven match. I was pinned down by his right hand and the weight of his body. Frail was no longer an adjective I'd ever use to describe him again. I felt him working his penis around my panties, looking to insert it.

My heart pounded so loudly that I actually attempted to reach up and plug my ears before realizing my predicament. My emotions and thoughts were swept up by a fearless tornado that pummeled my insides. As violently as the tornado came, it softly left; it was instantly slurped down into tiny saltwater pellets that fell from my eyes.

I sobbed heavily and then relaxed. I had completely capitulated.

*Take it, you dirty bastard.*

I'm not sure why Alberto recoiled, if it was the lack of fight

94

or the painful cry, or neither. Maybe he knew that that was not the way. But why did he do it in the first place? The alcohol we had consumed? Perhaps he expected an intensely passionate reaction to flow from his victim? Possibly, his patience had just finally run out. Or maybe, I was lucky and the entire plan was to rape and kill me, throw my body into the ocean, and let the sharks have their way.

In any event, I wasn't deeply troubled by the attack. I was, however, troubled by the fact that I was not troubled by the attack. Some sick part of me justified the action as his meltdown—I had driven him mad. My success as a man-melter was again proven.

Alberto's bedroom door slammed shut. I slowly rose from the couch, walking lazily to my room, no longer in danger. I stopped briefly to take in the ocean's roar. It was particularly loud. I wanted the pounding waves to shut the hell up. Little did I know they were on my side, rooting for a sensible decision to arise in lieu of what had just occurred. I went through a situation evaluation exercise. Despite the ocean's attempt to warn me of my own stupidity, I made the decision to stay. The shore became peaceful; the ocean was pouting. My gut feelings remained ignored.

Neither he nor I ever mentioned the occurrence. It was erased, forgotten; I sucked it up. Still, I remained exhilarated by all the power that I possessed. Was I now polishing skills that I somehow knew I would need later in life?

Even after the attempt at forced sex, Alberto didn't really threaten me. I teased him without ever thinking we'd be sexual. I played innocent, wounded, hurt, and most convincingly, naive. He took care of me like a loving parent takes care of an ill child, but I knew the status quo could not and would not hold steady. He had issues that were always just below the surface, festering until they would one day erupt.

We focused on our respective positions in our game of cat and mouse, changing too often to know who was which. I was lost but not losing. I believed he was the same. I was sucked in to trying to win with no real goal. His goal was winning me. I remained in the game for the thrill of the mindfuck and all the unanswered questions that needed answering. I wanted to wake up with the unpredictability of a new day; to know what would become of me once Gizel returned; to challenge; to win; to see where this game would lead. These were also the reasons that I could not simply walk away.

That attack was just the beginning. It was only a matter of time before I would have to make a life changing choice. And before I knew it, Alberto crept into my room one morning. He slowly and calmly inched his way into my bed. I had heard the door open, but chose to remain lying on my side, still and silent. He was naked. I could feel his heavy breathing on my neck. He was trying something new—his last attempt. It was time for me to make my decision.

I rolled over onto my back with my head turned away from him. I set my boundaries non-verbally by showing him what I would and would not do. Kissing was out of the question. I pulled up my gown and opened my legs for his hand to fondle me, but no other penetration. I remained motionless, while he rubbed his penis up and down my outer thigh. My brain shut out the current happenings and floated back to a time in my childhood.

*I'm ten, hiding behind the curtain, watching my cousin, Joy, kiss a boy from my neighborhood. She's supposed to be babysitting me but really just used my mom's house to carry out her need to feel like a "normal" teen girl. I don't mind. I like watching her, blissful and volatile. She doesn't mind either. She would say, "Just watch. Don't make a sound or you'll have to go to bed." No problem. I have a crush on her boyfriend. I want to kiss him too. And when I do finally go to bed, I fantasize about it.*

The soft hairs on Alberto's chest tickled my skin. I snapped back to the moment with the need to throw up. Approximately seven minutes later, he was leaving just as quietly as he had entered. I turned onto my side and cried into the pillow.

The same shit started to go on every morning. We never talked about it, and in time, I stopped crying. I learned to make myself numb. I learned that the cost of such an exchange sometimes came at a high price, and it was at a price point that was obviously still within my moral and psychological budget.

I discounted the cost by reasoning; as long as I was the one who allowed the ritual to take place, I remained in control. I could mentally disappear. He wouldn't know of the absence.

*Ha. Take that! You can't get in my head.*

In actuality, I had become a pro at convincing myself that I was the one in control. Yes, I was allowing the act to take place, but did that mean that I was in control? Or was he in control because I did not reject his advances?

I decided that I *could* leave eventually, thus affirming that I was truly the one in power. But what plagued me was: *could he throw me out?* That was the question that I knew needed an answer. I had to know the power of my hold. I could make men melt, but could I torment him to the point of no return? Break his heart? The time had come when I would get my answer. Gizel was en route to our home.

The morning before her arrival, I got my period, ironically. I was irritable. Alberto was nearing my bed when I announced my circumstances. He paced my room for ten minutes or more pondering the situation. I fell back asleep but was awakened when he sat on my bed and began reciting a story that began with his only daughter turning fifteen.

There was a question of whether Alberto's daughter was actually his biological offspring and a rumor was floating around the club that she was his lover. The times I spent with the both of them didn't suggest anything more than a mutual respectful adoration between father and daughter… then came an audacious statement.

"It is a father's duty to teach his child how to make a man feel love," he explained. "I could not leave something so important to a silly teenaged boy."

He had shown his own child "how to make love in many ways." He told me I should have learned years ago.

"I will be the one to show you," he continued.

I didn't really get the full understanding of his relationship with his daughter, but I was disgusted by his words.

"I'm on my period!"

"You lie, Savannah," was all I heard even though he ranted on.

I flew from the bed, grabbed the trash can from the bathroom, and emptied the contents—a bloodied tampon wrapped in toilet paper and two applicators—onto his lap.

*No "learning how to make love many ways" for me today, you nasty, incestuous parasite.*

He left the room in a tirade. I was off the hook. It was the first time that I had been excited about the homecoming of his true mistress. Once she returned, he'd have no need to molest me anymore. It was her turn to solidify her place in his life and in this cuckoo's nest.

The next day, I overheard the maid talking to her sister about Gizel's return and discovered the reason the maid was so vehemently opposed to my presence was that she was an aunt and ally of Gizel's. You'd think Alberto would have mentioned that, especially since I had twice been witness to his reprimanding her for being rude to me. She had her reasons; this was her sister's daughter's house. I was out of order for asking her to "freshen up" my shower when she was related to the woman who really lived here. She probably felt sick that she couldn't warn Gizel. That betrayal would surely have meant her job. She, like me, had to deal with the cards she had been given.

"G-day" was spent cleaning and preparing a superb welcome-home meal. By this time, I could cook up pretty respectable Italian fare. I made fettuccine Alfredo with peas and prosciutto while Alberto handled the antipasti and dessert.

I felt obligated out of some kind of sick solicitude, a deeply rooted sisterhood, to make an apology of sorts. Maybe if she liked me, this would work.

*Don't be delusional, Savannah!*

She would loathe me, no matter how sweetly I presented myself, how many flowers I bought, or how humbly I dressed. Like her aunt, Gizel had every right. I'd be damned if I was willfully leaving or letting her kick me out, though. Only Alberto had that power. I was betting that he didn't have the nerve.

As Alberto and I moved about the kitchen, I noticed how my enthusiasm for Gizel's return might have been a tad perplexing to him. He was fooling himself with thoughts of threesomes, a harem perhaps. Nope, she would hate my guts.

Alberto hadn't mentioned me to her prior to her walking into the kitchen. She took one look and knew right away that I was not the sous chef. Alberto didn't acknowledge her anger. He smiled as if the thought never crossed his mind that she may not be so happy to see a young beauty in her house. He introduced us with the same ignorance, or perhaps he didn't care how she felt.

My extended hand would have fallen off from rot before she would return a shake. She turned from me and walked to their bedroom. Alberto followed, but not like a lost puppy dog; he remained stoic with a smile of confusion (or manipulative evil) creeping onto his face. I sat down and ate, thinking that it could possibly be my last meal at the Manninos' lovely abode.

Gizel squealed something about me sleeping in her bed

before I decided to eat outside on the patio. I finished and set out for a night walk.

The house was situated on a long, winding road. It was extremely dangerous to walk it during the day and just plain stupid at night, as the drivers of all the speeding cars could not see you. Any amount of danger beat staying there.

I got to the bottom without incident and made my way to the local bar. I didn't want to get drunk for fear of being run over on my walk home.

No sooner had I finished my first drink than Alberto, with Gizel in tow, was standing in front of me. With a complete turnaround, Gizel held out her hand for me to shake and plastered a huge fake smirk on her boney face. Alberto was determined to make this little arrangement work. I wondered what he had said to persuade her to be kind.

My mind had made Gizel out to be striking. I had envisioned a graceful debutante with perfect features to qualify her for any Western pageant: long, flowing hair; perfect teeth; perky C-cup boobs; and a frame to die for, coinciding with her name. At best, she was average. She had flawed skin, buckteeth, hair in desperate need of a salon professional, and an Olive Oyl figure. Her appearance begged the question, "What the hell do you do with your time and money?" I felt my anxiety disappear.

She shook my hand (a bit too hard, squeezing my knuckles together), and the trepidation returned. The look in her eyes said, "It's on. Watch your back!"

Since it was indeed on, I added salt to the already open wounds.

"Give me a hug," I said. I squeezed her a bit too hard. "I've heard so much about you. Sit down, you guys. Let's have a drink."

Of course, Gizel whined about how late it was and even though she had traveled in first class, how she was so tired from her trip. I was relentless. I could not let her triumph. She could not win one measly battle—no matter how insignificant. From this day forward, I promised myself, since Alberto had convinced her of this ludicrous arrangement, I wouldn't let him down.

More so, I would not let her get one up.

"C'mon. Just one," I coaxed.

I ordered Alberto's favorite, a Cabernet. The fact that I had such detailed knowledge of his likes had to hurt. She didn't have a drink, of course. Gizel probably wanted tequila shots, but she'd just as soon slit her wrist than raise a glass of cheer with me.

Everything that night was a fight. Gizel was ready to leave before we had finished our drinks. No problem. I went to the restroom and took five minutes longer than necessary—just killing time to taunt her. Alberto forgot his glasses, so she quickly made the move to the driver's side of the car, thinking Alberto would ride shotgun, putting me in the backseat. I was light years ahead of her. Alberto wouldn't dare put me in the back. He already knew I was easily made sick by the motion. So she and I sat side by side on the way up the hill to our home, both knowing the one in the back seat had full control.

During the quick trip, I made a mental note: *maintain financial independence, or at least be able to check into a hotel for an extended stay on a moment's notice, especially when your rich boyfriend brings a third party to the household without your approval.*

Joe had told me all about Gizel. He said Gizel had grown up on St. Thomas. Her family was poor and remained poor while she dated and lived with Alberto, a multimillionaire. She and Alberto had met when she was only sixteen years old. Now that she was twenty-four, she was past her prime, old by Alberto's standards. He said she lived an amazing life.

The days that followed were strenuous at best. Gizel became a master at attempting to make me feel two inches tall. She dismissed her auntie for a week and gave me a list of things to clean. Even though we were playing tug-of-war in the beginning, I truly did just want to get along with her, so I did the chores.

Her attempt at imitating the wicked stepmother backfired twofold. First, I made a much better cleaning lady than her aunt did and second, when Alberto found out (because I told him), he was so angry that he didn't speak to Gizel for days.

Gizel also liked to flaunt her expensive jewelry and tell me in which part of the world each piece was acquired. She spoke Italian to Alberto, excluding me from the conversation, but Alberto would respond in English.

I had my tricks too. I invited Alberto to the restaurants that he and Gizel frequented. I prepaid the tab because I knew that generosity meant brownie points. Soon, her acquaintances were calling her with the news about lunch and the bill (news travels fast on an island), along with every other minute detail. She brought it up to me as if to say, "You're not slick." To foil her, I would simply invite her to join us.

This hateful routine of tit for tat was getting old quickly. Enough was enough. I was exhausted from not working. I needed a job and to be out of the house and away from all the futile, subtle bickering. It was mentally disturbing. I was nineteen and feuding with a twenty-four-year-old woman over a man whom I didn't even like, let alone want. Gizel and I were living in the same house but I did not have to be there. Two stay-athome nemesis tarts couldn't be good for anyone. So I found a job.

Work was my respite. Alberto, of course, was against it. I didn't care. But he was stern. If it was money I needed, he could and would provide it, anything to keep me from being away from him. But like the hot wings at Palm Tree Way: Nothing in life was free; taking his money surely had its price.

Alberto tried continuously to hand me ten thousand dollars, but I refused. The last thing I wanted was to be indebted to the Mannino crime family. Not to mention that a jealous and territorial Mannino girlfriend already had me in her sights.

Alberto attempted several times to leave the money in my room after his morning grope sessions, which didn't stop when Gizel returned home. The money was always back in his possession by the day's end. I'd rather slave away at a low-paying, menial job than be paid for what he did to me.

My not accepting money would be the catalyst that sealed the deal on Alberto's infatuation and pushed him over the edge into true admiration. Floating around his delusional mind was the thought that I loved him, and it was not because of his money. Sometimes greater benefits are gained from leaving the money on the table. I just had to figure out what they were.

While Alberto was planning the rest of our lives together, Gizel was planning my ruin. She changed the locks when she took him on a weekend getaway to St. Bart's. Of course, she "forgot" to give me a key. I spent the nights on campus with Dawn and some of my old classmates. I had so much fun being away that even after their return and my key was given to me, I would stay there frequently, which of course Alberto hated, primarily because that meant no morning fondling but also because he wasn't in control of me when I wasn't in his house. He didn't know where I was or with whom I was spending my time.

An argument forced me to reveal my refuge. After that, he would call to check my whereabouts or show up in person, so I stopped going altogether. My world shrank; we both knew it was a calculated maneuver on his part, yet I did nothing to change things.

Alberto cooked for Gizel and me. We felt obligated to sit cordially, even if our geniality was phony. One night, I asked Alberto if I should pay rent. He was flabbergasted.

"Of course not, Savannah. You work hard. I should pay you."

"I just don't want to be a bother. You guys have been so kind to me."

"No, we like you here. You are no bother. Right, Gizel?" he asked.

Thank God it was rhetorical. He didn't wait for a reply; he just kept on spewing compliments. I know from her eyes that Gizel wanted to pull my spleen out with her pasta fork.

A week after that exchange, Gizel told me that I would have to pay her five hundred dollars a month. That same evening at dinner, I gave Alberto two hundred and fifty, swearing to pay the rest as soon as I could. Gizel was livid. Again, her game was sloppy. It had backfired. Alberto knew the request for payment was the evil workings of Gizel. Alberto cursed her in Italian, sending her flying from the table.

I played innocent as Alberto explained why Gizel was upset with me. Her story was that I was using them and she wanted to make sure that he knew what kind of person I really was. She accused me of having a boyfriend and said that I really didn't like Alberto. (Half of that was true.) Alberto assured me that he was on my side and that Gizel would have to learn to live with our situation. I reassured him that I did not have a boyfriend and that I worked so hard so as not to be a burden. He didn't even want me to explain. He knew she was crazy with jealousy but he simply did not care. Plus, even if there was truth behind her words, he was blindly in love and she was stupid for not seeing it.

My new employment sparked a streak of kindness in Gizel aimed solely at Alberto. She would occupy his time when I was at work. She would plan trips, lunch dates, and boat outings, things that he and I had done all summer. I didn't mind. She needed to concentrate on getting her man to (at least) like her again. It was wasted effort trying to break me, as all attempts proved.

The weeks turned into months. Gizel was neither smart nor cunning, but she had become the most vindictive person I had ever met. She had time and energy to waste on trying to make me dejected enough to pack up and move. But I refused to let her win.

My stubbornness could be an asset, but I still had no idea why I wouldn't abandon them. I wasn't happy, and I was destroying her mental stability and my own. The fact that I was there with no plan was beginning to infuriate me. I was leaving my fate up to chance and circumstance, and I was not taking control of my destiny.

Alberto was indifferent to Gizel's pleas, threats of leaving him, tantrums, and sobbing. He promised that I could stay as long as I wanted, and with our physical "relationship" intact, he had no reason to kick me out. I ignored my gut that was warning me to do the contrary, and I stayed.

I changed my schedule so that I worked part-time. That made Alberto happy and Gizel despondent. She moped about the house, not speaking to either of us but that didn't bother me. We rarely exchanged words anyhow. I think Alberto found it refreshing. He mistook her silence for acceptance and did nothing to challenge that theory. Nothing Gizel did worked to produce a favorable reaction. Even weeks of giving Alberto her "best girlfriend" act did nothing to persuade him to once again be fully and solely committed to her. He was in love with my demonstrative ways. At the same time, he was punishing her for her summer infidelity. The choice of accepting her newfound role did not cross her mind, nor did leaving. I felt sorry for her again.

The whole situation was heartbreaking. We were all involved in a game where everyone was bound to lose in one way or another.

At the end of August, I walked in on a massive squabble

that was taking place behind their closed bedroom door. I eavesdropped to see who would arise victorious. Gizel was shouting at the top of her lungs.

"If you don't love me anymore, then pay for me to have my own apartment!"

*Point for Gizel.*

"I met you at your mother's. Go to your mother's!"

That was futile on his part. Going to live with her mother in a roach-infested, cement shack was not an option.

*But why's her mama still residing in squalor? Why didn't Gizel move her into plusher surroundings with an extra bedroom for times like this?*

One of her Versace outfits would have paid the rent on that shit hole for one year. She was wrong for that.

*Point for Alberto.*

Then, just as I was about to leave them to it, a cold chill raced up my spine and I actually jerked.

"You are not my problem!" he exclaimed.

After years of taking care of her every need, years of making her accustomed to a high-class lifestyle, grooming her to be exactly what he wanted, occupying her youth, forcing dependency on her in a way that I had witnessed with my own mother, "You are not my problem?" He was wrong.

It was time for me to exercise plan B, which I came up with at that exact moment. I strolled into their bedroom, thinking of how to say what had to be said. Gizel stopped yelling, and Alberto stood to greet me, bright-eyed and bushy-tailed.

I realized how sick and tortured he made her feel. She looked away as she often did, so as not to witness his excitement for her archenemy.

"I'm leaving. I'm going to school back in Minnesota."

Gizel turned and watched as Alberto made no attempt to conceal his devastation. Her diffidence pissed me off.

*See, I told you she didn't love you, you silly old fool,* was what Gizel was probably thinking. I wished she had the strength to turn her thoughts into words, cuss his lame ass out, and turn the tables.

I had given her the weapon, but she still could not pull the trigger. She just stood there, hoping I'd say that I was leaving tomorrow so that she could have her man and life back. Just like that, she let Alberto off the hook, wiped the slate clean, and started all over, powerless once more.

Joe was wrong; Gizel's life was not amazing. I thought she was sad and lonely, devoid of identity and love. She'd be lost if she was ever set free. I knew I had to leave and set myself free while I still could.

Alberto professed his fondness for me and spoke as if Gizel did not exist. Emphatically, he tried to convince me to stay.

"Please, I beg you, Savannah, do not do this."

Moisture gathered in his wrinkled, red sockets. Doing *this* was the only way to win.

Gizel and I stared at each other while Alberto had his little outburst of emotion. We understood that I had ceded the grand prize of Alberto, but she would never know why or care. She also did not know that Alberto would eventually take all his frustrations out on her. He would blame her for his loss and depression. Conditioned like an abused wife, she too would stay and take it like the battered woman she was. She was too broken to see that winning him was not a victory but a sentence to life imprisonment. Gizel thanked me with her eyes and scurried away to book my flight, my going-away gift—Gizel and Alberto together, again.

# five

I flew home to the welcoming hearts of my family and loving arms of my mother. She had been worried about her daughter who had dropped out of school to live a life of ignorance and bliss. The details of what I had been doing were narrowed down to "working." I sent my money home. Questions were asked, but the answer was always some derivative of the word *work*.

My mother knew that I was indeed an employment magnet and finally accepted things at that. As I said before, my family wasn't the confrontational, inquisitive type. They were the trusting, complacent sort. My mother was enamored with the idea of me being back home and even more excited that I would enroll in school; it was more important than learning the truth about what I'd been up to. Some things were better left unsaid.

After I paid the first and last months' rent for my off-campus apartment at St. Cloud State University and the tuition, then bought books, groceries, and winter clothes, I was nearly back to being broke. In hindsight, I should have seriously considered taking Alberto's ten thousand dollars.

In need of money, I went out in Minneapolis the weekend before classes began and hooked up with my old flame, drug dealing Thomas. We met at the local place to be. I walked in glamorous and matured from my stint away. I knew what I had come for.

Thomas had become a hardened street criminal. He knew nothing else. Even though half our hood and his brother were locked up, that wasn't a deterrent to keep him from hustling; in fact, he took advantage and his status on the drug totem pole was raised. He was the star addicted to the limelight. We sat at the bar reminiscing. He brought up the lady who had sold her lamps. He told me that I made him question his morals and about his nightmares starring that woman. He confessed that he never sold drugs to end-users again. I listened intently as he detailed his life as a drug dealer.

Giving my audience what they needed came as second nature. Whether it was a convincing tantrum, emotional cries, giddy small talk, or square innocence, I was capable of all of it. After Thomas purged himself, it was my turn. Thomas respected me. I was innocent in his eyes and incapable of hustling, so it was easy to convince him that the small bills from his drug sales should be set aside for charity.

Thomas' petty cash was bequeathed to the new "Girl in College Fund." Those small bills amounted to six hundred dollars or more a week. Thomas "flossed" (showed off) at clubs or other social events with the tens and twenties. The fifties and hundreds were for "stacking" (hiding money from any accountable, taxable situation). It was rumored that he stacked hundreds of thousands of dollars each month.

Thomas and I hung out when we could, but he was a man of the streets. He didn't want or need me for sex. He wanted me to stay sweet and become something great. He was aiding me in my education, and that made him proud of at least one thing that he was doing. I adored him for that.

I found it a tad disturbing how quickly and seamlessly I merged from one life to another—Alberto to Thomas to college to life at St. Cloud State. But that ability made it possible for me to live life like a chameleon, morphing and altering myself to fit my surroundings.

I hooked up with the boy I had been writing during my first year in college, Brian, my "other man." He knew that I was coming. Brian and I were an instant couple, brought together by lusty letters of unadulterated, animalistic sex. We experimented with every form of copulation imaginable. He even went down on me whilst I was menstruating. Nasty was his name, and I loved it. Fucking three times a day was normal. It was a wonder that I got anything accomplished and didn't develop a severe case of bowed legs. My sexual ceiling was raised to new heights because of Brian, and I was officially uninhibited.

St. Cloud was known as the party school. Going out drinking was just as common as going to class. There were more bars in a three-block radius than anywhere else in the state. It was the norm to bounce from bar to bar meeting friends or strangers to party the night away. I was new to their scene but drinking and partying didn't require me to know a soul.

After hours of vodka, shots of tequila, and flirting, I allowed three newly acquired drinking buddies to walk me home. We stumbled down a dimly lit back street. I fell and one of the guys picked me up, then kissed me. It was good. I felt my arm being pulled, and then I was being kissed by the next boy and then again by the third. I blurted in slurred words that number one had won, and I laughed hysterically as we continued toward my apartment. The smell of cologne mixed in the night air with the stench of liquor and my own barbecue breath from the wings we had consumed earlier. I don't recall taking my keys out and opening my door; one of them must have done that. I was laughing and kissing the first guy, "The Winner."

The winner and I were nearly naked when his friends came into the bedroom. I asked them to leave while they unzipped their pants. I got very upset, started cussing them out and was quickly put in my place—my place as a chick that was going to get gang-raped by her new drinking buddies. Before I even knew what was happening, I was lying face down in my own blood while they had their way. I cried and begged them to stop. I was punched in the face. I could only lie there, head throbbing, tasting blood, snot, and tears while being raped by guys whom I did not know and who were not wearing condoms.

The next day, hung over, swollen, and pillaged, I drug myself from the sticky and bloodied sheets. I ran a tub full of scalding water and removed the last article of clothing that still remained on my body—the bloody bra—tossing it into the trashcan. I wanted to set fire to it until all that remained was a small pile of ash.

The bath water was too hot. I winced but continued the plunge. My skin instantly turned red. I rested my head on the rear edge of the tub and froze in that one position from the pain, both physical and psychological. The teardrops that fell disturbed the otherwise calm, steamy water. As one ripple faded away, another took its place. I studied the water.

I closed my eyes, knowing I could not blink anything away.

Setting fire to the bra, to everything, crossed my mind. But how could I burn out the horrendously painful images, my achy body, and my crushed spirit. How could I set ablaze my damaged psyche? I thought about a raging flame turning it all to ash, as I remained submerged and still until the water was ice cold and I was shivering.

The same scene repeated for three days. Day four, I ate stale bread with peanut butter and showered obsessively, trying to wash away my guilt for the role I played in my own assault. I was a victim of bad choices, and my shame was only outweighed by my loneliness. I had no one to hug. The tears fell, dawn to dusk, from the memories of not only the recent event, but from all the bad memories that had accumulated in my short nineteen years on earth.

The assault gave me a reason to abruptly leave St. Cloud. I decided that I would return to Beautiful Isla.

I protected my mother from the truth, just as I had done many years before. I told her jealous girls had jumped me. My mother accepted my answer, but I believed she knew instinctively that this wasn't true. How can a mother shield her baby from all the evils in the world? And if she didn't, what would she think of

111

herself? How could a child tell her mother of the evils that had befallen her? I didn't know, but I knew not to tell her. The truth would have hurt her heart forever and have made it twice as hard for her to allow me to venture out again into the big, bad world.

My decision to vacate school, yet again, upset her, but she knew that I was searching for my place in life. She knew that I would not be happy cooped up or nailed down, and that if faraway places beckoned, I should answer. She let me learn and explore for myself. It had to be hard to let her only daughter go.

Alberto was simply the key to unlocking a unique and thrilling lifestyle. He, without hesitation, sent me a plane ticket when I contacted him. He had professed his love over and over in pages of heartfelt letters since I left, and I hadn't replied to one of them. I could not for the life of me appreciate Alberto's feelings. I didn't know how deep they were, and even if I had, I surely would never have been able to reciprocate. I was young, unwilling, and unable to mentally grasp the idea of falling in love with someone my grandfather's age. And why would I want to? It was totally out of the question. So my return to the island was probably another bad choice, but I was restless, in need of warm weather, and quite frankly, bored. School and my life were slow and monotonous; even sex with Brian had become predictable. The drudgery of another day, topped with the harsh event, revealed an unnerving need to leave it all behind as if none of it had ever happened.

My dear friend, Dawn, and Alberto were the only ones I told about the assault. I never felt a need to dwell on it; a do-over was not possible. Bad things happened. I was guilty of leaving others to control my situation. I gave them a green light. No means no, but when you are too drunk to make healthy decisions, whose fault was it that the light turned yellow in the midst of cruising through and you got caught fighting the moving violation?

To my surprise, Alberto was not at the airport, perched and

waiting. I had to take a cab to his house. The fare would be fifty dollars. I only had forty. I hoped he was home. He was, and he took care of the cab and carried my bags to the guest room, which was located next to his/theirs. It was clear; the choice was not up to me.

Alberto was playing his cards differently. He was much cooler, more carefree, less accommodating. It gave me the feeling that he was less in love and less willing to put up with my bullshit. I was vulnerable and felt obligated to obey him. Suddenly, I was walking on thin ice. I was made to feel appreciative and humbled by two actions; his not picking me up when I arrived and his sending Gizel away. I felt the power shift. I was coming to him because I felt that had nowhere else to turn, but would he use that to his advantage? Was he cunning enough to manipulate the situation to his sole benefit? I would have to figure out very soon if this was a game I was even capable of playing anymore. I had counted on his undying affection and if it wasn't there, then what?

The few months of living in the States showed in my loss of weight, brittle hair, pale and sun-deprived skin, and the bruises that hadn't completely disappeared. Alberto expressed concern by forcing me to see Dr. Sloan, a psychologist.

Dr. Sloan was a lumbering, gentle giant who spoke softly in a bit of a monotone. I didn't like that. It felt passive and condescending. Her office was clean, charming, and decorated in comforting earth tones. I sat in the plush leather chair next to her, and I felt my unease heighten, regardless of the color schemes. She put me off somehow, and it soon became clear why.

"So, Savannah, how are you today?" she asked as she cupped her hands over mine. "Fine. Thanks," I replied, removing my hands from underneath hers. "Is there anything you want to talk about? Alberto cares a lot about you and wants to make sure you're doing okay after what happened."

*Ah. So that's it.*

She hadn't even let me answer the question before bringing up Alberto. And the fact that she already knew what had happened made me worry. I followed my instincts and steered clear of divulging any details about anything that had to do with me. She wasn't out to help me; she was trying to help Alberto.

"I'm good, Doc. Just keeping things where they belong, in the past. No need for a recall. Bad things happen. Thanks for your time."

I got up and walked out. In that one ten-minute session, I knew that the doctor of mental affairs could not be trusted and my innermost secrets were not safe. She was a good friend of Alberto's and probably a paid informant.

Alberto would not be privy to the inside scoop. I think it bothered him.

The days went by, and I began to look and feel human again. The sleep and delicious meals worked. The speedboat was calling my name.

After we spent a magical day zipping around on the ocean, Alberto came into my room. He stood in the darkness, listening and waiting, not knowing whether or not I was awake. I kept my inhaling and exhaling steady, hoping to convince him of my deep slumber.

I laid there thinking of an article I read in one of my college psychology journals. It was about the 're-victimization' of victims of sexual abuse. Basically, a clinical social worker said, "Once you've been the victim of sexual abuse, potential perpetrators can smell it on you." In other words, they seek you out, always ready to pounce and always waiting for the day you get too comfortable. I was too comfortable. I felt him closing in.

Suddenly, Alberto pounced in a full on attack. He ripped away the blanket and smothered my body with his. My fighting instinct awoke. I kicked him off of me and ran across the slippery marble floor in socks and a nightgown to the kitchen to look for a very large, sharp object. I screamed repeatedly as he kept inching toward me. Instead of a knife, I grabbed the phone and dialed 9-1-1.

When he tried to take the phone, it fell to the floor. I could hear the operator.

Time slowed. It was as if I were underwater; sound echoed and the weight of the water made it hard to move.

I shouted, "Help! Help!"

The words blurted out, but I didn't feel as though they made any sense and I didn't know if the operator heard me. I saw every detail of his spindly, hairy, naked body as he closed in. I just wanted him to go away.

My own crying and ear-piercing howls brought the moment to clarity as if I had quickly surfaced; still, I couldn't decipher what he was saying. He was creeping closer, and again, I freaked out.

I grabbed a knife from its place in the wooden block and stabbed toward him in an attempt to back him up rather than to cut him. I needed to get to the security of the bathroom and lock the door behind me. He was blocking my path.

His words got louder. Suddenly, things became clear, as if I had shaken the water from my ears. Was he pleading with me? I tried to listen, but I was too loud. I started to calm down.

"I am so sorry, Savannah. Please put down the knife," he was saying.

When the police arrived, I had calmed down entirely, but my hands still clutched the knife so hard that my knuckles were beet red. I had snapped. My mind, body, and soul were exhausted. I wanted to sleep for twenty-four hours. But first things first, and I had to deal with the cops and Alberto.

As Alberto stood at the door in his smoking robe explaining the "misunderstanding" to two pompous police officers, I felt insignificant. The cops were clearly on his side. I knew that if it were truly an emergency, they wouldn't and couldn't help me anyways. They knew who and what he was. They left without taking notes or even saying, "Fuck off," to the victim who had solicited their aid. I hoped for their consciences nothing happened to me. I prayed the same for myself.

Instead of locking myself in the bathroom and sleeping in the tub, I curled up on the couch with my head in Alberto's lap, still holding the knife.

To accept this picture as normal would be the acceptance of insanity and I knew it. Things were unraveling very quickly and I had no control. But I still asked myself silly questions:

*What is with him and beautiful days spent on the water? Didn't my recent ordeal affect him enough to keep his hands off me? What the hell is wrong with me? His penis should be chopped into sections and strewn about his own living room. Why am I resting comfortably upon it?*

I let out a simple sigh—too many questions and too few answers. I was a repeat victim and he a repeat offender, both lost on what to do now.

Gizel returned from her mother's house to find me there, again. My queenship was revoked and I was demoted to princess. I was sent down to the maid's quarters to accommodate Alberto, so that he could resume his pattern of fucking Gizel and having "near" fornication with me. All was right in the bizarre world of the Manninos.

We spent the holidays like a cozy family. That would be the first and only Christmas that I ever spent away from my mom. I was miserable. Mikey and my mother sent me a package of wrapped presents that affected me the way a letter would an inmate on mail day. I treasured each gift and knew they were the kind I'd keep for years.

The Christmas season crept by lethargically. I couldn't wait to begin a fresh start by hurling the past year into history.

Our estranged threesome played host to a New Year's Eve bash with over one hundred invited choice guests. The house and patio looked amazing with well-placed white candles to illuminate the festive décor. A chef was even flown in from Italy to prepare the food and a disc jockey hired to spin dance music. Gizel bought a ball gown that reminded me of something Queen Elizabeth would sport. It was beautifully constructed with beads and embroidery so tasteful that the dress looked like it cost a small fortune. I almost forgot that it did—three thousand dollars.

I didn't accept the gown Alberto chose for me. My taste in clothing was far less extravagant, even meretricious, but I worked all four ounces of the $24.99 Lycra material. Gizel couldn't move in all her gorgeous layers of raw silk and had to take the position of stiff socialite, while I, on the other hand, dropped it like it was hot until 11:50 PM, at which time I quietly disappeared to my room.

I was a great believer that where you were and who you were with at the stroke of midnight provided insight into the year at hand. I didn't wish to taint the upcoming year by being in the presence of Gizel's jealous glare or Leonardo Peccati and his cronies. So I sat on my bed listening to the ocean out shout the partiers upstairs. I quietly waited for the precious moment to pass.

My plan was foiled when Alberto, at 11:59 and a half, walked in with two glasses of champagne. I made room on my bed. We raised our glasses, took a few swallows, and counted down five, four, three, two, one …

"Happy New Year!"

That was the first and only time Alberto and I ever kissed. There was no hesitation or feeling of disgust on my part. It seemed like the natural thing to do. It was so passionate and effortless that I, for a split second, forgot who he and where I was. Thankfully, Gizel was standing in the doorway to remind me.

My once hopeful New Year was ill-fated and doomed.

The very next morning and start of my new year, I was throwing up, only not from the exorbitant amount of libations. As if my life wasn't already in disarray...

I was pregnant.

Devastated, miserable, and probably more depressed than anyone could have imagined, I still had no one to hug.

I had successfully put the horrid memory of the rape from my mind, but like a broken dam, it came flooding back. The whole ordeal, which I had blocked out, was in the forefront of my thoughts, in full color, relentless. How could I handle dealing with an even worse residual effect from the crime than the fucking memories of it?

I was a child myself, not remotely ready for the responsibility of raising one. It hadn't crossed my mind to abort on the grounds of not knowing who the father was, but I wanted to primarily on the grounds of the welfare of the baby and my inability to take care of myself, let alone someone else. I felt the only route was abortion. My heart ached with excruciating pain from what I believed to be the best decision.

Alberto was the first to learn of my circumstances and of my subsequent choice. He quickly organized the island's finest doctor for the abortion. Gizel was again shipped off to her mother's.

Empathy and compassion like I had never seen came pouring from Alberto's new persona. The day before the procedure, I was ill. He brought home all of my favorite foods.

He held cold compresses to my forehead and tenderly stroked my hair while I rested on the couch. I had mentally muted my favorite programming, BET's Video Soul, and realized that Alberto was suffering through it. I was nervous. What was the catch? He hated music videos.

On the day of reckoning, Dawn was by my side to comfort me. As I lay on the bed looking up at the harsh institutional lighting, waiting for the low-dose sedative to kick in, listened to my quietly eked out prayer and cried with me.

"Dear God, I'm so sorry. This was not in my plans. I love life. But this baby's life belongs to you. Please watch over... him..." I knew in my heart it was a boy. "Until I get to heaven."

Tears rolled from my eyes, into my ears, and off the sides of my face, making sounds when they hit the thin paper pillowcase under my head.

I closed my eyes and thought maybe God would take me too. When I opened them again, I was without child. I lay in the clinic bed for hours after, not wanting to move or to speak to anyone. The staff tried to physically remove me. I was weak, but fought them back. I needed just a little more time in the place where I killed my baby boy.

"It's over, Savannah. We have to go now."

Dawn carried me to her car, and I cried for two hours, drenching her clothes.

I returned from the clinic, and Alberto was there once again to nurse me back to health. Something was different. I'm not sure if it was the New Year's kiss or my complete dependence on him, but he was changed and I began to relax. All suspicions of his strange behavior were put out of my mind. I actually enjoyed his caress and let myself unwind under his gentle, sincere touch. He was illuminated under a less critical light because of his genuine compassion toward me. Our actions became reciprocal, all from one tragic event.

*Yes, he's been stellar in caretaking; we had watched movies, went on dates, he had rubbed my back, and cooked my meals. But hadn't he also sent the ticket, tried to buy me with a wad of cash, just playing savior? ... All from one tragic event?* My apprehension returned.

*Had he planned the rape? Did he manipulate my world so as to force me to come running back to him? Could his felonious arm reach as far as St. Cloud State in rural Minnesota?*

The stories of Mafia influences were true. I saw how everyone tiptoed around Alberto, how they acceded to his every inclination. I was aware of the things money could buy, including private detectives in South America, psychiatrists, and clandestine abortion doctors. He had notorious wealth and an ignominious repute that made people respect and fear him. He was without boundaries and ungovernable, making it easily possible for him to orchestrate a crime against me.

But even while I questioned his involvement, I felt I owed him kindness.

*Am I going insane, becoming one of life's casualties?*

Maybe me going crazy was also a part of his deranged plan. But still, he could not have prophesized a pregnancy.

I fell asleep curled up on my bed, wrapped in Alberto's arms, wondering where the rollercoaster was headed.

Something had changed with Gizel as well. I had pushed her to the point of no return. She finally got one hundred percent pissed off and desperate, a dreadful combination. Her new plan was to give Alberto a reason to kick me out. She was thinking so deceptively that the suggestions had to be emanating from a much wiser source.

It turned out I was right. One of the Italian ladies from the club that night, one of the group who had been drinking frozen fruity drinks, was her trusted advisor. Her new strategist would try to help Gizel win the gold.

My body healed, and over the next few months, so did my mind. With the ordeal tucked squarely behind me, I focused on securing work and enjoying the islands. I left my woes behind the doors of the Mannino household every time I walked out.

I rented a sad-looking car. That oozing pustule of an automobile, and holding down a day job at a trendy ice cream parlor and an evening hostess gig at a fine French restaurant, gave me freedom. I started living life outside of the Mannino household again, at least when the stupid car started.

I found the card of the scuba instructor who gave Dawn and I the bumpy ride into town. He was elated that I had finally called. I smashed any hope of a love affair by being completely honest about my involvement with a demented psychopath. He reluctantly denied his attraction but remained committed to seeing that I received scuba-diving certification.

The first time out diving, I panicked. The process that my brain went through to convince itself that it was okay to breathe underwater was a huge ordeal. Actual breathing underwater was cause for me to hyperventilate. I went into complete panic mode; my life flashed before my eyes and all instruction flew from my memory. Water filled my mask, which in my state, I had knocked lopsided. I was trying to hold my breath to no avail. I was fighting for my life just feet below the surface.

My instructor must have been used to first-time idiots and took control. With one grab to the back of my neck, he pulled me to the surface, saving my life. I calmed down and regained a halfway decent breathing pattern. We stayed on top of the ocean bobbing like buoys.

"Are you ready to try again?" he asked.

The dagger look I gave him should have warned him of my lack of interest in continuing.

*This sadist is nuts!*

He was also persistent.

I did try again. After a few more attempts, I was addicted.

I learned to work the equipment, trusted my guide, and let go. Even after the sun had dipped below the horizon and the ocean was nearly black, I didn't want to come to the surface. I wanted the ocean to lull me into a deep sleep and carry me away into its subterranean vastness.

Diving calmed my spirit. The unease of day-to-day living in a crazy house with no sure future was instantly erased and replaced with physical sensations of the exotic underworld. The ocean hugged me. It made me forget about the recent pregnancy resulting from a brutal rape and the subsequent abortion; it made me forget that I was a concubine for an Italian mobster, whose main squeeze was probably plotting my death by way of adding arsenic poisoning to the cannoli or worse. It made me forget that I was a clueless and wayward nineteen-year-old with no goals. The warm, coddling ocean and scenery like no other place on dry earth made me almost forget that I had dinner plans with a new hopeful candidate.

*Don*

I came to know of Mr. Donald P. Keller through a monopolizing and extremely shrewd Arabian businessman named Yasir. Yasir owned the majority of the island's novelty shops. He was wealthy many times over but cheap as penny candy. Wanting to get on the good side of Don, a richer and worldlier individual, envisioning big business deals in his future, he needed a bargaining chip—payola, so to speak. I was it. Don had owned the island's communication system before selling it to EF Hutton. He had one of the nicest houses on the island and took private planes down to bask his pale ass in the therapeutic sun as often as he could.

Yasir arranged for me to go to dinner with Don. I felt prostituted and decided that it was an awful feeling. Who was he to arrange a dinner for me? Why didn't I protest the whole idea? Why did I accept, if the whole setup was insulting?

My car stalled, and my scuba instructor dropped me off at Mr. Keller's lavish doorstep. I was early and looked like something the cat had dragged in. My hair was a massive curly mess. My skin, not yet re-plumped, was still a bit pruney and ashy from being submerged in salt water all day, and my bikini top and short shorts had "silly" written all over them.

The good Mr. Keller's expression, words, and thoughts could not have been less in synch. He looked entirely taken aback by the wild boar poised in front of him.

"It's so nice to finally meet you," he said while likely thinking, *Why the heck did I make reservations at Chez Cruso? I can't take this chick anywhere!*

He was pleasant and gracious when I explained my extenuating circumstances and asked to use his restroom. I pulled out a sexy black dress and a pair of pumps from my beach bag. I took a shower, pulled my hair into a nice neat bun, dolled up my face and forty-five minutes later, I emerged looking like a million bucks. His expression said it all.

He, on the other hand, looked more like hot shit (literally) with an obvious toupee. I could overlook the fake hair, sagging face, and even saggier ass if he was the one to spring me from Cell Block M.

I had recently been hired at Chez Cruso as a hostess and was still in training. It was my night off. We were greeted by my manager and shown to the best table located near an open window overlooking the ocean. I hadn't gotten a chance to view any of the food yet and was excited about eating it. The Chez Cruso owner was an eccentric but talented restaurateur. It was known that he had the best of the best in food and beverages on the island. It was the most expensive and elegant dining establishment we had.

The crisp white tablecloth and stiff white napkins folded into the shape of a swan were new to me, as were the plethora of silverware and numerous wine glasses. I was perplexed by all of the formality coming from our waiter.

"Would you like an aperitif?"

*What is a frickin' aperitif?*

"No. Thank you," I answered.

It was a different feeling working in such a fine place from being its patron. My excitement was replaced with worry and a lack of confidence. I wasn't even sure of my ability to eat as I scanned the menu of unpronounceable and unknown words. Don took control as I sat extra upright, smiling and attempting not to look out of place.

The spotlight lit the shore and the candlelight hit my face, accenting my high cheekbones and long eyelashes. Don commented on my beauty for the third time since my transformation occurred in his bathroom.

I was nineteen. Don was nearly sixty. Of course I would be overwhelmingly attractive to him. He had hit the jackpot. I just didn't know that that was how he was feeling at the time. I was more concerned about how I could impress, and then use, him. There was something to that saying, "With age comes wisdom," because the fact that I had shown up was impressive enough for him.

We connected immediately. His youthful outlook on life, interesting tales of business ventures, and blunt way of communicating made things relaxed. He explained the menu with the same simple ease.

I found a new passion; I wanted to taste food from every culture, experience unfamiliar vegetables, and dine in restaurants on yummy morsels that I couldn't pronounce. My mind was ready; my taste buds tuned to adventure, and then the appetizer of escargots arrived.

Those little bastards were ugly as hell. I wasn't so sure after viewing their appearance that my mind, or my mouth, was ready for snails. Couldn't I be eased in, with perhaps veal? Don reassured me, as he pushed one into his mouth, that I would forever remember the first time I tried and fell in love with escargots. And so I did.

I was dumbfounded at how different French food was from Italian. Weren't the countries next door to each other?

When I had left home, the most exotic food I had ever eaten was boiled pig's feet. I could count the number of times my family had dined out on one hand, and even then, it was worlds away from star-rated places. My mother occasionally fried smelt; that, and my trip to Red Lobster with Antonio, was the extent of my seafood knowledge. So to me, everything was a mystery, even un-fried shrimp. Food took on a whole different meaning; I suddenly catapulted from nourishing and filling meals consumed because I needed to live to a menu of pure existential enjoyment.

*Yes. The food is exquisite, Savannah, but why are you here?*

If any of Alberto's friends (or worse, Gizel's friends) saw us, it would be a matter of seconds before Alberto would burst through the restaurant doors, snatch me from the table, and whisk me off through the open window to his faraway fortress to be strictly guarded under twenty-four hour surveillance by heavily armed personnel, but not before putting a bullet between the eyes of Donald P. Keller.

I was not sure when things had gotten so bad in my head. I was paranoid in my thoughts and glanced unintentionally towards the door far too often. Don inquired about my nervousness. I didn't know why, but I told him half the story. I left Gizel out. To add her to the anecdote would just make me angry and I would lose the empathy coming from my very concerned admirer.

Then, I found the answer to my question as to why I was having dinner with Don. Just like that, he too asked the question, "What can I do for you?" He went from admirer to savior in six words.

My way of thinking strategically was surprising even to me. I had grown used to using people for what they could offer in my times of need. It worked. I wondered if other people were so savvy; life was a seemingly easy breeze. Why had so many people who I had known made life seem so difficult to navigate? The hard part was finding someone with means; after that, it was all downhill. Don had means, and a plan was developing on the spot.

We finished up our meal and my escape from Alberto, Gizel, and all things island was plotted over crème brûlée, which beat out tiramisu as my new favorite dessert. He was more into it than I was. Every detail was worked out, down to scheduling a taxicab to take me from his house to the airport. I had to make my way from Alberto's to Don's with my bags and my rental car, which I would store at his home.

In case of any hiccups, I suggested we should travel separately to the airport and that he should wait for me at the gate. Those words made him unsure of my willingness to actually go through with the plan. I assured him that if he bought the ticket, I would be at that gate. The flight would depart in four days.

That was our first date.


Back on the home front, the situation had deteriorated even more. Alberto was no longer the kind caretaker of my person. Maybe my attitude of disgust returned all too quickly for his taste. My misery was tenfold. Not only was I dealing with Gizel, but also Alberto was becoming ridiculously controlling and more sexual, but with a tinge of negativity. It was no longer as simple as him coming to fondle me and rubbing his penis around my thigh; he began kissing my neck and sucking my nipples while pushing his penis against my pelvic bone. I was still stiff as a board with my head turned away and my mind in another place. His whole demeanor suggested that he no longer found joy in the molesting. String by string, he was unraveling. I feared another sexual attack in the making.

The following night, Chez Cruso was once again my place of employment, fairy tale over. My boss was happy that I had come in and tried the food. He was probably more excited because my date spent approximately five hundred dollars on the feast. Alberto showed up at Chez Cruso to drive me home. He and the owner, for reasons mysterious to me, hated one another's guts, so at least my secret date was safe.

About halfway home, Alberto had a burning urge to finger me. He fumbled with my panties, nervously and urgently pushing my thighs apart like each of his fingers had perverted minds of their own. His pointer found its target, dove in, and squirmed around. I sat looking out of the window at the white lines whizzing by and pretended that nothing was happening.

*Why do I let him do these things?*

I had evidently become numb to the events in that debauched symbiotic relationship. I told myself that it wasn't that bad, but I felt dirty, used, and far from being in control. The tides had turned. Alberto had gained ground. My instinct to accept an arranged date with Don proved that I was aware I was losing ground, just as I had known with Paco and accepted a lunch date with Alberto; I was always plotting the next phases of a peripatetic lifestyle. Our very lengthy cat and mouse game was nearing its end. Either he would break me and force me to submit to his will or I would have to get the hell out. There was no middle ground.

I played peek-a-boo with the ocean as we passed the waterfront buildings.

Even with all the contemplation, my most prominent thought was, *I hope his fuckin' fingers are clean.*

# six

Don and I were scheduled to leave for Europe in three days.

Days on an island, while counting the seconds to a new life, seemed like an eternity. I tried to act as normally as possible so as not to alert Alberto of my intentions. I got my car fixed. I still went to work and behaved as I would normally have. I even planned a boat outing for a week in advance. I did it all in the event Don changed his mind about taking me, or I changed my mind about leaving with him (after all, I was young and plans could change at a moment's notice).

At our fairly customary breakfast, Gizel, who had been giving me the silent treatment, finally spoke to me.

"Savannah, would you like to do some shopping, maybe run some girly errands?"

I looked at Alberto; his smile read, *Gizel is finally coming around.* He seemed proud of her progress. His naïveté killed me.

"Okay," I said and smiled at Alberto, confirming to him that I too was willing to play nice.

Gizel went shopping. She bought thousands of dollars of tacky, brand name clothes as I trailed behind her, acting the part of her lowly servant. It was a game I played unbeknownst to her. I had to let her think that she was abusing me so that when I made my move, it would hurt twice as much. Hadn't she caught on? It had worked exactly like that so many times before.

We went from expensive boutique to expensive boutique. She needed tons of bags to make me feel deprived and envious. Her friend (and partner in scheming my downfall) suddenly appeared. They had some amusement in subtly taunting me, acrimoniously asking questions.

"What did you buy?" Gizel's friend asked. But before I could respond, she continued the inquisition. "Aren't you a shopper?

All real women love shopping. Is that a polyester dress you're wearing?" The questions were followed by their giggles.

The Italian-wifey chick was so exquisite that I ignored most of the digs. I was truly in awe of the details of her wardrobe and person—nails, feet, both perfect. Hair, wow! Makeup, flawless! Her shoes had not one scratch! Her slacks, nary a wrinkle! She smelled scrumptious and moved fluidly. She looked as if the 85-degree weather had no detrimental effect on her clothing or armpits. I put her age at about fifty or so, but she looked thirty-ish—youthful and vibrant. Everything about this woman was pure perfection. Even the Versace-clad Gizel was banal in comparison. They mindlessly followed me into my favorite store.

Even though the Italian woman was snide, I complimented her. It couldn't be helped. She deserved it. I wanted to be like her: polished, graceful, and perfect. Her wealth was reflected in more than a name-brand handbag. She was born into it, an aristocrat. I wondered if *it* could be learned. Gizel was not a hopeful example.

"You are beautiful," I said with all sincerity.

My flattering remark tailspun her into another dimension, throwing Gizel off balance. There was nothing for Gizel to do but watch her comrade spin away. Until those words left my mouth, she was ready to break me down, humiliate me, and question my relationship with Alberto, my morals, and my character, until I finally tapped out.

My admiration brought her back to her place as a regal and principled woman of a higher class of human being who would no longer involve herself in the petty dealings of two dimwitted girls. The realization hit. It was not my intention; it just worked out. The Italian empress was much too good for Gizel's paltry bullshit.

As I flipped through a sale rack, Gizel desperately tried to continue their daunting game, grasping, hoping to spark the once-burning revenge flame, but it was all for naught. Gizel could only be heard like background noise, but neither I, nor the empress, paid attention. The admiration had been reciprocated.

I spotted the ideal dress and strolled to the counter, sandwiched by the tag team gone sour. I pulled out a gob of cash,ten thousand dollars to be exact. It was the same cash Gizel's man (and mine) had bestowed upon me earlier that morning when he had come to gratify himself.

I peeled off a one-hundred-dollar bill and waited for the three twenties and change that I would get back from my inexpensive purchase. The saleslady slowly bagged the cheap,black Lycra mini tank dress with the sides cut out and the pair of neon-pink clip-on hoop earrings. I stuffed the money back into my jean purse and turned away from the catty and thoroughly stunned duo, then I exited the store.

*Fuck you both.*

Gizel got home and toted two trips worth of junk from her car. She arrived before me and had to explain to Alberto why we weren't together. I stepped out of the cab and walked through the door moments after her lies were told with my single little bag. I handed him his money and thanked him while dangling my purchase. Gizel almost cried. I'm not sure why. Maybe, it was the fact that she had spent so much on crap to make me mad and it had backfired, or that Alberto had given me gobs of money or that my sexy black dress may eventually be worn for her man or all of the above…or simply because I had won, again.

Then, two nights later, I came home from my job at Chez Cruso around 11:00 PM to find a note taped to my bedroom door.

*Please remove your things from our home and leave immediately, Alberto.*

I was shocked. Had Gizel done that or had he really wanted me out? It was clearly his signature. I didn't care either way.

I went to pack my belongings. The timing couldn't have been better because the very next day, Don was leaving for Europe. Until that note, I hadn't fully committed to the fact that I was really leaving with a complete stranger with whom I had had only one date. I wanted to indulge my sense of curiosity, but I was scared both of leaving and staying. My decision would have been spontaneous, going in either direction, until that note. That one line gave me the strength and extra push that I needed. I'd be damned if I would not be on that flight. The next morning, I would abandon the psych ward at Hospital Hellhole.

The ocean smiled at my decision by way of soft waves slapping against the shore. I smiled back.

Alberto crept into my room about 6:00 AM, earlier than normal.

I was startled.

*Does he know of my plan? Is he coming to kill me? Why is he here? Isn't he upset and angry with me for some odd reason? Doesn't he want me gone?*

Apparently, he had changed his mind. He came to beg me not to leave. What in the world was going on?

"You and Gizel don't really want me here. I'll be fine," I said with a combination of sadness and bitterness.

"Savannah, you must stay. I was so upset. You have to understand, I didn't want to tell you to go."

"I know. So you put a note on my door."

"No. I mean I did not want you to leave. I *do* not… Savannah, I love you. But I am a jealous man. Forgive me."

*Uh-oh! What did he do? What should I forgive him for? Why is he jealous? I haven't spoken to Don. Is Don still alive or swimming with the fishes?*

"Jealous of what? Work? That's all I do."

He placed some very nice panties and earrings on my bed.

"These are for me?" I asked as I looked at the items.

"These are yours." He corrected himself, "Are they yours?"

"No."

"But I found them in your car!" He was almost yelling.

"And?"

"They were in *your* car. You are the one to tell me *and*!"

"*And* I don't wear Christian Dior underwear, nor a size medium, nor do I have holes in my ears to wear these kinds of earrings."

He took in my answer, turning crimson. He knew that I was not lying, so my answer elated him.

"I'm still going to leave."

*Oops! Deflated.*

"I'm not welcome. Gizel hates me and… and you don't trust me." My words cut like a dagger through his heart. It was over… but it wasn't that simple.

Alberto stormed upstairs.

I considered the situation. A better question was how had he come across underwear that was obviously planted in my car? Gizel had to know he was sticking his nose in my belongings.

*My God! She's evolving!*

She was even more devious than I had given her credit for. She was exploiting his weakness.

*All points go to Gizel!*

Except I was much too smart to leave evidence of any wrongdoing lying around or hidden anywhere on the compound. I had known he looked through drawers and such because he was an amateur at sleuthing (a trade I had mastered), but my car? Alberto had hit a new low.

Alberto was obsessed and his obsession took him to a mind-set that I hoped to God I would never venture near. He was looking for any and all incriminating evidence so that I, like Gizel, would feel beholden, guilty, remorseful, and trapped. He would hang "it" over my head, persecute and punish, until his request for sex and love was satisfied—an insecure, jealous, and controlling man indeed.

I had spent many months trying to figure out this strange life. The answer was clear. I needed to leave. What was stopping me from just picking up my bags and walking out?

Suddenly ...

BAM!

Alberto pounded my door. It opened so forcefully that it dented the back wall. I jumped, not knowing what was happening. He flung Gizel into a corner chair like a rag doll. He must have hit her very hard because her left eye had already begun to swell.

"You put those things in Savannah's car!"

He accused her of the exact crime that she unquestionably had perpetrated and told her to pack her things and leave. But she did not state the obvious—*Why were you searching Savannah's car?*—and neither did I. We could not reverse the accusations, putting him on the defense. We knew our place and we feared his anger, and that was the reason I couldn't simply walk away.

"This is Savannah's house now! You will leave immediately!"

*My house? God, no. What have I done?*

Instead of accepting defeat, Gizel dropped to her knees and begged for my forgiveness. She wept so heavily that all I could do was hold her. I don't know why I showed her any compassion. All that time, she never once tried to befriend me. She may have had an ally. She may have been surprised that I was only a frightened, young girl flailing around with no harmful intentions, just playing silly games because I had nothing better to do in the world. She may have found that there was so much that I needed to learn from her. But instead, she made me her enemy.

I sat there holding her, because I was her; we were the same animal...no better, no worse, just two girls in need of love and a sincere hug. I knew it, even if she didn't. I rubbed her back; it was the touch of someone who cared.

133

Alberto, not so forgiving, ranted and raved in Italian for ten more minutes. He was playing his part in this ridiculous game—threatening to kick her out when he had no intention of letting her go anywhere. His enraged machismo display was to keep me from leaving, but my seeming alliance with her egged him on. He probably thought that maybe he could have us both after all.

I so badly wanted to whisper into her ear, "It will all be over soon. I'm getting the hell out of here and you two nutcases can have each other." But I held back. It was clear; the only way that I could leave safely would be without Alberto or Gizel's knowledge of my plans. Alberto had come too far in this game and was much too in love to simply let me go. Gizel's knowing and not telling Alberto of my getaway would make her an accessory and thus a liability to me—not worth the possible repercussions. She would jeopardize the safety of us both. So, I diligently kept quiet.

That day, Alberto all but followed me around. He was everywhere I was. It was infuriating. The time I needed to leave, in order to make it to Don's and then to the airport, was nearing. I had to remain calm because Alberto was on edge. I feared he'd whip out handcuffs and yell, "You're never going to leave here!"

The day before, I had emptied my bank account and pierced one ear so that I could use the store credit that I had at the jewelry store (it was either that or buy a smaller, cheaper set, but I wanted a one-carat stud like the Italian empress). I also said my good-byes to a few key people.

*Did too many people on this bitsy rock know? Did the information regarding my departure leak back to him?*

I was nervous.

*How am I going to transport my bags from my room to my car without Alberto seeing me? What will be my excuse to leave? It is my day off; is Alberto planning an outing?*

*Think...*

*Dawn!*

I had to sneak a call from the landline. The phone in the kitchen was the best option.

I casually went up to get water from the fridge. I poured and was sipping from the glass while I was closing the door, only to find Alberto standing there. I jumped, splashing water on my face.

"Geez, you scared me. Want some water?"

I abandoned the plan to snatch up the cordless, rush to the bathroom, lock the door, and punch in Dawn's number. It was a stupid idea anyway. Then it came to me: maybe I should just ask.

I had rarely used the phone. So as not to draw suspicion, I told Alberto that Dawn and I had planned a beach day and that she was coming to pick me up. Although he was disappointed, he understood.

"Hey, Alberto, can we have fettuccine alfredo tonight? And can Dawn join us?"

He relaxed and smiled.

"That's a good idea," he said.

"Can I call Dawn and tell her to give me a few extra minutes so that I can unpack?"

"Yes. Of course, Savannah."

When I had said everything that he needed to hear, he left me the hell alone.

*Dawn, please be home.*

Praying had never seemed so important before that moment. At times like that, what else does one do?

It was about a fifty-fifty chance that she'd be in. The phone rang. No answer. I tried again; on the second ring, the phone was picked up. It was her roommate. My heart skipped a beat. If her roomie answered, that meant Dawn wasn't there, but I asked anyways.

"Is Dawn there?"

"She's in the shower."

"It's Savannah. Get her now; tell her it's an emergency."

Thirty-two seconds later...

"Hello."

Dawn was at Alberto's in nineteen minutes, a record. It was at least thirty minutes from campus. She pulled into the driveway and I quickly prepped her on the situation.

She averted and widened her eyes. I stopped talking and turned to find Alberto hovering behind me.

"Hello, Dawn," Alberto said.

"Hello, Alberto," she casually replied without any hesitation. He had always liked her. As they made small talk, I went to my room to grab what was important. I stuffed the knickknacks like makeup and jewelry into a small beach bag. I checked for his whereabouts.

I had hidden my passport and occasionally moved it in the event he found its resting spot. I couldn't remember where I'd put it last. My heartbeat sped up.

I looked behind the bathroom vanity mirror. Not there.

Checked lining of my luggage...

*Shit.*

Not there, either.

I started moving the bed out from the wall. I had cut a slit in the mattress and stuffed it in there, once.

*Is it still here?*

I was on the floor fishing for it when I heard Dawn coughing. It was a warning. He was on his way down. My sleeve got caught on the bed frame. I yanked a few times. It wasn't budging.

*Stop worrying about your freakin' shirt... Is it there?*

I forced my way in further. Just as I was about to give up, my fingertips barely felt the corner of the thick cover. I jammed my hand in, dislodged it, and pulled my sleeve from the frame causing it to tear. I quickly got to my bag and tossed my ticket to freedom safely inside.

My eyes darted toward the open door. My heartbeat slowed up a notch.

I protectively strapped the bag across my body and pushed the bed into place. Just as I was turning to leave the "Room of Bad Memories," I felt his undeniable presence. He was stalking me, toying with me until I broke. His gut was warning him. His eyes were wild and suspicious.

He glanced down at my bags.

"Savannah, you didn't unpack."

"I know. I'll do it tomorrow. I decided to read."

He zeroed in on the nightstand. Thank God I hadn't thrown the book into my bag.

"Gizel and I are going to the market for dinner things," he calmly said.

"Okay. Can you get tiramisu?" I said as I batted my eyes hoping to ease his mind.

"Savannah. For you, anything."

Alberto gave me a hug, something he never did. Maybe I was just paranoid but in my mind, it signified the end of a very turbulent relationship. With me there, we would have all been certifiably insane within months. By leaving, I was saving us all, especially Gizel.

I returned the hug, the unspoken good-bye. I watched him exit my bedroom like so many times before, but this time with the knowledge that it was the last.

Dawn and I waited impatiently for a few minutes, fearing an untimely return. Then I bolted to my car, lugging my bags. I loaded up the trunk. I'd be damned if the piece of shit didn't start. Dawn, who had already backed down the driveway, was just about to turn the corner when she saw Alberto and Gizel heading back to the house. She put her car into reverse and gunned it, backing up the hill. She almost took me out! I had already exited my car and was sprinting toward her. She stopped, and I slid into the passenger seat.

"It wouldn't start…the car," I said out of breath.

We plastered on smiles as they turned casually into the driveway. Gizel had forgotten the shopping list.

*Is she messing with me too?*

Gizel's lackluster eyes met mine as she passed Dawn's car. *Bye,* I blinked.

She understood and blinked her reply, *Good riddance! You home-wrecking jezebel. Thank you for giving me my life back.*

"Forget your car. It's rented. He'll return it. I'll come back to pick up your things. Let's go!" Dawn said, not so calmly.

"No. You go. Go pee."

She smiled and hopped out of the car, trailing Gizel inside. That bought us time until they left, again. I moved the bags from my car to hers.

Speeding through town, running lights, and passing slow-moving cars, we got to the airport with no time to spare. I quickly hugged and kissed my friend. She didn't ask any questions.

"Call me when you can, and *be careful,*" she added with emphasis. The way she said it scared me. I hadn't thought about anything much but getting the hell away.

*Be careful,* in the *watch your back, don't get killed* sense never crossed my mind; it had only crossed it in a, *don't get caught* kind of way. And now that she had said it with such dread, not dying was all I could think about.

Don wasn't at ticketing. I waited and waited. I looked around nervously. My palms were sweating. Then I remembered…

We agreed to meet at the gate!

Everything seemed to be played out in slow motion. I wanted to push fast forward. I finally got to the counter and showed my passport. The attendant took longer than necessary. I became nervous. I hadn't bothered to find out whether or not a ticket was purchased, or even if he were indeed leaving that day. My heart rate sped up, and many, many thoughts raced through my mind.

"Got it. One way to Köln, Germany?" she said.

"Yes!" I said almost screaming at her.

*Hurry up and give me the damned boarding pass.*

She told me the gate and informed me that they were boarding my flight, Flight 49.

My teeth chattered. My body shivered. My nerves were shot. I estimated from the timing that if Alberto had deduced that his gut was correct and found my bags missing, it would be right about the time that I got halfway across to the other side of the airport, where I had to go through security, when he would pull up to the curb in search of his fleeing concubine—just in time to spot me through the windowed wall.

Then I saw Don heading my way. His smile took over his repugnant, swollen face. He made me ill at that moment. His whole demeanor was irritating.

*Why is this old-ass man so excited about taking an underdeveloped nineteen-year-old out of the country? Shouldn't he be ashamed of himself?*

Something told me to be patient and not go to the gate with Don. Don't get caught in the middle of the airport with nowhere to hide. Just wait.

*Be careful.*

Don was elated that I had decided to show. He was telling me about his apprehension of leaving a paid-for, first-class ticket without talking to me since our date, but he believed in fate. Just then, I heard tires slightly screech. I saw a black Range Rover pull up to the curb. My mouth dropped.

"Meet you at the gate," I said.

139

My abruptness didn't worry him. He was on cloud nine, glad that I had made it. He ventured off toward security. He and Alberto unsuspectingly passed one another. It was like a scene from a highly dramatic film noir. The slow motion kicked in as I witnessed Don's corny smile colliding with Alberto's hardened glower. Thankfully, Alberto didn't catch a glimpse of me as I ducked into a bathroom. Even so, I stared frightfully at the door, hoping that he was not so brazen as to check the ladies' room.

My heart palpitated. I held my breath trying not to hyperventilate like I did the first time I went scuba diving. As a matter of fact, except for the water, it felt exactly the same; as if I were fighting for my life and my reprieve was just a few feet away.

I decided against hiding in the stall. I needed room to fight. I fished a pen from my bag and secured it between my fingers. I was nearing a state of panic. I felt the nausea lump into my throat. Maybe I should just run for it. Again, for the second time that day, I prayed.

*God, please get me off this rock safely.*

Someone came into the bathroom; sweat instantly formed on my brow as the door closed. I planted my feet and held my breath as the person rounded the corner.

*Whew.* It wasn't Gizel or Alberto.

Then I heard my name.

"Savannah?"

An older, black island woman looked me up and down, smiling.

"Ex…excuse me?" I stuttered. I almost threw up. He must have sent her in here!

*Oh, God.*

He had described me, so I didn't lie. I broke down quietly. The tears were real, and they fell without prompting from my manipulative theatrical side.

"I'm running away from the guy out there. If he knows I'm in here… I don't know what he will do to me," I told her. "I'm scared," I added.

That was obvious, but I felt she needed to hear it. She gave me a quick pat on the back and left the restroom. I fiddled for some money. My hands trembled like crazy. I could hear Alberto's voice with nothing between us but a door.

*Be careful,* repeated in my mind. *Be careful.*

I decided that I would not miss the flight! Even if I had to sprint to the security gate with an old, crazy-assed Italian mob boss hot on my tail.

I waited five minutes, ten minutes. The bathroom door opened. The lady returned.

"Da coast is clear. He and dat woman left in a dark-colored truck."

Her island-accented words were music to my ears. I thanked her profusely, placed a one-hundred-dollar bill into her hand, and took off running.

Free!

I made it just as the doors were about to close. Don was standing in the aisle talking to an attendant about waiting a few more minutes when I showed up. Relief fell over his face and I gave the best smile that I could muster. I felt a persistent uneasiness. My shoulders were tense and I couldn't concentrate on my plush first class surroundings, Don, or the attendant who was hounding me about a cocktail. It wasn't until we were in flight that I let out a sigh of relief, relaxed, and actually smiled genuinely at my travel companion. I guzzled down two glasses of champagne. I wanted to shout until the breaking point of my vocal cords, "Free at last, free at last, thank God Almighty, I'm free at last!"

I was liberated from one situation and was blindly leaping headfirst into another. It was probably stupidity at its best, but

I was content and open to what adventures might lay ahead. My attitude was "bring it on." After the last two years, I could survive anything. I had done it! I had run away from Alberto Mannino. My life was intact.

*I will never return to that wretched island ever again.*

The flight was nothing less than spectacular; it was Lufthansa, first class to Köln, Germany. I didn't know such luxury existed on an aircraft. The service was impeccable, and the food was unbelievable—all-you-can-eat caviar, exotic fruits, and delicious wines. The amenities blew me away. When they brought a down comforter at bedtime, I was floored! We also received pajamas, socks, and a much-needed toiletry pouch; a purse and the beach bag with a change of clothes was all that I had managed to gather up.

Don and I talked nearly the entire trip. The other passengers were so far away that our conversation was private and did not disturb anyone—unlike flying coach where travelers were allotted three inches between their knees and the seat backs and were nearly stacked on top of one another, making conversation illegal.

Our very sentimental bonding occurred en route to Germany. Don was frank. He was married and had no intentions of divorcing after forty years, three children, and a tribe of grandchildren. I understood. He proposed that I be his mistress.

"What do you expect?" he asked.

I was new to the kept life and hadn't quite figured that out yet. I was living day-to-day without a plan. I hadn't thought about much more than surviving, messing up Gizel's (and by default Alberto's) life, and more recently, getting away from them altogether. What did I expect? I was dumbfounded by the question, but not dumb enough to say something stupid.

"Can I think about it?"

He accepted that, and we drifted off to sleep. At least he

did. Making mental lists of all that I wanted and needed came remarkably easy. By the time he awoke, I was prepared, and before he could fully open his eyes, I started listing my demands.

"I want a monthly allowance, a car, and a place to live. I don't mind working, but my money won't be used for paying bills. I expect you to take care of me, buy me nice stuff, take me on trips and to nice restaurants, and expose me to new things."

"Done," he said.

I rolled over, feeling triumphant, and fell into the deepest sleep that I had had in months.

When Don and I arrived at the hotel room, the phone was ringing. Don answered. Shrill vocals emanated from the receiver. I figured it was his lovely wife. *That's what forty years will do.* I left them to work it out and headed to the giant bathroom to bathe.

I couldn't help but think of that poor shell of a soul I had left behind, Gizel. Even though she was an enemy of sorts, I wondered where her life path would take her even more than I did about my own. My wonderings brought me to the conclusion that her fate could have easily been mine if I hadn't been cut from stronger cloth.

Just as I was starting to enjoy myself, rapid knocks on the bathroom door echoed, signaling urgency. I opened the door to find an ashen and solemn face.

"It was Alberto. He told me he was going to cut off my balls and stuff them down my throat."

I laughed and thought, *This Don character is hilarious.* But he had his luggage and was heading toward the door.

"We're moving to an undisclosed location. Get your things."

I spent the rest of the day trying to convince Don that Alberto was all talk. He kept asking me stupid, unanswerable questions.

"How do you suppose Alberto found us? He called me Donald and said that I was 'no Don.' What did he mean? Will he know we moved to this hotel? What if he knows where my family lives?"

These were all questions that I refused to dwell on out loud, but of course thought about intensely.

*What have I done?*

The only bit of reassurance was that Alberto did not assassinate Gizel, his longtime girlfriend, after his hired detectives brought him damaging evidence of her foreign-soil love affair. He let her live, and she meant much more to him than I did, right? Or maybe it was because I meant nothing to him that he would kill me? Or maybe he would simply kill the non-Don, transport me back within his clutches, and dare me to attempt another escape.

After a few days of serious fretting and ordering every meal from room service, we forgot about the Italian bully/stalker planting bombs in the very taxi that we were going to sequester, waiting for just the right moment to push the detonator, blowing us to smithereens. We forgot that we were fugitives and ignored the threat to all whom we loved.

We were two careless "newlyweds" on a European vacation, traipsing in and out of neighboring cities and countries, eateries, boutiques, theaters, bars, and nightclubs, drinking heavily and having a blast. Don too was an alcohol abuser, and we spent days in oblivion. He managed to squeeze in some business. While he did that, I shopped my drunken ass off.

I yearned to dress like the Italian empress. I paid attention to quality, choosing silks, wools, and cotton blends. I bought exquisitely designed and manufactured shoes. I let the sales staff dress me and talk me into ridiculous frivolities. Hotel spas quickly became another new favorite pastime.

Don surprised me with all-new Louis Vuitton luggage. I had mentally abandoned the suitcases of clothes and trivial possessions that Dawn harbored.

I was made new. Don had transformed me. He was very proud, not unlike Antonio and his brother Cori before him. But as the story goes, every good thing must come to an end.

After three weeks, it was time to head home to detoxify, snap back to reality, and focus on my future. We had determined that I would go home for a visit and then move to Miami to work at one of his companies. The subject of sex had yet to be broached.

The night before we left Germany, I had to solidify my standing as the mistress of Donald P. Keller. He made it clear that it was give and take. It definitely was my turn to give.

I gave him one minute and nine seconds of oral pleasure. And that was that.

# seven

When I arrived in the States, I called my mother. She had been at her wits' end for three weeks. Apparently, Alberto had called looking for me. She had no clue where I was. I hadn't thought to notify her of my whereabouts because one, I wasn't proud of Don's age, our relationship, or my decision to abscond with a man whom I had just met and two, I didn't want to worry her about why I had left the island and Alberto Mannino.

My reasoning was stupid on both accounts. She was my mother and had every right to know I had left the country, with whom, and the reason for my abrupt departure. After Alberto's call, her thoughts of what had happened must have been horrifying. The conversation with her was the worst that I had ever had in my life. My mother's voice was a mixture of relief and scorn. But within seconds, she was yelling at me, and then suddenly, she lost it. My mother's heaves made tears well along the lids of my eyes.

"You are selfish little girl. You have no idea what I have been thinking! No idea of how I felt, not knowing where my child was. I had to wake up every day for twenty-one days not knowing…I had to…" She could barely speak. "I had to go to bed and wake up not knowing what happened to my baby."

I had no words. A huge lump blocked my throat. Tears flowed uncontrollably down my cheeks, and for the first time in a long time, they were full of remorse.

As I stood at the JFK phone booth, I could no longer contain my emotions. I let out a loud, mournful yowl. I was weeping like a baby. All I wanted was to hold my mommy and tell her that I was sorry over and over.

My insensitivity was appalling. I felt so ashamed. I was apologetic, but it didn't seem to make a dent. I had made my mother suffer and worry until she was sick. The word *sorry* was lame and had lost all potency. While I was having the time of my life, she endured the same three weeks quite differently; she had three weeks of not sleeping, of calling everyone I knew or who might have known me, and contacting unhelpful police, hospitals, and finally, morgues. She spent the weeks wondering whether or not her baby girl was dead—three terribly long, heart-wrenching weeks.


*Aaron*

My trip home was long overdue. Mary picked me up and we didn't waste time. We went to the place where our former high school classmates would be congregating. It had only been two years since I had graduated, but it seemed like an eternity. I was astounded how little they had progressed. I kept the details of my life fairly guarded while listening to their boring tales of local dish. My experiences since graduation clearly ran circles around all of theirs collectively. I was living in the fast lane but could slow down enough to appreciate the mundane.

As Mary and I were saying our goodbyes, the very handsome deejay approached me.

"Hi, I'm Aaron."

"Hey." I tried very hard not to give him any energy. It was difficult. My eyes were drawn to his face, my ears to his voice, and my soul to his heart.

He was so intuitive and smooth; he was confident, and unlike most guys, he wasn't intimidated. He turned and walked away from my game of "not giving him any energy." I found myself searching the room so that I could give him my number. When I found him, he was talking to a cute girl. I slid him my number and left.

Both Mikey and my mother were thrilled to spend time with me even though I had made the announcement of my plans to relocate to Miami. I cherished every moment with them; however, I couldn't keep my thoughts off of Miami. The eighty-degree, sunshiny days and sexy nightlife were awaiting my return.

Aaron didn't call.

Miami welcomed me back with outstretched palm tree arms. I was home.

Don took me car shopping and purchased an Audi on his credit card. I was impressed by the buying power of good credit. I made a mental note to aspire to such creditworthy heights. He deposited twenty-five thousand into an account and left me to make a life in Miami. He would return in two weeks to spend time with me for my twentieth birthday and to introduce me to my new job.

I had two weeks to live it up. I rented a furnished apartment around Sixth Avenue and 110th Street, just a few blocks from the ocean. I stocked the food cabinets with liquor. I scouted the hottest hangouts. My residual worries were completely forgotten, as were Alberto and Gizel. The intrigue of my new life was my new focus.

The Miami nightclub clientele was extremely transient. Acquired friends would stick around for a few days, maybe weeks, and then I wouldn't see them again. I had become accustomed to meeting and bidding farewell to "friends" all in the same night. I was not a drug user, which proved to be seriously detrimental to rubbing elbows with the who's who. Many Miami socialites were cocaine abusers, and I wouldn't succumb to the pressure. Besides, I had to keep my wits about me if I were to advance in this world. So I was excluded from private parties held on yachts and the multi-million dollar estates, but was pulled into the VIP circle at nightclubs by young partiers. The stresses connected with being the plaything of an elitist weren't attractive. I preferred waking up in my own bed. I was content with drinking and having fun, and for a while, that sufficed.

Don appeared right on schedule. He brought a diamond necklace for my twentieth birthday. His kindness was a refreshing character trait in comparison with the fly-by-night boys in the Miami scene. He took me to a fabulous restaurant that boasted of having the best alligator. Alligator?

*Who eats that shit?*

It was delicious.

After we returned to the hoity-toity hotel, Don did a very strange thing. He began licking me—not just my privates, but my arms, legs, ass, and face. I didn't know if that was something I had missed in my sex education. I thought it was gross.

As his tongue slid over my flesh, the air expelled from his nostrils cooled the moist area, sending an unwanted sensation through my nerve endings. It was annoying. I counted each of the thirteen minutes it took for him cover every inch of my body.

I toyed with Don's cock until he came. I am fairly sure I would have to be near comatose to stomach actual sex with him. First, I was going to have to get over the whole licking thing. He was satisfied, and that was all that mattered to him and to me. I could not wait to shower.

The next morning, Don and I met at Second and Biscayne. That was where TeleComm Inc. was located. The day had come for me to mainstream into a traditional work environment.

I had serious reservations about whether or not I was capable of such an act. And I was right. My problems started with my attire. I quickly learned that not every outfit can be worn everywhere. My colorful silk short sets seemed conservative and appropriate to me. I guess in corporate actuality, they were considered beachwear or casual at best. Don would have to take me shopping, again.

As user-friendly as technology was supposed to be, I, for the life of me, could not figure out how the hell a fax machine was able to transport documents from one place to another! I was so bowled over that I called my mother, from my up-front -and-center reception desk and in a voice just above a whisper, asked her to explain the magic. Asking anyone at the job would probably be grounds for my immediate resignation, as that would have been enough evidence that I was not qualified for the position and would point to the probability that I was involved with the boss.

I was thrown into a secretarial/receptionist position with no prior knowledge, experience, or even idea of what the job entailed. The sales office housed four men: the site boss, a technical person, and two salesmen. Their gender was the only reason I made it for as long as I did: three whole months. Four women probably would have eaten me alive, belittling me for my lack of skills and palpable ignorance. The men just goggled and I flirted back. Men equaled job security; it was sad but true.

During my stint, I learned the corporate milieu and was no longer intimidated by faxes or busy phone lines, business attire, or a coffeemaker. I could, if I wanted to, survive and excel in that environment, but I had other plans.

Exhausted from late nights, early mornings, drinking incessantly, and a mundane work life, I needed a break, a vacation, or a change of pace. To satisfy the anxiety, I quit working and enrolled at Florida Memorial, a small college.

I pillaged the sanity of my male colleagues. After accumulating collateral damage on the campus, I took my show on the road. I hit the clubs. Drug dealers didn't impress me. I had had my fill with Thomas and Xander. I had Don's deep pockets, so my dating agenda wasn't about finding a rich guy. I was looking for normalcy in a handsome and exciting man.

Dating for me was unsuccessful; everyone ended up a friend.

There were no sexual sparks, just platonic relationships. I couldn't stop thinking about Aaron.

Don showed up once a month to orally harass me. He left satisfied, but still, we were "sex" free. I wondered what the thrill really was for either of us. The relationship didn't make much sense; he was forking over around seven thousand dollars a month and did so happily. He spent most of his time conducting business in foreign countries and I was left flapping in the wind, trying to make sense of my life.

I was bored with school, friends, dating, and being a mistress. Don felt my unease and wasn't quite ready for things to cease, so he bought me a condo on the bay.

*A new home is a charming pacifier.*

Of course, I stayed.

I was wide open and ready for adventure and romance; my soul was searching for something more—anything.


My place was spectacular. Everything was new: furniture, pots, blankets, the works. My newfangled accoutrements deluded me into believing I was renewed. Maybe I was, for a while. But there's nothing like love to make you feel brand spanking new.

Aaron called!

He was coming to visit. I cancelled all of my plans to prepare for the next day arrival of a man who I had only met once, briefly, and before that call, didn't have any communication with.

My excitement could barely be contained. I blasted music and danced around my beautiful condo. Just as I started to calm down, I would be overcome with joy. I leapt onto my elevated queen bed and jumped fervently. *Aaron is coming! Aaron is coming!* I fell into my fluffy pillows with a huge smile and said it out loud, "Aaron is coming."

Aaron and I held hands, kissed, and behaved as if we had been together for years. Our comfort and infatuation was mutual. We adored each other. I took him to my favorite spots but it was he who showed me Miami. He was adventurous and took me places that I had never thought to explore, like a day-cruise to the Bahamas.

Aaron also took me to hood hangouts. That was where he felt most comfortable. We ate at Caribbean, Cuban, and soul-food restaurants. It was a 100 percent turnaround from the divine, profanely priced dining experiences with Don. I loved it all the same, even more so because of whom I was with.

We spent 24 hours a day together for nearly two weeks and I didn't want to spend another day without him. Aaron was the one that I had been searching for. He was the kind of man who was instantly remembered and adored by everyone he met. He was genuinely kind-hearted and routinely went out of the way to offer a kind word to a stranger or help to someone in need.

On a dank, stay-in kind of night nearing the end of his visit, Aaron insisted on taking me out when I would have preferred to order Chinese delivery. We went to a scary area, not the cool little restaurants or club scenes that I was familiar with, but some foul, fucked-up place. The war-torn Overtown neighborhood looked as if the actual residents had been violently murdered and then devoured by heinous creatures that roamed the streets looking for their next victims.

"What the hell are we doing over here?" I asked him, concerned.

"It's all good, baby," he reassured me as he pulled up to a wayward soul.

Aaron reached out and handed the stranger a crumpled twenty-dollar bill. For a fleeting second, I thought Aaron was doing some charitable work, like giving to the homeless, nothing outside of his character and my heart felt relieved.

Then the man slid him something in return. My heart ceased to beat for what felt like a full minute. I took a deep, exaggerated breath. I knew.

My stomach immediately ached, my head spun, and my world was turned upside down. I wanted one of those creatures to bust out our windows, drag us from the car as we struggled to get away, and eat us both for being so stupid.

That night in my living room, my beautiful knight inhaled the sweet, putrid smelling fumes from a Coke can turned homemade crack pipe.

Aaron tried to explain to me that he only used crack "every blue moon." I locked my bedroom door and cried myself to sleep. Aaron was becoming a creature, and that distinct aroma haunted me.

The next morning with no stammering, no vacillation, I said, "Just get out of my house." I loved that I was strong when I needed to be. He left in a cab with my heart.

Aaron sent a tape with just one song: Howard Hewitt's "Show Me."

*You've got to let me know*
*Just how far to let this go*
*Help me (Darling please show me)*
*Show me (How to love you)*

*You've got to take my hand*
*Show me that you'll understand*
*Help me*
*Show me*

He sang it very passionately into my answering machine three times a day. He bombarded me with that song until I was forced to listen.

Weeks later, I picked up the phone. To his surprise, I listened to him.

"Baby, we are destined. You know it. Forgive me and believe me when I say that I love you. I love you, Savannah May Lovely. I love you."

He profusely claimed that he was in love. I believed him, because I needed to. No turning back, I was all-in.

We dated long distance, until one gorgeous summer day, I slammed the book shut on Miami, the condo, the non-Don, his mollifying money, and all that was left of that chapter and raced off with reckless abandon, devoting my life to the man of my dreams—a mendacious crack addict.

# eight

*Month One*

As the saying goes, it takes many nails to build a crib but one screw to fill it.

Against my grandmother's wishes, Aaron and I rented a beautiful apartment in the downtown area and moved in together. Our twenty-fifth floor pad had a spectacular view of trillions of twinkling city lights. They consoled me just as the ocean had before them. I was happy.

It was the first of August. By the twenty-seventh day of August, my grandma's cautious predictions had manifested. I went to the hospital for a routine yeast infection.

"Do you know that you're pregnant?" the doctor asked. It felt like a Mack truck had hit me and then backed up over my paralyzed body to make sure I understood the gravity of the situation.

*Excuse me, what the hell did you say, you ignorant asshole?*

He repeated the cursed words so matter-of-factly. It was just as if he had said, "Your life is over; get dressed for your funeral." I was so distraught that the doctor didn't feel right leaving the room, not even to get a nurse.

"Are you okay?" he asked.

*No!*

The question was answered when he saw the tears in my eyes. He did what anyone would do; he patted my leg. I needed a hug. I finally caught my breath and gathered myself.

"Are you going to be all right?" he asked one more time.

"I don't know," I replied honestly.

Aaron and I were very much in love. I told him about the yeast infection turned "You're going to be a father" office visit.

155

He actually smiled. I didn't know what to make of his reaction: was it a good thing or was he high?

I was on birth control pills and hadn't foreseen that missing a pill would make me wind up with child. I was devastated.

Aaron and I went back and forth on the subject of abortion for two weeks. I didn't want to be pregnant, but how could I justify aborting? I knew and loved, very deeply, the father and more important, I was mentally and physically capable. I wasn't a teenager anymore.

I stopped by my mom's house to visit. My family (like most) gathered in the kitchen. My mother was home alone.

I opened the fridge.

"Do you have any pickles?" I asked.

"Are you pregnant?" she responded.

My mother's loving, insightful question was what I needed; my fetus was free of a doomed fate. Thanks to my mom, motherhood was inevitable and celebrated. She gave me a much-needed hug. It was a loving sweet gesture passed from mother to soon-to-be mother.

I told Aaron the good news as if I had just found out that I was pregnant all over again. Suddenly, the tide shifted, and I was overly ecstatic.

"We are going to have a baby!"

His cocked smile divulged worry. We both pretended that it didn't.

Aaron had a not-so-secret secret: he wasn't just a blue moon crack user. He was full-on a drug abuser, and the pressure of being a head-of-household provider for his pregnant woman would prove to be too much.

I was working as a waitress, going to a local community college, and taking care of our home, while he ran the streets, apparently looking for a "come up" to fund his next high. He was a road manager for a famous recording artist and that only exacerbated his abuse and depressive mind state, as that artist was also a drug addict. Almost nightly, I cried myself to sleep. I lived in fear that he would wind up dead in a desolate, drug-infested house.

A recurring nightmare would replace my dreams: Aaron convincing me to join him in smoking crack, me getting so high that I'd ignore the contractions, keep smoking, and deliver my stillborn baby on a filthy, crack-house floor.


*Month Five*


At 4:00 AM, Aaron crept into our home. He came to steal money that he knew I had tucked away. I had been educated months prior about Aaron and my cash. But I guess he thought I was still stupid. I heard him rifling through my purse and then fumbling in my usual hiding places. Then, he entered our room. My heart was pounding. I knew he had been smoking all night because he was with his boss. I was also sure they had exhausted their ATM's hours after the clock struck 12:00, and I was their last resort.

I played sleep until he shook me hard enough to know I was faking.

*"What?"* I was pissed off.

"I need to borrow…"

"No!"

He looked cracked out, a crackhead at his worst, the kind that scares you. The skeletal remains of the walking dead.

As he violently began tearing up the house, I watched in disbelief as the romantic, fun, caring, and generous man I knew on the trips to Miami was literally disappearing before my eyes.

I moved about the apartment, disgusted by his lack of care for our things. Finally, I sat on the couch and waited for his tantrum to subside. I said out loud, "Funny, how I so eagerly wanted you to come and now I can't wait for you to leave."

He looked at me and, for a split second, I thought he'd abandon the search mission and fall into my lap, weeping away his sins. He did not. He emptied the linen-turned-baby closet and left receiving blankets, rattles, and onesies scattered on the floor.

I wanted to unzip the back of the stuffed animal, retrieve the cash, and throw it into his face; paying him off so that I could move on with my life.

"Go fuck yourself!" I shouted. I wasn't ready to let go.

I didn't give him one cent. Aaron walked out with a jug of pennies that I had been collecting. He had become that lady who gave up her lamps for a hit. She said good-bye to light in exchange for the darkness of drugs. Just as Aaron was now turning in his dignity for a jar of pennies, that would soon become a tiny vile of crack cocaine. It didn't have to be this way. He was the father of my child and unfortunately a pathetic looser.

I picked up the onesies and used them to wipe the tears from my face.


*Month Six*


Aaron rarely came around and when he did, we argued. He was an unreliable, burdensome home wrecker. But I loved him and was too emotional to make any sane sense. My primary argument was that he didn't spend time with me. I questioned his love. I accused him of infidelities. Made him make promises that he was sure to break. I so badly wanted to be loved that I ignored his disrespectful ways, made excuses for his abuse of me, and denied his atrocious behavior. I pardoned his nasty addiction to crack. Once again, I was living a complicated, filthy lie.

*Month Seven*

It was out of financial desperation, after Aaron had cleaned out my savings account and disappeared for a week, that I called Don. I was broke and had nowhere else to turn. Don wanted to see me, and he was the last person I wanted to see. I hung up the phone and realized that I was nauseous; disgusted with the fact that selling myself had become all too easy. But rent and all the other bills were past due.

I flew to Chicago and made out with Don for a few thousand dollars and a used car that he needed to off-load. I drove home, tears dripping onto my round belly the entire way. What would the baby inside think of its protector who had let a stranger lick the roof of its home?

When Aaron finally came around, I told him what I had done, hoping for a reprimand or, at least, empathy for the way I was feeling—dirty.

"You had to do what you had to do," he said.

In a way, he was right. But I hated him for saying it. Didn't he love me? Didn't it bother him?

I learned that street rules are different, and Aaron was street. Of course he loved me; of course it bothered him. But, I did what I had to do. He was okay with me surviving by any means necessary. He was also the last person who could, because of his own heinousness, judge me, and I knew that. His guilt for his own behavior could only be forgiven, if he forgave me.

He told me he was proud because I was his bitch and I could hold it down no matter what, and that my strength was what he loved about me. We washed each other's sins away by making passionate love that night... and I was his bitch.

The next morning, my mother came to visit. She saw me, and then the tears poured from her eyes. Her mother, my grandmother, had died. I held my mom for a very long time while we expressed our sorrow. My child wouldn't get to meet one of the strongest women I had ever known but God Almighty would.

Aaron sobered up enough to get me through the days leading up to her burial. I promised my grandmother that I would make an attempt at strength and try to make things work with Aaron. She and my grandfather were married for sixty years, committed, even through countless trials and tribulations.

*Month Eight*

During the remainder of my pregnancy, I thought I would help my man get healthy and get us back on track. I so desperately wanted to change Aaron, to make him whole and help him overcome his addiction. My inherited strength would see us through. I had to do it for our family, our baby.

It seemed the harder I tried, the worse he got. In my attempt at being a gallant rescuer, I had become a useless enabler. I believed his obvious lies, cleaned up his messes, made excuses to his family and mine, and coddled him through bad choice after bad choice.

My life had amounted to a huge pile of stress compounded with hellacious hemorrhoids, anemia, and itching that made me want to scrape off my palms.

More often than not, I was left alone, sobbing. I was depressed and couldn't tell anyone the reasons for my miserable state. I blamed the pregnancy because my family had already formed their opinions regarding Aaron, and I didn't want to aggravate the fragile relationship between them by exposing his tormenting ways. Dawn and Mary kept saying that I could do better and to leave him, but they were both in horrific relationships themselves. Who were they to judge? If they couldn't follow their own advice, why the hell should I trust them? With no one to confide in, I was left to sit with my pain and suck it up.

I would sit in pain until the day Ava (a combination of Aaron and Savannah) would bless my life; depression and heartache would be replaced with fear, anxiety, and hope.

I couldn't be Aaron's bitch any longer. I would be a bitch of new breed—a mother.


*Month Nine*


After a twenty-four-hour labor and a three-hour delivery, I was blessed with Ava. She was a six-pound-nine-ounce beauty. She was instantly the light of my life. She gazed into my eyes, and I knew that absolutely nothing or no one else mattered. I placed the gold band that was first her uncle Mikey's on her finger.

"Will you marry me precious little angel?" I kissed her forehead.

It would be her and me against the world, always and forever.

My child needed me to be strong. So I gave up on Aaron. He was no longer worth fixing; plus, he weakened me.

It was as if Ava's birth was the birth of a new person in me, the real me, and the only reason I existed. I cried, but this time the wetness was cleansing and healing. I wanted to cry a tubful of the remedial agent and bathe in its strengthening power. Ava's birth clarified my being.

I lay in the hospital bed dreaming of the possibilities for her life. I did not want her to grow up poor, stuck with limited options. I wanted her to have the world at her feet. I wanted the best in education, the best of the best of everything.

Uncle Mikey came to visit and left behind a newspaper.

I flipped through and read a few discouraging articles and panicked. What did the world have to offer? How would I be able to give Ava the best of the best? Was I delusional in thinking it was even possible?

Just before crumbling and tossing the special Monday edition of bad news into a garbage can across the room, a small article caught my eye. Some crazy was claiming that every household in America would have at least one computer. For some reason, I wanted to talk to the man with the ludicrous claims. I called his office in Seattle.

"Hello. Mr. Gates' office. How may I assist you?" said the receptionist.

"Hello. Can I speak to Mr. Gates?"

I was transferred. Pleasant music played and then his secretary asked who I was and what the call was pertaining to.

"Savannah Lovely. It's personal."

She patched me through.

I wasn't a person who pestered people, so when he answered, I simply asked him about his theory of *everyone* having computers in their homes. He laughed.

"We'll just have to see."

He wasn't coo coo. He was ingenious and confident. That turned me on.

I invited Mr. William Gates to Minnesota to dine with me. He said the next time he was in town, he would call; I knew they were nice words to get off the phone with a silly, oblivious groupie.

The reason I called took a turn the moment I realized that he was serious. I invited him out because my sights were set high. It was my innate ingenuity kicking in. I guess I figured

162

it was just a matter of time before I would need to get Ava and myself the hell out of this life, and why not via some crazy genius named Bill Gates? I took a shot with nothing to lose.

My restlessness, like so many other times, was forcing a grandiose change. Life as a broke, twenty-two year old, Midwestern, mothering nobody wasn't cutting it.


Aaron bought, or shall I say brought, me a ring and asked me to marry him.

There was a time when I would have jumped for joy, professing my love from the highest of mountaintops, but when he asked, I almost laughed aloud. Not the type of change I was looking for.

Where had Aaron been? Didn't he know that I was dying a slow death from this day-in, day-out mundane existence? Didn't he see my reverse Cinderella saga play out? Riches to Rags. Or, that I was tired and rundown from being a single, working parent? Hadn't he witnessed my transformation into motherhood?

Of course he knew all of that. The insecurity that my change caused in our relationship made him forgo getting high long enough to pose the question with a ring in hand.

"Will you marry me, Savannah?"

I accepted the ring—thinking I may need the cash later for formula or diapers. However, there was no way I could accept his proposal.

I left Aaron, sad and depressed, just as he had done to me so many times before. I had bigger problems, like how I was going to get my life back so that I could build a life for our baby—my baby. How would I manage as a single mother?

I moved into my mother's house.

It was the first time that I saw having money as an addiction.

For months, I worried about not having enough money, not being able to afford non-sale items, cutting coupons, and price comparing. It was the first time since those early days in the Virgin Islands that I felt poor. I missed being free from the burden of poverty and free from worry. The lack of money caused problems, having money solved problems; at least, that was how it appeared. Then it finally clicked; I had to use the resources that I had that didn't require calling random people from news articles or fishing through the Forbes Fortune 500, simply hoping that someone wanted to hook up.

I called Don.

Don had to be convinced that I was eager to see him and not just desperate. I painted the picture by telling him what he wanted and needed to hear, which was that he was my savior and that, although things were going well for me, I missed his company, blah, blah, blah. He questioned me about my relationship with Aaron, and I told him the truth; we were done. After a few hour-long defensive and explanatory conversations, Don suggested we meet in Las Vegas. I had never been to the City of Sin, and I couldn't wait. Don and I solidified a date to rendezvous.

Ava was a little over twelve months old and probably wouldn't miss me too much as my mother was catering to her every need. I jetted off to Vegas. It was my first trip away from my daughter; I missed her more than I had ever imagined, but I justified: my decision would ultimately have a positive impact on her.

*Dr. Gunther Wydler*

No sooner had I walked into Caesar's Palace and taken a seat in the grand entrance than an aging gentleman asked if I'd like to have a drink with him at the bar. It was one hundred degrees outside; I was thirsty. In addition, I had some time to kill before Don arrived, a dangerous combination of circumstances for a bird like me.

"Sure," I smiled.

It turns out that the drink proposal was a cleverly disguised proposition. He wanted me to go to his suite and copulate for currency. How much, I didn't know. Possibly, if I would have inquired, things may have turned out a lot differently—everyone has a price. However, I wasn't willing to explore my financial ceiling or the possibility of prostitution at that moment. In my state of disappointment, I couldn't even make eye contact.

*Do I look like a run-of-the-mill prostitute? Can't he see that I am more than that? I have a carat diamond in the ear that faced him. How dare he?*

When I finally looked at him again, I saw Antonio, Badi, Dr. Wilson, Paco, Alberto, and Don. He was all of them wrapped up as one big trick! My clit jittered; I was on to something. So I gave him a serious study. He was a dorky man of means and an eager server of pleasure. I could spot those types from a mile away. He was instantly infatuated, shown in his perky pupils and his prolonged nervous smile. I trusted my instincts and snatched his business card before he could completely remove it from his pocket.

*Doctor? Hmph.*

He begged my forgiveness. He did not mean to insult me. I played wounded until I clearly heard him announce that he would like me to accompany him to Vegas some time and to call if I'd ever like to take him up on the offer. He had asked without using the words, "What can I do for you?" The old man-melting Savannah was back! Old fool.

Don appeared just after I had said goodbye to the doctor. We checked in and made our way through the casino to our room.

Vegas was the Mecca for the new, exciting, and different. I was in awe—the pulsating lights, the dinging of the slot machines, and the people milling around hoping to walk away the lucky winner. Everywhere I looked—the bar, the bellhop desk, the tables, the cage—I saw money. Money seemed to be oozing out from every crevice. I started mentally planning a way to get my hands on some.

Once inside our room, I sat on the huge bed checking out the outstanding decor. Don immediately started to undress me. He remained fully clothed. He was the same old, same old—predictable. He spent ten minutes licking the bottom of my foot and suckling my big toe. I wanted to pull my knee to my chest and let it go with all my strength into his face, sending him flying out the window of our fifteenth-floor suite. But like any tiresome routine, it was endured. His fetish was part of the deal. Our deal. But my instincts told me that "our deal" had become obsolete the moment I met Gunther Wydler.


After my return from the weekend with Don, I was able to put thirty-five hundred dollars into my safe-deposit box.

Money represents different things to each person, such as status, frivolity, freedom, ability to impress others, family/generational wealth distribution, and philanthropy; for me, it simply represented security. It was my backup money, in case things became dire. It was my "Help me! I'm drowning," safety net money. It felt good knowing it was there, if I truly needed it.

I went about life a bit more secure, but still things were difficult. I was out of work. My sole job was mothering and maintaining my mother's home, not an easy task with a very active and intrusive toddler and little parenting skills. She scratched and stained the walls and floors, left a mess every place that she set foot, obsessed over emptying contents of everything;

the refrigerator, cabinets, purses and her favorite: the dirt from potted plants. As soon as I finished cleaning up one mess, she was creating another. More often than not, I let the house fall into near ruin before setting about the grueling task of clean up—and not during naptime because when Ava napped so did I. She was exhausting. I dreaded the thought of working. I was by nature organized, typically a bit of a clean freak, and full of energy, but if I couldn't handle things now, how could I possibly throw a full-time job into the mix? The answer was depressing. I couldn't.

I dug out a business card. It read, "Dr. Gunther Wydler." It might as well have said, "When you have nothing, you have nothing to lose. Call me."

Don left from Vegas to spend the summer vacationing with his wife, and Aaron started disappearing for weeks on end. Aaron and I weren't physically together, nor were we totally emotionally separate. I was confused and angry, and it would take years to sort out all these feelings I could and would do what I had to do to survive. Aaron was the one who had instilled that message. So I did what I knew, what I was good at, and what would provide me with immediate gratification.

I dialed the number on the card.

Dr. Wydler was ecstatic to hear from me.

"What would it take for you to visit me in California?" he asked.

*Wow.*

The pattern was clearly developing: calls to wealthy men who could "help" me.

I had island-hopped with influential people. I had dined exquisitely on a first-class flight to Köln. I had gone to see *Madame Butterfly* at the Opera Garnier in Paris, France. I gambled fifty dollars a hand at Caesar's Palace. I had eaten escargots, for Pete's sake! Who was I? What had I become? I was living at my mama's house, depressed and clipping coupons.

I had had enough self-pity. It was time to regain my life. Innately, I knew destiny was looking me in the face; now it was up to me to decide. The questions were already answered.

"Send $1200 cash and a round-trip plane ticket. And I need my own hotel room."

The next day, a FedEx package arrived. Inside were fifteen crispy one-hundred-dollar bills, a first-class plane ticket, a hotel reservation confirmation number, and a note.

*Dear Savannah, I look forward to a great time.*

*Have a safe trip, GW*

I could have pocketed the money and chalked him up as a sucker, but somewhere deep down I knew this was a chance of a lifetime. It was exactly what my life had been about and what it was destined to be about. I knew the rules and how to apply, manipulate, and benefit from them. What did I have to lose? No, that was not the question floating around in my mind. I was focused on what could be gained.

I didn't sugarcoat it. He would be my third sugar daddy.

Ava was a handful but my mother had raised two. It was evident in her effortless attention paid to everything at once, something that I admired and had not yet learned. As my mother ran a bath, put the dishes away, loaded the dishwasher with the breakfast dishes, pulled out Ava's clothes, undressed Ava from her pajamas, cleaned up toys, submerged her, and washed her hair while she played with toys that my mother remembered to add to the sudsy water, I asked if she'd watch Ava for the weekend. My mother just looked at me and said, "Sure." She didn't ask any questions and, if she had, I would have lied.

I felt at ease knowing Ava was in good hands as the jet took off, carrying me to meet an unfamiliar man. A man who was more than twenty years my senior. I was square with my decision to go and excited about what lay ahead. But as I analyzed the situation, questions kept disturbing my calm state.

*What does a grown man have in common with a skinny single mother from Minnesota? He's a doctor, a worldly businessman, and a traveler. What's making him take risks (beyond hiring an hourly hooker) to fly me across the country and spend a few days entertaining me? Is he lonely? Bored? Is he like Alberto and Don who aggressively sought out a young mistress? Is this a part of everyday normal relationships, or am I somehow drawn to these types of men? How could I have such adventures and not know one other person who had had them? Am I classy by nature, able to pull off what others like the Italian empress were born into? Something about me is attractive to older, accomplished men. What is it? How do I prune it to perfection?*

I was in for a long flight as the questions of the dynamics of being kept plaguing my brain until I stumbled on the chief question:

*If it is that I am to be kept, what should I do differently that I hadn't done with Alberto or Don?*

*What do you want, Savannah?*

The flight to San Diego lasted an eternity. Deep in thought, I found it remarkably easy to block out a screaming little girl seated about six rows behind me.

I sat in my seat even after the first class passengers exited, thinking about what lay ahead. I took deep breaths, gave myself an inner pep talk.

After deplaning, I thought that maybe that the screaming child was a warning sign, not unlike all of the other signs that had been subtly displayed and ignored throughout my life. I looked around for another glimpse at the little girl in hopes of finding clarification.

I played a game of "if/then." *If* she were still a distraught mess, *then* I'd forget about any long-term plans with Gunther and become a "normal" worker bee mother and settle into my ordinary Midwestern life.

I spotted the girl and her mother coming from the restroom. The girl had done a 180-degree turnaround. She was wobbling behind her mother, happy as a clam. As they walked past me, I whispered, "yes!"

# nine

Dr. Gunther Wydler was waiting at the baggage claim with a man dressed in a black suit. Gunther was just as homely as I remembered. He greeted me with a handshake and a warm smile as if I were a visiting business associate. I didn't mind. That pace was far better than him sticking his tongue down my throat or pressing my little breasts to his chest.

The man in black was the driver. He took my bags. I followed him and Dr. Wydler. With each step, I moved further away from my past and closer to what would become my future.

When I reached the stretched town car, the driver opened the door as Gunther walked around to the other side; it was the first time I had ridden in a limousine and I could not contain my curiosity. I slid open a lid and saw ice; another housed drinks of all sorts. I pushed a button that opened the roof and warm rays lit up the dark interior. Gunther smiled. I caught myself and resumed my place on the leather seat. I didn't want to look green to the high life but it was too late; he knew I was no expert, but my inexperience, naivety, and innocence were exactly what turned him on.

I found myself on familiar territory—in a game.

It was a bright and sunny day with one daunting cloud that hung ominously in the sky. I watched it for a while from the sunroof, and then slowly it dissipated just as we pulled into the hotel's carport.

Gunther had cleverly arranged adjoining suites. The bellhop, who was toting my solitary roll-on bag, followed us to our rooms even after I had told him several times that I could manage. He practically forced me to release the handle and I quickly learned why. The tip was substantial. The good doctor was generous, and the bellhop was far from being the bored moron I had assumed him to be.

Dr. Wydler and I didn't go through any awkward moments. We were eager to learn about one another, and the conversation was easy and informative. I asked about his career, the Northern California town where he had grown up, his life, and future. Then he performed the same inquisitive interview on me.

That night we went to a lovely restaurant. I enjoyed his company more than I had any other man under these obviously structured conditions. He was unintimidating, very humble, gracious, and a true gentleman. If he had been younger or if I had been attracted to him, or if there had been a smidgen of chemistry, he would have been an ideal mate. But none of those were the case. Our relationship would be an arrangement.

I had arrived on a Wednesday. We spent two days sightseeing in the beautiful, tranquil city with trips to Coronado, downtown, Pacific Beach, the La Jolla Cove, and Del Mar. I knew from all of the scenically stunning places I had seen that San Diego was the best in America. City life, fused with the ocean under the umbrella of small town values, was quite appealing to me. I immediately wanted to live there. The weather was like no other place I'd ever been, and the cleanliness and hominess made it a place where I could envision raising my child. I soaked in every detail.

The weekend was a surprise. Gunther asked me to accompany him to Vegas. I was thrilled; he could see it in my eyes. We left that Friday afternoon on a first-class American flight, returning to the scene of the crime.

By nature, Gunther was a nurturer. He didn't ask; he just did what he knew to be the right thing. He did all of the typical chivalrous things, but then he went beyond as his generosity was a big part of who he was. If I wanted a Coke, he'd give me a twenty-dollar bill to go get it. When I came back with change, he would refuse it. If I were torn between two entrées, he would tell the waiter to bring them both. He bought primo tickets and tipped handsomely. He took limos, not cabs; we sat first class, not coach.

He was accustomed to the best of the best, and this was extended to me as well. I felt special around him—valued.

I took things slowly. I wasn't looking to strike any deals during that trip. I wanted something more than a quick vacation and something less than living with him as his woman. I was looking for the ideal situation. And since I hadn't yet plotted that out, I had to be patient. Time would help me see the light. Plus, it wasn't just about me. I had Ava to consider. She changed the way I handled everything, especially Gunther.

I went back home wealthy by hood standards. I had the original fifteen hundred plus thirty two hundred from gambling—well, acquiring was what I called it. Gunther would give me gambling chips and leave me while he chose to gamble in solitude. I didn't like the whole, give your money to the person with cards and years of card dealing experience, or the loud money-sucking slot machines. I decided to pocket the chips and cash them in during a "bathroom break." I accumulated about twenty-two hundred and Gunther sent me home with another thousand.

The trip back was long and tedious. I was anxious to see Ava.

Ava screamed, "Mama!" and started to cry when I walked in the house. She dropped her toys as I bent down to pick her up. I held her tightly as I nestled my nose into her neck. She wrapped her tiny arms around me and would not let go. I sat on the couch holding my baby for about fifteen minutes. Her willingness to sit that long conveyed what she could not say—she had missed her mommy.

The home phone rang and the caller ID told me that it was Aaron. I didn't answer.

Aaron and I were still stuck in an on-again, off-again relationship. He was a hard habit to break. Our success teetered on his use of crack. The times he was sober, we would talk about getting a house and I'd dream about the white picket fence surrounding it. We went as far as to attend a few open houses.

We picked out Ava's room and discussed what changes we should make. We had even convinced my mother to come with us and check out a home that we really loved near a beautiful lake. Then, she, being a homeowner and non-delusional, would point out the obvious, and reality would slap us in the face, shaking us from our fantasy. We had no credit and bad credit; we had no money, no jobs, and no job history. We were in debt, and for good measure, she would remind us that we had a child. Maintaining a house when we couldn't even maintain an apartment... on and on.

She was right, of course. I was crazy to think such thoughts, but even though the possibility seemed grim, I knew I could have it. I could have it all. I also knew it would not be Aaron who would give it to me.

A few days after I settled back in, a feeling of contamination swept over me. I'd vacillate between praising myself for a job well done and self-reproach. I'd think about Ava's hug and then question my parental aptitude. I was ridden with guilt for leaving, but excited by what the future may hold.

I needed to talk to someone about my feelings regarding the Gunther trip, so I sought solace in the only person I knew would tell me what a brave and money-gettin' hustler I was, the only man who would boost my confidence and have me believe I was a "bad muthafucka" for puttin' the "smack down" on that "trick" and then not giving him shit in return.

Aaron.

After my detailed rendition of my experience, after I confessed that I felt dirty and less than worthy of bearing the name Lovely; after I expressed the plaguing, guilty feeling that consumed my motherly heart, he did what I needed him to do; he convinced me that I was a "down-ass bitch" and Ava would be better off because of it. After his pep talk, in my mind, I was indeed "the shit."

Then as slickly as any smooth operator I had ever known, he honed in on the money. He etched a story that was so well

174

constructed that it made complete sense as to why I should give him twenty-five hundred dollars. He capitalized on my vulnerability and need for a friend, and then spun his words to boost my esteem. Once I was in our corner rooting for Team Savannah and Aaron, he made his move. I learned the hard way—by giving Aaron the money.

I stood with my sober man in a delusional dreamland again; maybe with a few bucks, he could make something happen. He could flip a pound of marijuana, doubling his money and then do it again and again until we were financially secure, buying him time to find gainful, legitimate employment. He claimed he knew the person he would get the brick from and he had plenty of clients lined up. It was just weed. There was no risk. We could buy that duplex. It would be easy money; it was all lies.

I didn't see Aaron for a month. I sadly learned that he figured out how to gain access to my safe-deposit box and cleaned that out as well. I was devastated. I was left broke once again; thus, I couldn't afford the bail when he called from jail. Somehow, Aaron found a way to post.

After months of waiting, the time came for Aaron to go to serve out his six-month sentence. Prison was not a part of either Aaron's or my experience. We were both scared. I forgave him for stealing the money and promised I'd be in his corner through the ordeal. Maybe jail was for the best. Maybe he would use the experience at rock bottom and turn his life around. Maybe jail would break him of his drug habit and reform his soul. I did what I could to keep my promise and that was to go visit.

With child in tow, I took the trip to the men's correctional facility outside of the city, sitting in the dingy waiting area like all of the other stupid girlfriends to see my man. The visit depressed me. Aaron looked thin and beat down. He was hardened and disconnected from his child, the outside world, and me. He was learning to survive, and it was not an easy task. His new world had new rules, and he had to focus so as not to miss a lesson. My trivial updates on the Gunther situation or Ava's latest new feat went in one ear and out the other.

He was vacant.

I cried all the way home, wondering why I didn't stay away—far away—from his contagious smile and slick maneuvers. Why hadn't I adhered to the off-again from the onset? Why had I so desperately given him permission to drag me down? Why did I feel so obligated under a stupid street code to stand by my felon? The only reason that kept popping up was that I loved him. I loved him deeply. I had room in my heart for him and Ava, if I could only just change him.

There were letters and visits, and then one day, I rode two hours through a snowstorm on a public bus to visit. I waited and waited in the receiving room, and then visiting hours were over. Aaron didn't come out. I panicked, but the guards assured me that he was fine. If he had been killed, they would have alerted his family.

A week went by before he was able to call. He told me that he had managed to get into trouble and was sent to solitary confinement. I was angry that he didn't understand everything that I had to go through—getting Ava and myself ready, the bus ride, the search, the gates, the waiting, the disappointment, the ride back, all while weathering a dual storm of nature and nurture.

He didn't care. He had bigger problems, like not attaching a life sentence for murder to his six-month bid, or worse, not surviving it, so I kept the details of my life to myself.

Aaron got out. He and I never recovered from his jail stint, but the separation proved to be a good thing for my mental state. We had almost settled on being friends, except that we still had sex from time to time; well, we did until I found a used condom in his bed. Somehow, his deceit was an eye-opener, proving nothing I could do or say would change him. I didn't cry or mourn our breakup. I simply moved on.

Plus, my life had already taken its unconventional course. I purposefully had developed my second life, leaving frequently to visit Don on occasion, but mainly Gunther.

I had come to terms with doing what I had to do, and I did it.

# ten

Ava was a bit over two. She was my world. I didn't understand
why so many people thought she was spoiled. Perhaps they were
jealous that my two-year-old only wore designer clothes, had
every toy imaginable, and was doted on constantly. She was clever
and gorgeous, and I was there to make sure she wanted for nary a
thing. Thanks to Don and Gunther, my socio-economic status was
slowly heading into the black. I was spending their money—turned
my money—just as quickly as it was coming in. I was thrilled to
have that problem.

Gunther was CEO of a startup company called Sovium, a
seller of biochemicals and research reagents. After things were
underway with financing, he asked if I would move to San Diego
and open the United States headquarters. I couldn't have said "yes"
fast enough.

I was sure the year of "dating" had somehow lured him into
the trap of having the need to bring me closer to him. I was
equally as confident that the move would set me up for success, if
manipulated correctly. I was also certain that Gunther would not
and could not hang me out to dry. Like Alberto, he was in love.
I would once again solidify my standing as a kept woman. I was
accustomed to the routine. I had been summoned by the Major
League to play with the big dogs. I was going pro in area code 619.

I told my mother. She wasn't surprised. She had uprooted
and replanted for a fresh start herself; she knew how necessary
that process could be to a stifled life. My mother had been there
when I needed her and would be there if I ever needed her again.
We didn't talk much about my plan, thankfully, because I really
didn't know what I would have said. I was leaving to find my idea
of a better life, only with a keen instinct that that was what was
awaiting me—us.

It was a steamy August day when Mikey and my mother took Ava and I to the airport. We said so-long to Minnesota, to Aaron, and to the mundane. However, it was very difficult to say goodbye to my mother.

"You can come visit as soon as we get settled." I could feel the ball of emotion get caught in my throat.

Mikey punched me in my shoulder, vowing to visit. My mother kissed Ava and me and walked away so that I couldn't see the painful wince of my mother's eye, left forlorn once again when her baby waved goodbye.

Ava and I moved into a swanky hotel in Torrey Pines. The day we were checking in, Elizabeth Taylor walked right past us followed by her entourage carrying a sea of Louis Vuitton suitcases.

*Wow!*

Ava got a kick out of ordering room service and scribbling her "signature" on the room charge bill. We lounged around the pool drinking virgin coladas as if we were on a tropical vacation. That was our life. We were treated like royalty. The staff bent over backwards to make us feel at home, and for three weeks, it truly was our home.

I rented a car and traipsed all over La Jolla and Del Mar searching for the perfect place to live. It was the valet who told me about the Golden Triangle. The name was appropriate. It was an area between major freeways that formed a triangle and housed some of San Diego's elite. Centrally located, it was a jewel of a community.

A brand-new complex had been built: the Villas of Renaissance. It was a stunning oasis with plenty of palm trees, birds of paradise, fountains, and pools. The property was fashioned to be a contemporary Venetian retreat. I sent the prospectus to Gunther; he sent the money for deposits on two apartments:

his and mine. I made sure that the units were not too close in proximity to one another. I needed my space, and he made it clear that he did too. It was indeed going to be an interesting arrangement.

We both were in high spirits. Gunther and I still hadn't done much in the way of consummating our relationship. I had no idea what I had gotten myself into. Prior to my move, on one of the earlier trips, I had professed that I was a lesbian. Gunther seemed not to mind. I believe that it posed a unique opportunity in his mind; he would not have to compete with men, making his life much less complicated. But I was worried about how the whole lesbian thing would play out, as I was not a lesbian. I had to be crafty each and every step of the way so as not to let on, but more important, I had to find a way to secure the lie and affix it so there was no skepticism.

My mind was at work. My survival instincts were on autopilot.

In the spirit of Johnny Ray and Aaron, I pimped myself. I created an inner-dialog monster. But those constant pep talks (which I called "pimp talks") made a difference.

*Make that motherfucker pay. You got to get it while you can. Stack chips!*

Gunther was in for a hell of a ride.

My three-bedroom, top-floor apartment was where I wanted to be. It was huge and had vaulted ceilings, making it look and feel twice its size.

Again, I shopped for everything new, including my first home computer.

*Touché, Mr. Gates, touché!*

I went to modern furniture stores. Ungodly price tags were attached to the uniquely crafted furnishings that screamed my name. I had a great sense of decor, and with unlimited funds, decorating was pleasurable. I spent over fifty thousand dollars and my place was fabulous. Gunther's place wasn't nearly the labor of love mine had been. All of Gunther's utensils, bedding, and bath items came from Target. I bought him cheap, traditional furniture, conservative and bland. The vast deferential was that my apartment was my primary home and his was his third. He was happy that I was eager to do the work, which he had rather not.

I loved the Villas, with their newness and the amenities. Aside from offering the usual things—pool, Jacuzzi, workout room— they organized parties, picnics, and brunches. They provided arts and crafts for the kids, a concierge service that basically did everything from dry cleaning pick-up and drop-off to house cleaning. I took advantage of it all.

After a month of organizing our personal lives, including furnishing Gunther's apartment, securing a monthly rental car, opening checking and savings accounts for Ava, Gunther, and me, paying off all my debt, including all of my student loans, it was time to establish the U.S. office.

Gunther performed according to a checklist system. But his line items were so general that I had to create sub-lists and break down and rearrange things into practical to-do lists. I had never started a business, but was determined to figure it out. The City of San Diego Small Business Association (SBA) was helpful. They provided a plethora of information for start-ups. I followed their step-by-step instructions. It was a grueling but not an impossible task. I was proud of what I had learned and how I systematically went about setting up the business.

I scheduled meetings and did the bulk of the groundwork prior to Gunther's return; I did everything from acquiring the correct permits to arranging meetings with accountants, bankers, insurance companies, the Better Business Bureau, and the Chamber of Commerce.

By the time Gunther returned from Europe, an entire two weeks were booked with important dates. He was impressed, and I was pleased.

We settled on one of four locations that I had diligently scouted with the commercial realtor. We received the keys to the U.S. headquarters; Sovium was up and soon to be running.

As Gunther and I walked around the 2,500-square-foot space inspecting every detail, I was thinking out loud about what desk should go where in one of the back offices, when he reached for my blouse, gently pulling it from the waistband, lifting it to reveal a white lace bra. His plan of getting me alone to meet his primary object worked.

I played along on the very familiar territory, my stage. He clumsily moved in. He pulled one side of the bra cup over my breast and began to suck the exposed nipple. He concurrently navigated the other hand up my skirt, rubbing my inner thighs and then vagina.

He thought he was Casanova, but his hands were slightly moist and cool. He was nervous and jittery. It felt like making out with a virgin boy in high school. I let out a sigh, but not of boredom or disgust. It had a dual meaning; for me, it was: *Here we go with this again.* He interpreted it as a sigh of passion. He was obviously turned on by the noise and sucked even harder.

I was numb again and somewhat sad that I had found myself in a passionless, non-reciprocating position. It was what it was.

It was at that moment that I learned the art of "faking it." With my head tilted back, I squeaked out a sound that set him off further. I unbuttoned my own blouse, suggesting to him that I wanted him and lifted my skirt. He handled my breasts roughly before dropping to his knees. I thrust his head between my legs and moaned wildly. The sounds got higher in pitch as I climaxed and faked an orgasm. After I caught my phony loss of breath, I reached for his belt buckle. He moved away.

"That was for you," he said. And once again I spoke in a low whisper to the Lord as Gunther searched for the light switch.

"Thank you, Jesus."

Gunther was serious about his pleasing. It made me realize that he truly wanted to see me happy. It was not his fault that anything sexual from him could not do the trick; in actuality, it did the opposite. I was a paid professional performer, and he would never know it. I just had to make him think he was pleasing me, and he would continue to try his best.

He went to one bathroom, I to another. Thankfully, there was no mirror. I could not bear seeing my reflection. Again, I sighed.

That night, Gunther surprised me with another trip to Vegas. With Ava in tow, we headed off to our very familiar stomping grounds. I arranged for the hotel babysitting service to stay with Ava while Gunther and I went to dinner, a show, and gambled.

The routine was basically the same; Gunther would give me about two thousand dollars in chips and cash, and then he would leave me alone. I had become immune to losing money, as I knew it would be replenished when I tracked the ATM (Gunther) down. I had an endless bankroll and became quite the black jack and baccarat player.

The second night in Vegas, Gunther and I had an expensive French dinner at Bally's. Gunther ordered. When the frog legs arrived, they smelled just as scrumptious as the escargot I had had on my first date with Don and had the identical effect. Frog legs became one of my favorite delicacies.

Over dinner, I asked Gunther why he didn't like to gamble with me. He was surprised by my question. He had always thought that it was I who preferred to gamble alone because of what people might think. I knew what people thought: I was a skanky trull, whoring my body and time for the cheap thrill of gambling and a couple of bucks. I didn't care. I had long ago stopped caring about what other people had going on inside of their heads.

From then on, we sat next to one another at the tables. Every night, I performed the one-woman act of faking an orgasm.

Things had become predictable and routine (in our version of sex). He'd go down; I'd come. On few a drunken occasions, it was real, but mostly, it was not. He'd jerk his own penis until he was satisfied, ejaculating on to his own stomach, like an epileptic frog.

I never sucked, kissed, or licked his smaller-than-average sized man part. I didn't want to, and he didn't allow it, so why would I attempt to change things? I believed that he was staying on the safe side of any full-on sexual encounters with me so as not to disturb the possible heterosexual within. Trying to stick his pee-pee where it didn't belong might prompt me to run off with a man half his age. He was thrilled with the way things were, and I had conveniently convinced myself that I was too, in a loveless, sexless relationship.

On the last day of our trip, Gunther took Ava and me shopping. Ava got chic gear for school, and I got a whole new business wardrobe. The clothes were dazzling. I looked forward to going to work. Ava couldn't wait to go to anywhere.

Money took on a different meaning in my life. I was no longer frugal or financially stressed. Sovium was paying me five thousand dollars a month, and Gunther another ten thousand along with anywhere from five to ten thousand dollars from our repeated gambling trips to Vegas. Gunther paid my rent, BMW car note, and the insurance. I stopped shopping by price at grocery and department stores. My housekeeper placed fresh, beautiful bouquets in every room weekly. I pampered myself with manicures and pedicures, and had a standing weekly hair appointment. When my friends had birthdays, I sent five hundred dollars. If my family needed anything, I gave it freely, without expectation of repayment. My accounts were plush. Money was no longer an issue; my need for security had been more than met.

My life was good, very good—except for the nagging

thought that our fairy-tale life was an outright lie. I pretended to like Gunther. I convinced everyone that we were just friends (including my daughter and mother).

I developed a self-loathing every time I had to play the role of dedicated girlfriend, every time we had our version of sex, and every time I looked in the mirror. It was a hard realization that I was simply a very highly paid plaything.

I could easily put the negative reminders out of my head with alcohol, partying with my peers, or spending money. But how long would those temporary fixes last? When would I have to face the truth that I was not happy?

My only comfort was the fact that Gunther didn't live in southern California, yet. He still had his home in San Francisco. Plus, he was establishing his business overseas and was gone much of the time. Without that respite, we would never have made it past three months.


From Vegas, Gunther flew off to Europe, and Ava and I returned to San Diego.

The Sovium office was waiting for me. It took thirty days to get it operational. Again, I shopped; I purchased the carpet, phone system, computers, fax, coffee and postal machines, lobby desks and chairs, pictures, shelves, file cabinets, plants, company signage, office supplies, letterhead, and furniture for accounting, reception, the break room, and three offices. I needed help.

Ava the diva didn't like the temporary day care where I left her while I ran around town. So I called her dad in to babysit. It was the least he could do.

Aaron was totally astonished by my living conditions. He looked around my apartment at all of the nice things, studying the artwork and praising me on the modern, colorful décor. It pissed me off. Why was he surprised? When he met me, I was living in sky-rise, ocean-view luxury. With him, I had tried to build a home overlooking the city of Minneapolis.

*Does he think that I don't deserve this?*

It was with Aaron that my standards had dropped to an all-time low. With him, I floated just above the poverty level trying to get ahead only to be brought back down by his lowly, selfish ways. He was toxic.

Ava was thrilled to see her dad. She wouldn't let go of his hand. She took him to her room to show off her princess bed and her very own TV. While Aaron sat on her bed, Ava put on her favorite swimsuit.

"You mind if we go swimming?" Aaron shouted.

"Not at all. I have some things to do."

While they were gone, I went about the necessary task of hiding all bank information, keys, codes, and anything tied to any money in my safe deposit box; I prayed for strength. The light came on…

It wasn't Aaron. It was I! I was the idiot who let all the atrocities occur. He was who he was. I had changed! I had convinced myself that he brought me down, when in actuality, I had done everything to myself. I made bad and costly decisions. I gave him power, knowing that he was a drug addict. I allowed myself to wallow in self-pity and to become depressed. It was all done entirely by myself. I, I,

*I* …

I decided to buy Aaron new clothes and shoes. My thinking was that if he felt good and was included in my success, he wouldn't do anything to mess it up, like steal the lamps and pennies and disappear on a week-long binge in search for "the answer" via a crack pipe. In return, I expected him to treat my home with respect.

He did.

Every day, I came home from work to find Aaron, Ava, and the house spit-shined with dinner on the table.

Aaron's attempts to rekindle any kind of feelings and his desperate effort to be more than friends/less than lovers were transparent. They had come much too late. The days of crying myself to sleep and praying for miracles were long gone. All I wanted was for Aaron to cherish his daughter and be a great father even if I had to be his guide, pay for plane tickets, and forgo child support. I would no longer badger Aaron about his shortcomings; I would accept them and move on.

My mind was clear. I was in charge of my own destiny, even as it applied to Gunther. I had to find the happy medium of being kept and all that it entailed, and maintain respect for myself. I was in a fortunate position and needed to figure out how to take huge advantage. That would be the only way to survive this life. I needed balance to live without regret and self-hatred.

# eleven

Aaron left and it was back to single motherhood. Long days of exertion at Sovium and catering to Gunther took their tolls. The reason I managed was because of one word: duplicity.

In order to reconcile my self-analyzing thoughts with the frightening reality that I was once again a mere concubine, and for the sake of my sanity in raising a lawless two-year-old, my dual life had to be developed—the loving *Savannah* my friends and family knew and *Vannah*, the loveless, money-mongering bitch out to get hers at all costs.

Ava too had developed duplicitous ways. My quiet and obedient angel could change into the spawn of the devil at will. I was scared. I should have known things were getting out of hand when she started barking orders and throwing tantrums. I didn't know that it was the beginning of a one-year sentence to the insane asylum.

My ability to manage a mouthy toddler was nil. Ava had a favorite saying, and she used it relentlessly. It was shouted at me after a long day of work, twenty times a night.

"Don't tell me no; tell me yes!"

It was triggered every time she heard the word *no*. And for a toddler, that was pretty much all the time. *No*, we cannot have McDonald's again. *No*, don't throw the couch pillows off the balcony. *No*, you may not watch *Beauty and the Beast* again tonight. *No*, you may not paint the television with pink lipstick.

I was trying to get her ready for bed when she wiggled free. I chased her sticker-clad body from her room down the hall and into the master bathroom. She slammed the door and locked it. I repeatedly asked her to open it. She refused. I found the metal key, poked it through the hole, and pushed the door open. She stood there with her hands on her naked hips. She screamed, "Don't tell me no; tell me *yes!*"

I took a deep breath and shut the door. I left her in the bathroom. If I had not, it would have been the first time I, Vannah, would have beaten Ava. My nerves and patience were shot.

Ava stayed in the bathroom. When she came out, I, Savannah, was asleep on the couch. Already covered from head to toe in stickers, Ava had added lipstick, mascara, blush, and eyeliner (all used incorrectly). She snuggled up to me and we, the duplicitous mother and child, slept.


*Tristan*

The next day, I took off work and spent the day at a La Jolla spa pampering myself with a moisturizing facial, sugar scrub, and seaweed wrap, topped off with a manicure and pedicure and a trip to the hair salon. That night, I called the sitter and blew off plans with Gunther. I hit my favorite Friday nightspot, The Red Lion hotel's lobby bar/night club.

The place was extremely popular, and I had everyone on the bankroll; the valet who parked my car up front and let me hang on to my own keys, fifty bucks; the doorman who let me skip the long entry line, a hundred bucks; the bartender who kept 'em comin', another hundred bucks. Club Hitz had prepared me well. I knew what made those people tick; it was the same thing that made me tick: cold hard cash.

A tall handsome man watched me as I got out of my car, breezed into the club, and gave a nod to the bar back who then whispered into the bartender's ear and moments later brought me a drink. I didn't see that man again until much later. And when I saw him, I saw stars rain down from the ceiling and felt my clitoris performing summersaults; the female version of a hard-on.

He was standing amongst the big, chest-out guys in the "playas' corner." I pretended not to notice the NFL players when

I approached. My eyes were locked in, a ploy to make one feel special. The DJ blasted out song after song of up-tempo dance tunes, coaxing people to the dance floor. I asked the jock if he'd like to dance.

"No."

I turned to walk away.

He tugged at my arm.

"Where you going?" he shouted.

"I want to dance, and you don't. So why should I stay?"

"My ankle's sprung."

"Oh, how'd that happen?"

*Football practice?*

"Work."

"What do you do?"

"I'm a firefighter."

*Yeah, right you are, Tristan Henderson, number 23 of the San Diego Chargers.*

I was a professional clubber; I was well aware of the athletes' watering holes, who they were, how much they made, and who was getting cut. I knew which ones had tiny sticks and which ones were hung with tree trunks. I probably knew more about them than they knew about themselves.

Many of the girls who were in that particular club did too. The difference was I was a classy, nonchalant, manipulating hustler and they were young, dumb, gold-digging groupies—each one a clone of the other.

"Whew. I'm glad you didn't say football player! You can buy me a drink then," I said, convincing him of my gullibility.

Tristan and I hit it off. We made googly eyes for most of the night even across the club and through the barrage of females that wanted his attention and the host of men that wanted mine.

We were honed in to each other; our minds were made up.

The very next day, Tristan and I met for lunch at a casual

restaurant in Mission Valley. We had a nice conversation; there was a lot of flirting and lip licking, but he was nervous. I thought for sure it was because I didn't date football players, and he would have to eventually come clean.

"Look, I play for the San Diego Chargers. Is that gonna be a problem?"

*Yep. I was right, and no, that certainly is not a problem.*

I gasped and played coy.

"Okay, I'll let it slide, if you kiss me," I said as I leaned into him.

We spent every day of that first week together doing nothing other than the nasty. My body had never known that kind of treatment. I was sore from head to toe, but that didn't stop me from craving him insatiably. His smooth, youthful mocha skin; godly physique; and huge cock was a far cry from the ghastly white, soft, limp flesh of the aging Gunther.

Tristan was four years younger that I was; I began to see the attractiveness of youth to the old. I had rounded the corner. There was a time when the men I dated were older. However, I was getting older and wanted the fresh innocence of youthful men. Once you get a taste of youth, it is difficult to go back, clarifying why older men were drawn to me.

Tristan was the remedy for my life. I had struck a balance; I had a sexual outlet that could withstand Gunther and my life as a kept woman.

As long as Tristan and I had a clear understanding of my two simple, unbreakable, heavily-punishable-if-broken laws, things would work out fabulously:

1) Gunther comes first.
2) Don't ever reveal yourself to Gunther. He's my job/money.

Tristan was cool with the rules. All I wanted was for him to make love to me as often as possible. We didn't even have to talk.

Gunther returned from Europe. Tristan played his part and stayed away while I played mine, entertaining Gunther.

During Gunther's stay in San Diego, we worked hard, made out in accounting, went to Vegas on the weekends, and enjoyed San Diego's finest restaurants. It was then that we discovered Mille Fleur, an exquisite restaurant that made me replace Italian with French food as my favorite cuisine.

We ate large portions of caviar with homemade blinis, frog legs, lobster salad with citrus crème dressing, sweet breads, foie gras, and black truffle mashed potatoes that made you want to slap someone.

With Gunther, I became well versed in wines: the reds, like cabernet sauvignon, pinot noir, Chianti, Bordeaux; and the whites, like chardonnay, Sancerre, Gewurztraminer, pinot blanc, pinot grigio, and Riesling. He educated me on which selections tasted better with which foods.

We often ate at restaurants where there were wine pairings; it was an absolute treat, because you were poured a different sampling of wine with each delicious course.

Mille Fleur was our home. It was where the wealthiest of patrons spent their Friday and Saturday evenings. Their piano bar was equipped with a skilled piano man, a master on the ebony and ivory, and an overall crowd-pleaser.

Gunther and I were settling into our situation. But after the first few weeks following his return, I was bored. I didn't want to go to Vegas or make out in the accounting department. I didn't want to get dolled up and go to Mille Fleur, paste a fake smile across my face, and sing heartrending storytelling songs from the '70s, like "Mr. Bojangles," with people three times my age or better.

I wanted Tristan.

It was Friday night; we were finishing up at Sovium and the staff was talking about their weekend plans. Gunther was passively infuriated with me and avoided any conversation on the subject. That was the first time that while he was in town that I hadn't made plans with him.

Once we were alone, away from our minions, he attempted to get me to commit to something but I used Ava as an excuse, claiming that she needed me to stay home for a few nights and spend time with her. I also said that it was going to be hard to get a babysitter with such late notice because there was a huge music festival going on in Pacific Beach, blah, blah, blah—lies.

He was suspicious, but I did my best to reassure him that we could make plans for the next weekend. With that, I dialed Tristan.

No answer. I left him a message instructing him to leave me a message on my home phone, letting me know whether or not he was available to come over and if so, at what time. Before I left work, I picked up my desk phone and checked my home messages. It was on: Tristan cock at ten o'clock.

With so much prepping to be done, I rushed out, almost forgetting to say good-bye to Gunther.

My housekeeper came on Fridays, so I was good there—grocery store: check; Victoria's Secret: check; spend time with Ava before her sleepover at my neighbor's house: check. Try to get Ava out of the princess outfit that she'd had on for two days: no check…okay, three days. By 9:30, I was good to go.

My place was beautiful. Calla lilies, lilacs, and Stargazers adorned the glass tables. I had beverages and appetizing snack items on hand in case my man needed nourishing. The sheets were just out of the dryer, and I was just out of the shower with Victoria's Secret laciness under jeans and a silk blouse. All was right.

When Tristan came through the door dressed in brand-new clothes, smelling subtly of soap, it was as if a year had passed. I couldn't wait to get at him. He was turned on by my eagerness;

we ripped at one another's clothes until we got to the bed. Not a word was needed. He pulled my small frame over his muscular torso, and we passionately kissed.

My phone rang. I paused. It stopped and rang again, and then again and again.

We both knew who it was.

As we lay there, both frozen, listening to the nagging ringing, we knew that we had messed up. I answered the phone on the third ring of the fifth call.

Tristan sat up, concerned. I put my finger to my lips. He rolled his eyes to say, "No duh."

I used my best sleeping voice. Gunther immediately accused me of fucking around. He was shouting at the top of his lungs.

"You are a disaster and have no idea what you are doing!"

"Leave me in peace for one weekend or forever! I don't give a damn! It's your choice!" I screamed back.

I slammed the phone down on the cradle. Then I removed it. If he called back, I didn't want to hear the noise.

*Shoot! Did I blow my lesbo cover? What have I just done?*

I didn't care. I had a very sexy, naked man with a huge hard-on to tend to. I pulled back the sheet and put his penis in my mouth, and all our immediate concerns were sucked away.

The next day, Tristan and I were eating breakfast when we heard a knock at the door.

"Don't answer it," Tristan said.

"I ain't that kind of girl."

If Gunther were coming to drop the financial jackhammer, I wouldn't run. If he wanted it over, so be it.

*Say it to my face and carry on.*

I briefly pictured Gunther with his marshmallow knuckles, back-handing Tristan for messing with his dame. I smiled at the visual. Tristan, a six foot two inch, 195-pound NFL player, looked panicked as if Gunther could do him bodily harm. I wondered if Gunther got violent if Tristan would kick his ass or cower in the corner.

"Who is it?" I asked from behind my locked door.

It was a floral deliveryman. Gunther was the only man who sent flowers.

The thought of the arrangement exploding as soon as the deliveryman was a safe distance away crossed my mind, but that was Alberto, not Gunther. Gunther was harmless.

The guy handed me an enormous bouquet with all my favorite varieties. I put it on the table and fished for the card. It read: *Have a nice weekend. GW.*

I was baffled. I read it four times. I didn't know what to make of it.

# twelve

My guilt for hurting Gunther was eased by my transformation
to a woman of docile, accommodating behaviors. I didn't want to
ruin my plush life for second-string Tristan dick. So for months,
I spent time with Gunther as often as he wanted to help reduce
his pain.

Simultaneously, I was creating a vast amount of pain in
myself. I hid any inkling of unhappiness by becoming quite
skilled at performing arts. Night after night, he planned events,
movies, and dinners. I was exhausted and sick to death of
Gunther. Acting proved overwhelming.

On the fifth night, I halfheartedly dressed for yet another
night out with Gunther. Ava was now three. She was crying
because she didn't want me to leave. I had to. It was my
unspoken contractual obligation as a kept woman.

As I wiped her tears away, I looked around at all the
expensive things that I had acquired for Ava and myself—
things that I had paid for with my time, body, and spirit even
when I didn't want to. Those things beat out my happiness. Her
happiness.

My staying with Gunther could only be explained by
obscenely selfish greed coupled with years of mental and moral
reconditioning. I loved the lifestyle, the accumulated cash that
afforded me all of our pretty little things. I was young, with
money and living a life that most people could only dream about.
I brushed on more blush.

*Stop whining and suck it up, Savannah. Where the hell is hard
hearted Vannah when you need her?*

Gunther picked me up. I was one minute late and he made a
point to act irritated.

I went about the evening on autopilot. Feelings of loathing

for everyone and everything surfaced, including people and things associated with his restaurant of choice.

By the end of the night, I was ready to go home, home to my daughter. But still on auto, I headed to Gunther's apartment. I had almost worked up the nerve to say good night, when he pulled out a wad of temptation, my pacifier, the reason I was there. He wiped away any thoughts of an upheaval. I stayed. I did what was expected.

As his fumbling hands drunkenly moved over my body, I pretended. I acted. I faked. I had been doing it for years.

*Hurry up, before I smash your trachea with my thighs.*

I had disappointed myself.

When I returned home, saddened by my choice and lack of courage, I paid the sitter and went to wash the nastiness away. Ava came into the bathroom and gently hugged my bare legs. Her soft fingertips unknowingly caressed my thigh. I bent down removed her beloved princess crown and kissed her forehead in the same place I did when I had left earlier.

She smiled.

Her smiles always melted my heart and brought me away from negative thoughts to a place where I could take a breath and see that things weren't so bad. My angel's glorious smile meant all was right in the world.

Then with one sentence, she took it all away. Her words pierced my brain like a ball bearing that had dropped from a skyscraper.

"Mama, why does your butt smell like Gunther?"

I couldn't believe it. My daughter knew that the smell was undeniably of Gunther's cologne. I prayed her young mind couldn't imagine anything beyond what I replied.

What had I done? Were my life choices subtly deranging hers?

I fought back the emotionally induced tears.

"He spilled his cologne on his car seat and Mama sat in it."

But nothing could stop the wave that moved through my being.

Nauseated. Hot. Dizzy. My knees buckled, and I fell to the floor, pulled myself up to the toilet, opened the lid, and puked up the whole evening.

Keeping Ava unsuspecting wouldn't last forever. She would grow up and ask even worse questions. I had to regain power. Answers to her questions couldn't come from a cowardly, powerless puppet.

That was the last night Gunther had power over me. I found my voice, and I'd be damned if he wasn't going to pay for each and every time in the past that I hadn't used it.

I was on a mission: find strength to make changes.

The next day, after recovering from the emotional breakdown and horrid hangover, I told Ava to pack some toys and swimsuits.

"Where are we going?"

"On an adventure, baby!"

"Adventure to where?"

"It's a surprise."

The girl couldn't hold water, and I didn't want her telling everyone our destination. I needed a real break.

I packed up the car with all our beach gear and headed south on interstate/highway 5, toward Mexico.

While Ava slept, I contemplated. There was no way I could sustain my lifestyle without Gunther. I could pay rent and bills, but for how long before the worry surfaced and the money ran out? I had a cushy life but was living it basically from month to month. What was it that I wanted? How could I make myself happy in this odd relationship?

When Ava and I arrived in Rosarito, I promised myself not to think about Gunther, money, or our future. My goal was simply to enjoy life and Ava.

La Paloma was more than a resort; it was respite, hospice, and rehab center rolled into a single, non-smoking, oceanfront room. The fresh breeze infiltrated our spirits, marking the beginning of a fun-filled adventure.

Ava was my doctor, medicine, and strength. We spent our days playing on the beach, horseback riding, eating freshly caught lobster, shopping, getting our hair bead braided, and laughing. She was my dinner date, friend, and massage therapist. I was her easygoing, silly, and loving mom.

After five days, I was ready to take on life. Only it would be under my command. Our trip marked the end of my complacency and Ava's obsession with princess outfits. We headed back to the real world.

It was the first of the month. Rent was due. Gunther was accustomed to handing me the check for my rent. I usually stopped by to pick it up, or I got it at work or over dinner, or sometimes he dropped it off at my place.

While we were gone, Gunther had been calling my house line fifty times a day trying to reach me. I walked through the door and went straight to the ringing phone. I took in a deep breath and finally picked up.

"I'm coming over," was all he said.

His tone told me that he was upset.

I sent Ava to my neighbors'. I tried to keep Ava and Gunther separated as much as possible. The combination just seemed wrong.

I was smiling at the memories of the past week as I put a load of summer clothes, swimsuits, and beach towels into the washing machine, and then he knocked. I shut the lid and went to answer the door.

My mind was different, my attitude adjusted. I could tell by my assuredness and demeanor that the scene would be the telltale of the path our relationship would take. I was ready.

I opened the door.

"Hello."

"Where were you?"

I invited him to sit on the couch.

"I took Ava to Mexico for a vacation. You know, with the money you gave me when you said 'spend some time with Ava'?"

"You disappeared! You said nothing! You didn't come to work! This is not acceptable!"

"What's done is done. What now?"

He sat quietly. His face contorted. He took my lack of remorse for insolence and did the only thing he knew he could to punish me; he withheld money.

With an outstretched arm, he held the rent check.

"Here's the rent money," he said.

When I reached for it, he pulled it away. He held it out again. But before he could pull it back, I snatched it from his slow hands. He dove, grabbed it, and then angrily ripped it into little pieces.

I balled up my fist and punched him in his ugly, screwed-up face. It felt good.

My hands, without mercy, pummeled his arms that were blocking his face and upper body. He fell off the couch into a defensive fetal position. I kicked his head and back with my heel to cause the most damage.

I was trying to physically hurt him, much like the way I believed him to be financially hurting me. I had built him up to be my puppeteer by allowing him to control me with money. At that moment, I wanted to strangle him with my strings.

My repressed anger emerged so uncontrollably that I didn't recall how I came to be holding a knife. My mind was set on slicing him from ear to ear or stabbing him repeatedly in the kidneys, or perhaps even gutting him.

The slight smirk that was strangely on his face when he raised his head was instantly erased as his eyes froze with terror.

"Vannah, please put down the knife."

The loud washing machine kicked in. Swoosh, swoosh, swoosh echoed around the apartment formulating the soundtrack to a possible homicide.

He said it again.

"Vannah! Put down the knife."

Images of a naked Alberto flashed through my mind. I dropped the knife.

"Get out!" I shouted as I walked to the door.

Swoosh, swoosh.

I was violently shaking as he slowly crawled toward me. I stood still watching and waiting as he inched his way across the living room. He was in pain. He finally reached the door. I opened it; he didn't stand up, and with his head down, he crawled out. I slammed the door and locked it.

"Oh, my God," I said out loud as I leaned against the wall. "Oh, my God."

I shook with disbelief. I had never felt so much rage. I had snapped and very well could have killed a human being! I paced the floor trying to calm myself down. I looked at the knife.

Swoosh, swoosh, swoosh.

I couldn't take the noise. Was it again a warning of sorts, like the ocean, the daunting cloud, the little girl on the plane? I flipped the lid open to stop the cycle all together. The load sat submerged in water. I slammed the laundry closet door.

*Oh, my God!*

I was sure that would be the last time Gunther and I ever spoke to one another.

Twenty minutes later, my phone rang. I removed my swollen hand from the bucket of ice. I was hoping it was my mother returning my call. I needed to tell her that I was probably moving back home.

"Hello."

"I apologize, Vannah." His voice frightened me.

I hung up. He called back and left a very rueful message. He called again and again. Gunther left message after message that begged for my forgiveness.

My mind could not fathom why he took so much abuse. When I had gotten to a point where physical abuse became an answer to solving a problem? Hadn't my trip to Mexico been for the purpose of a fresh start? What kind of start was this? How do I proceed? How do I go back?

Both Gunther and I were psychologically and systematically tearing the other to shreds. My beating him was equally as sick as his accepting it, apologizing for it, and blaming himself for it. I cried; I realized that I was abusive. I had always understood and basked in the fact that I could melt hearts; even that was a form of psychological abuse, but I had never physically beaten another person. My achy fist was a blatant reminder; but what about the permanent scars on my psyche? What kind of person was I?

I left Ava at the neighbors and got drunk, alone in my apartment.

*What are you gonna do now?*

It was clear Gunther wasn't ever going to leave me. No matter what I did, or did not do, he would be there. It wasn't sexual intercourse he desired after all. Gunther wanted to be kicked, punched, bitten, and shamed. We were the same. I was weak for money and Gunther was weak for humiliation. Where Gunther would not leave, Tristan would not stay. Tristan was busy with his job, so he said. The truth was he was bored playing back up to Gunther. He lost respect for me and despised my duplicitous lifestyle. He told me that I had no moral code and that I needed Jesus. Then, he stopped taking my calls. I was crushed. We had spent such intimate times together. He knew my life story—the true story. He was the only friend that I had in San Diego; he was the only one hugging me, even if it was preceded or followed by sex. Tristan left a void and without him around, I hit the streets. I started hanging out at swanky bars and meeting fascinating people. I acquired acquaintances, both male and female, trying to fill the void.

Gunther didn't like it. I didn't care. So began Gunther's obsession. He had lost control of his once submissive girl and was creatively inventing ways of gaining it back.

He made lunch and dinner plans with business associates. My work schedule was made to include traveling with him. The weekends were reserved for Vegas. I couldn't escape him for one moment. Our arguments escalated.

Mentally and financially, I prepared to leave him. But he was crafty, and it was pretty easy for him to entice me back to a submissive mind state with even larger amounts of money. Every evening, we had dinner plans; afterwards, he'd give me money. Every weekend, we went to Vegas, where I always came home with money. Money was the motivation behind everything. The more he gave me, the more I wanted. The more I got, the easier it was to do what he wanted. The more he saw that money was my motivation, the more he gave me—a continual circle of misguided values.

My so called glamorous life was unraveling. I was a cheerless marionette, even though I had vowed to make changes. The balancing act that I thought I was so equipped to handle was becoming overwhelming. I was depressed and mad that I hadn't changed, but I masked it beautifully, hiding behind the thrill of acquiring more money.

Gunther wasn't the man that I had dated for a year prior to moving. He had changed. He was in love with someone who could not exchange the sentiment. I had played my role so convincingly that he believed that, deep down, I had to have had feelings for him; plus, I had stayed with him, a sign of true love.

I knew that Gunther suffered from my actions, and yet I still continued on. I turned him into an insecure maniac just as I had done to Alberto.

Employment at Sovium was annoying on a good day. I dreaded going and purposefully half-assedly performed my managerial and secretarial duties. I truly hated seeing Gunther's face.

Thankfully, Vegas was a gratifying dressing. He sensed that, and we went often.

By my estimation, Gunther and I traveled to Sin City eighteen times in any twelve-month period. We saw every show, ate at every expensive restaurant, saw every hotel's premier suite (we moved around Caesar's, Rio, Bellagio, Mandalay Bay), and shopped at pricey boutiques. Vegas and the money acquisition never got old; it was just the company I kept. But with a little imagination and constant pimp talks, I could reinvent our relationship and convince myself life with Gunther was worthwhile and exciting.

My vivid imagery could spark the flame or create a mind-blowing fantasy for my otherwise unusual and depressing life. But Vegas would end. I'd deposit the cash. Gunther would commence driving me crazy again.

His trips away were getting shorter and further apart; most of his time was being spent breathing down my neck. At work, I couldn't move an inch without looking up to find him leaning over my shoulder. He thought it was cute, foreplay for when the last employee left and he'd head off to the accounting office, anxiously waiting for and expecting me to trail him. The whole scene was creepy and exasperating, and I told him as much. In the aftermath of that conversation, he continued his disturbing accounting room ritual.

Things worsened. On one of Gunther's brief trips away, I let myself into his apartment to do a little pillaging. I was certain that Gunther had obsessive-compulsive disorder (OCD) but was never professionally diagnosed. Everything about his clothes, his work, his car, his apartment, and his behavior suggested it. Nothing was ever out of place. When we sat down to dinner and he saw a fork or knife was crooked, he was compelled to straighten it. Everything had to be flawless. He put pressure on himself, his employees, and me to be perfect. Nothing could be dirty, disorganized, or have any errors.

Because of his idiosyncrasies, I believed that I could easily find what I was looking for. I stood at the door and analyzed his place—the carpet, which lights were on, the closed curtains. I had to be aware.

I carefully picked up stacks of neatly labeled and organized files and sifted through them. I scoured his credit card statements and a pile of miscellaneous paperwork. Nothing. Where was it? He wouldn't take it with him. It was there somewhere.

I slowly and meticulously searched through drawers, closets, under couch cushions—nothing.

*Where does he keep it?* I stopped. *Of course!*

I went to his bedroom.

I looked at the carpet around his nightstand.

*He is one slick fucker.*

Under his phone was a legal pad. I studied the pad's position and the position of the phone as it sat on the pad. I marked the exact location of the edges with tape and gently picked up the notebook, making sure nothing fell out. If something had and I had no idea which page, he'd know that I knew. I avoided sitting on the bed. Any crease would raise suspicion.

About halfway through, the notes began. The pages were organized by names, date, time of call, and message.

My mouth hit the floor. My heartbeat sped up.

I didn't know how deep his obsession went until I saw how

detailed the records were and realized the time and energy he spent tracking and logging my calls. He had a separate tally for the recurrent callers, including Tristan.

The very first log date wasn't surprising. Gunther had been keeping a record of my phone calls from the first time I spent the evening with Tristan while he was in town; he had known my voice mail pass code. I checked my home messages from my office line, giving him everything he needed to do the same.

The reason I was in his apartment was because I suspected something like that pad existed. I didn't change the code because somehow I wanted to use his deliberate infringement on my personal rights to privacy to my benefit. Like with Gizel, the game was on.

I went to Mail Boxes Etc. and copied the log. I returned the notebook to the exact spot. Then I used the same broom he used to set the trap and erased the indents in the carpet caused by my standing in his untouched radius. I turned off the only light I had turned on and left the apartment exactly the way he'd remember it.

Something sparked. I changed into a vengeful, manipulative asshole with the sole purpose of regaining my freedom and finding happiness while still stacking the easy money.

The first thing I did was quit working for Gunther, no more personal assisting and no more trips to accounting to be groped. I would miss the income but would gain some much-needed reprieve from his sickness and some time to formulate a plan.

I spent my days shopping habitually, buying the clothes that I desired. My huge closet was filled with outfits that Gunther and I had bought together, mostly in Vegas. My style had been stifled by Gunther's need to dress me how he saw fit. I left the conservative, drab, expensive garments neatly on their wooden hangers on one side of my enormous closet and displayed the dark, scanty attire on the other. My life was a direct reflection of my wardrobe.

During my gutsy metamorphosis, Gunther had graduated

from logging phone calls to tailing my every move—a jealous and controlling man indeed.

Almost nightly, after spending time with Ava, I went out seeking adventure, dressed always in black, knowing that my obsessed keeper was stalking me.

# fourteen

Once again, Gunther found a way to have all of his wishes
satisfied where I was concerned:

Travel.

By taking me away from men, parenting, nightlife, and
anything and everyone besides him, and any thoughts of leaving
him, he would triumph. My life was a carousel, with him the
center around which I spun. For the sake of seeing our bountiful
world, I didn't protest. Being constantly on the go would be a new
deterrent for the both of us.

Someone had once told me that I could fall in love with a rich
man just as easy as a poor one. I eagerly wanted to test the theory.
So I searched high and low for Mr. (Money) Right.

My socializing hit new heights as I flew east to hang out
with the guys from Boyz II Men and Mint Condition, and then
northwest to kick it with players from the Seattle Super Sonics.
I headed south to dine with a real estate tycoon and west to kiss
Denzel Washington at a restaurant on Melrose. Other times, I
stayed at home, up all night listening to Ken Caminiti spill his
guts about his regretful life of promiscuity and drug abuse. I even
exchanged lust-filled letters with Tupac Shakur, a musical genius
who was locked away at Clinton Correctional Facility.

I was young, adventurous, and ready for the next big thing.
If not for my daughter, I wouldn't have been so grounded in San
Diego. I would have made temporary loveless homes all over the
globe. In contrast, Ava was shuffled among friends, babysitters,
family, and her father, all while I was living my wayward life. Still,
I had a home where my heart was, and she was the beacon in my
life, the place to where I would always return.

My guilt had quadrupled, but Ava was always well cared for.
I balanced my selfish life of leisure and journeys with guilt gifts

and trips. I took Ava to St. Martin to visit Dawn. Ava and I spent quality time scuba diving in St. Bart's. I took her to Paradise Island in the Bahamas, Barcelona, the south of Spain, Paris, and the Greek Isles. We toured major cities in the United States like New York, New Orleans, San Francisco, Seattle, Atlanta, Portland, Las Vegas, and Miami. I sent her with her grandmother on vacations to Washington DC, Mexico, Belize, Denmark, and Germany.

Ava rarely complained about my absence because she knew no other way—Mom traveled—and because I made sure she wanted for nothing. I was unknowingly raising her to be a bold manipulator. If she said, "I miss you, Mama, come home," she knew my response would be along the lines of, "Okay, baby, I'll be home in a few days and then we can do whatever you'd like." She was a crafty child, but I loved spoiling her, so it didn't matter. She was mine to spoil.

I traveled to Africa, Chile, Argentina, Brazil, the south of France, Greece, London, Italy, Germany, and Mexico. I could not sit still. Traveling was my solace. My only worry was: where to next?

Gunther spared no expense when it came to vacationing. He made sure we had first-class flights. We lived like royalty. Through Holland, Belgium, the Netherlands, Germany, France, Switzerland, Austria, Italy, Hong Kong, Japan, Thailand, Korea, Greece, Tahiti, Martinique, and all of the Hawaiian Islands, we lodged in the most exclusive resorts and expensive hotels these places had to offer and dined in topnotch restaurants.

Gunther and I took a month-long trip through Europe where our goal was to follow the highest-rated establishments as laid out in the Michelin Guide and perform evaluations. It was the happiest that I had ever seen Gunther; he thought he had found his soul mate.

He draped me in the finest clothes, beautifying his mistress so that I got the attention that made Gunther feel so special. I was picturesque, easy on the eyes, but it pained me to pretend that I was happy.

I had played the role, but I frequently wished that I were with the person of my dreams experiencing these amazing things. Inside I was unhappy, but on the surface, I was having the time of my life. The conflicting feelings occasionally reared their heads, and I would act out like a spoiled child, becoming moody and critical for no apparent reason, with Gunther getting the brunt of it.

While we were in Marseille, I left him. I didn't know where I was going. I was simply propelled by the need to get away.

*Just disappear and you'll be okay.*

I walked about ten minutes and came across a small motel located in a perfectly seedy area. I knew it wasn't the type of area Gunther would venture into. I checked into a room the size of a Cracker Jack box and read myself to sleep.

The next night, I decided to sightsee. I ducked into the first lively bar I saw. A terrible band was playing terrible music, but after a few drinks I didn't care. An older Frenchman, dressed in drab colors except for a bright red ascot, asked me to dance. I shimmied my shoulders on the wooden make-shift dance floor. Gunther walked in and saw me being twirled by my partner. He went ballistic.

"What are you doing! Where have you been?"

"I'm dancing! I've been hangin' out in Marseille, just not with you!"

Gunther grabbed me by my arm and forced me from the dance floor. The man protested in French. Gunther replied to him in French. I picked up a glass and doused its contents on Gunther's face.

"Don't touch me!" I yelled.

It came out too loud as the music had stopped. Everyone in the room turned their attention to us, the stupid Americans. Not too many bar fights in those parts, I suspected. The bartender jumped over the bar and escorted us out.

After a few more verbal attacks, humor emerged. I laughed. Gunther was still upset, wiping red wine from his milky bald head. I looked at his smug face and cracked up. I laughed so hard that I fell to the ground. I couldn't catch my breath.

Gunther smiled. The insolent girl that he drug from the dance floor just moments before was replaced by the fun Vannah that he loved. My laughing lightened his mood. It was contagious.

Gunther chuckled.

For five minutes we tried to control the onset of the giddiness. He waved the bartender, who came out to check on us, away and kneeled next to me, awkwardly putting his hand on my shoulder.

"I thought I lost you, Vannah."

I had to express amusement to keep from crying; he, on the other hand, was overjoyed that he had found me. Our mind-sets were worlds apart.

He didn't even ask why I had left. I laughed it all off. There was no need for more words. We walked with linked arms to my motel to gather my things so that we could continue our trip.

I gave myself the pimp talk. "*Stop whining, you spoiled brat! What is wrong with you? Enjoy these times. They may end. Then what? Back to boontown waiting tables at Hooter's? Buck up. You're headed to Monte Carlo, bitch, to celebrate your twenty-seventh birthday.*"

I listened to my inner dialog and Gunther benefited. I was in my place, at his arm, turning heads and enjoying life. I was shopping in pricey boutiques, dining in classy restaurants, gambling with other wealthy Monaco vacationers, dancing at Jimmy Z, flirting behind Gunther's back, and lying nude under the sunlit sky while getting sloshed; I was living life freely and without care.

I didn't want to leave.

# fifteen

Gunther and I landed safely from our European travels. I returned to being a barfly and hanging in the hottest clubs. Gunther resumed stalking.

Two years of extensive canvassing of the world and nothing had changed. I was still not in love with him; he was still obsessed with me.

Gunther invited me to dinner. I accepted. He had been annoyed by my lack of enthusiasm for him. My acting skills were diminished, and I could no longer contain my true feelings. I detested what he represented, my keeper. I was tired of faking it. Tired of traveling. Tired of playing a losing game. He was right to feel anxious, even upset with me; I was not his domicile concubine accepting her role. I was slipping away, to where I did not know, perhaps to being unkept.

Somewhere around mid-entree, his true feelings emerged as well.

"Vannah, you are lazy—*sloth*—and do nothing to earn the money that I give and give."

"What are you saying?" I was used to the discussions. He would threaten my financial security in one way or another.

"I am saying that you are unappreciative."

"No, Gunther. You are unappreciative and manipulative."

"You need a job!"

"Really? How could I possibly keep a job if you require my presence every other week in foreign lands? How could I, after so many years of becoming accustomed to certain amounts of money, suddenly not need it? You provide this cushy lifestyle, but at the same time, you're upset that I enjoy it."

We sat in silence for a bite or two.

Thoughts of Gizel's dependency had scared me, so I made

sure Gunther could not pull the financial rug out from under me completely. I had been wise enough to save and would be able to at least move down a class or two into a more befitting lifestyle.

I excused myself from the table and made a beeline to the hostess' desk.

"Please see to it that the bald, old fuckface gets a cab."

I peeled off four crispy one hundred-dollar bills from my wad of cash, which was stuffed into a purse pocket.

"This is for the bill."

I left the restaurant and headed to a PF Chang's for a nightcap. As I drove, the scenario played out in my mind: Gunther would go home and call my number fifty to sixty times, frantically waiting for me to pick up. After two hours had passed and still no word, he would then proceed to leave resentful, hateful, and threatening messages, telling me what a selfish person I was and that he no longer wanted to take care of me; leaving the restaurant was proof of my selfishness. By morning, the messages would be sweet, offering a truce and detailed lunch plans. He would start begging for forgiveness, claiming that our argument was entirely his fault, if I had not responded by noon.

And so, it happened just as I had predicted.

Over the next months, the game of tug-o-war became our theme. He tugged and pulled at my emotional and financial strings and I pulled and tugged at his. He'd go from accommodating generosity to angry prudishness while trying to manipulate me into the woman of his dreams. I'd play along, friendly and available, and then suddenly snap, brimming with disgust for him and my contrived life. My attitude was always adjusted when he pulled out his checkbook or pacified me with neat piles of crispy large bills, sometimes with the paper band stating the amount neatly still on display around them.

The more money I got, the more I spent trying to pacify my loneliness. On one of my shopping trips, I met an exotic and interesting beauty.

We caught eyes over the latest cell phone gadgets at a kiosk counter in Fashion Valley mall. She spoke first in a dialogue that I hoped was destined to continue for a lifetime. She moved like a sleek game cat, a panther.

"I love your bag."

"Yours is hot, too."

"It's no Louis." It was a statement meant to compliment my taste, as well as inform me of her knowledge on such subjects. I liked her.

She moved to my side of the kiosk. Her perfectly proportioned body was heading right toward me. I got nervous for some reason. I watched her closely, hoping that that wasn't the end of our conversation.

"Do you know where to get a glass of wine around here?"

Her question was music to my ears. I liked her even more. I took her simple inquiry as an invitation. I would have taken anything she said as an invite. I was lonely and in need of a drink. The connection and understanding of each other's needs through a single glance was real.

"Yep." I wanted her to take my hand in hers and walk right out of there—away from it all. She paused, waiting for me to answer, but instead:

"Can I join you?"

"Sure." She smiled.

And just like that the beautiful Faye came into my life.

We settled on the loud, busy bar at Cheesecake Factory. After our first bottle of wine, I moved into the booth on her side of the table to sit next to her. Our intimacy had escalated.

Intellectually, I had met my match. I enjoyed the verbal volleying. The tête-à-tête through two bottles of wine and a subsequent dinner lasted three hours, mainly skimming over our lives to date. It was the first time I had ever spoken with such blunt openness to anyone.

"Have you ever been in love?" she asked.

*Hmmm…great friggin' question?*

Had I ever been in love? Tonio, Aaron, Tristan. I thought so at the time, but wouldn't true love still linger in my heart? Wouldn't my affections for those people drive me back to them? Was I even capable of the emotion?

I avoided answering by giving her my outlandishly negative view of the male species.

Talking shit about men became the pivotal point at which we collided. We embraced our mutual loathing and found joy in verbally bludgeoning the gender. She detested men and I had no reason to like them either.

From one drink turned dinner date, I felt as if I had met my kindred soul. Dawn and Mary were still dear friends; bonded by time, mutual respect, and simple disclosures. We were friends who didn't know any of the gritty details of one another's adult lives. My lifestyle wasn't easy to comprehend and the fewer who knew the better for me and for Ava. So I did not share. But Faye? She was different. Our friendship would be different too.

Faye had dated very wealthy men, so she was no stranger to money. She lived well, dressed and acted the part: the part that attracted wealth. She was well traveled and learned, but just below the surface, there was a dark side. My curiosity made me want to know more. I was drawn to her in more ways than one. I liked Faye and she liked me just the same. We not only had a dark side, we were living on the dark side. Faye reminded me of myself.

Faye quickly became trustworthy, fully understanding my issues with Gunther. She truly believed that Gunther was the fortunate one, so I even had an ally.

My evening hours were shared between hanging out with Faye and staying home with Ava. I spent my days volunteering in Ava's first grade classroom and shopping for the latest and greatest in name brand clothes, shoes, handbags, and everything electronics.

I was extremely conscientious of my every move, fully aware that Gunther was watching. I reluctantly spent time with him, hesitantly accepted dinner invitations and barely answered his calls, waiting sometimes up to two days to return a message. He sensed my unease and went overboard trying to regain my respect and our affinity. By increasing my monthly allowance to counter the fact that I had no job, he was on the right path. He knew money would keep me, and so it did. I knew he would never leave me. Our insecurities melded together, and the cycle continued.

As Faye and I had become very close, she confided in me secrets about the abuse she suffered at the hands of her family, mainly her mother. She told me of a child that she birthed at the age of eleven that had disappeared after delivery. She shared painful stories that made me feel fortunate for having an imperfect but loving family. I had shared a great deal about my life as well. She understood that my pain was just as significant. We cried and laughed, ate and talked until the sun came up. I loved Faye and she loved me.

It had been months before I let Faye in on my secret. We were at my place watching foreign films and eating caramelized onions and baked Brie with French bread. I told her to call my home phone and leave a message instructing me to meet her at The Flame, a bar in Hillcrest, which was a known gay and lesbian community.

We got dressed from my favorite side of the closet.

"Here." I handed her my car keys.

"Go lay on the floor in the back seat." She looked at me

quizzically and took the keys from my hand. She didn't ask. She knew that an explanation was on the horizon.

I turned off the apartment's lights and shut the curtains, a signal to Gunther that I was leaving the house. I slid into the driver's seat. As I was exiting the garage, Gunther's headlights lit up from the parking structuring in the opposing building. Faye patiently waited.

"Gunther stalks me. Any time I leave the house at night, he follows. He checks my home phone messages and knows what I'm doing. Since I quit working years ago, he has managed to tie up my life with travel and, when we are here, my days with trivial, irrelevant errands. He comes home from work, switches to a rental car, and waits for any movement. He doesn't go to sleep until he knows that I must be asleep. If I have lunch plans and he knows, he'll sabotage them. If someone leaves a message, all the details are logged. So far, I've been messing with him for shits and giggles, but I'm trying to figure out how this whole scenario is going to play out and work to my advantage. Any ideas?"

Her mind was reeling.

"Girl, this shit's been going on for years? Why didn't you tell me about this sooner?"

"I thought you'd think it was kinda sicko of me to stay with him."

"This type of espionage, sadistic, Gotham City stuff is right up my alley. He's the one who is sicko."

I had found the perfect partner.

We arrived at The Flame. The Flame was the most infamous lesbian nightclub in San Diego. Up and down the avenue, women were dressed ambiguously. You really had to look closely to notice they indeed were all women.

I pretended not to notice Gunther situating himself in a parking lot, kitty-corner from the front entrance with a clear view of the door. Faye rolled out the backseat and went one way around the building, undetected by our spy, while I went the other so that he saw me.

I fell in line, two dykes behind Faye. The big, black, don't -fuck-with-me-mama, checked the identification of all the queued women to ensure we were of legal drinking age. Then, she motioned for us to enter the club. Parting two heavy, carmine velvet curtains, we entered Lesbian-land.

Once inside, we took seats at the bar and shouted over the music our order for double rounds. Faye listened as I described Gunther.

"Gunther is narcissistic, OCD, and under no circumstances welcomes change or loss. He wants life to work, as he believes it should. Any rifts are disturbing, but contradictorily, they are also energizing. My anarchy and blatant disrespect is a strange turn-on, a highlight in contrast to his humdrum primary life. He systematically categorizes my calls and actions so that he can find out what makes me tick. He's fully aware that it isn't his ass," I explained.

"Does he know about me?"

"I suspect that he may have seen you, but that's about it."

"Is he married?"

"Maybe. It never concerned me, so I never asked."

"Hmmm…This knuckle-dragger has met his fucking match!" she exclaimed.

My heart reverberated, skipping to the beat of the blaring techno mayhem. I was elated. Her attention and fervor for my state of affairs sparked my desire to take swift and immediate action.

*Gunther has met his fucking match.*

With the conversation under our belts, we scanned the room, both intrigued by our surroundings. What I expected from a gay nightclub was far from what I got. I imagined women off in corners grinding and licking at each other. Or secret back rooms where you could go to participate in lesbian S & M sex. Instead, I found a club atmosphere no different than any heterosexual club I had ever been to.

We downed our drinks and looked at each other, thinking the same.

"Let's dance!" I shouted.

We fought our way through the thickness of the crowd. We reached the dance floor and began to conform to the music. Tightly gripping my hand, Faye moved with me in total rhythm, her body melting into mine like a second skin.

The dance floor was devoid of any light. It was completely dark with the exception of flashing red strobe lights attached to the ceiling. Around and around the red lights went, delivering just a hint of the figures moving on the dance floor. Coupled women were vibrantly dancing to Gloria Gaynor's "I Will Survive." Out loud they sang:

"At first I was afraid, I was petrified, just thinking I could never live without you by my side. But then I spent so many nights just thinking how you did me wrong and I grew strong! I learned how to carry on!"

It was like magic! The women sang so loudly their voices overpowered the song. Faye and I began to sing and dance with the crowd. We were home. Before long, our inhibitions had disappeared, and we took on the roles of a seasoned lesbian couple.

Two hours later, Faye and I left the bar arm in arm; with only a few drinks under our belts, we were not yet drunk but not fully sober. We stumbled and laughed, giving Gunther—who was still on duty—the impression that I had picked her up at the bar and that we were wasted.

On the wall, under the bright, red neon Flame signage, we passionately kissed. Faye pulled up my black, lacy, button-up shirt, exposing my nipple and sucked it seductively, as I ran my fingers through her silky hair. We were purposefully letting Gunther get an eyeful.

Faye rode back to my place, sitting high in the front seat. It was the beginning of a beautiful relationship.

# sixteen

"What if we invent a pill that looks exactly like that Viagra crap, but our pill makes dicks shrivel up and fall off?" Faye shouted to me from the kitchen.

I heard her voice and the oven door open, simultaneously. I was barely awake, sprawled across my couch, starving. She had been preparing a meal for what seemed like hours.

"Then what would we do with the puny penis punks?"

"Make them our furniture, of course! Couches, tables, and the fat fucks would be our beds."

"Of course. Is dinner ready?"

Faye was finishing a Master's degree in clinical psychology and had just begun culinary school. On most nights, Ava and I were her willing guinea pigs, subjecting ourselves to her psychological babble and her creative renditions of meals. Whatever she was concocting behind the partitioned wall made me salivate. I swallowed and thought to myself that Ava didn't know what she was missing tonight: dickless, human armoires and something very garlicky.

Ava was almost six, the age where the number of sleepovers you were invited to and attended determined your social status. Ava was gone nearly every Friday and Saturday night. Occasionally, I would host the event, but the more popular she became, the more her friends wanted to come to her sleepovers. The parents of her peers owned huge houses. Our apartment and I could only take so much.

My mind abruptly switched gears.

"I'm going to need a P.B. and J. pretty soon!"

"You're so spoiled and impatient. Relax!" She shouted as she brought me a glass of wine and an appetizer of lobster ravioli in a rich, white wine cream sauce.

It was extraordinary.

"Yeah. It's okay." It was an obvious lie. "Shit covered cardboard flakes would taste like heaven right about now."

"Funny. That's what that is." She smiled and headed back to the kitchen.

"I've been doing a lot of thinking about Gunther," she added.

"Me too."

"I think we should double team him. I know it's kinda crazy, but I think I would be better at extorting money from him."

"Hmmm… I was thinking we should leave him alone."

Faye peeked around the corner into the living room.

"Leave him alone? How?"

"I mean—he really isn't doing anything. I make a hundred and sixty grand a year or more doing nothing. So what if he stalks me? Stalking doesn't cause me any pain."

"That's only because you're immune to the pain and you think abuse is normal; it's insanity. It's not normal, Vannah. And that's not my point. My point is we could make him really pay. Pay for being born a man! He's giving you kibbles and bits. What about a condo? And that new Benzo you're always fantasizing about?"

Faye was right. Gunther's business had been doing well for years. He was in the process of yet another expansion. He would have subsidiaries in four countries by the years end. He kept me on a financially short rope because I never pushed him for more slack.

"Yeah, well, I'm not ready for him to pop your little blue pill quite yet. Let's start with that stupid ex of yours!"

I thought that I was cleverly switching the subject, but the look Faye gave me just before returning to the stove proved otherwise. The subject wasn't dead.

We dined almost in silence, if not for an occasional moan of ecstasy that was derived from mouthwatering white truffle risotto and fillet of sole, pan seared with a caper lemon sauce that made me want to pick up the plate and slide my tongue around until it squeaked.

That night we watched Bitchette in the *Last Seduction*. Faye looked at me with deep concern.

"We need to be fucking men up," she said.

It was the most romantic thing anyone had ever said to me. Faye knew me and that turned me on.

I'm not sure what made a smile engross my face. I had always been fucking men up. But Faye had wanted me to join her on a whole new level of fucking men up. She wanted to fuck up the whole population!

"Cool. But let's make a list, starting with your asshole ex."

Gunther would have to be off limits. Faye was reckless and my financial security needed coddling. I would protect Gunther from her wrath, but I had to be tactful about it so that she wouldn't deem me a lousy team player, or weak. Gunther only knew of Faye through his spying. I hadn't introduced them and wasn't so sure that I wanted to. Something told me to keep them separate. As for all her greatness, Faye was a ticking time bomb, a regular Kamikaze.

Faye and I went from verbally plotting ridiculous revenges on enemies (like hanging her ex over the Nobel Avenue bridge in a pink prom dress) to actually writing down a list of her sworn adversaries who needed punishing. Well, at least in her eyes.

Faye's creativity for the schemes bordered on pure ingenuity, raunchy decadence, and half-witted plans. On several alcohol-induced stupors, she'd try to convince me to streak across my courtyard or skinny dip in my complex's pool. I would just laugh and nurse us both back to sobriety without incident.

We'd spend hours berating our male counterparts or anyone pinned for payback. One night after she thoroughly ranted on about her former boyfriend, I suggested we egg his house.

"C'mon! It'll be fun." I slurred.

She was in the fridge grappling for eggs before I finished the complete thought.

I jumped up, prepping for action. I went to the closet and pulled out two, black, skintight body suits and laid them on the couch.

"This is perfect. He's never home on weekends!" she blurted loud enough for me to hear, but not truly addressed to me.

Faye returned to the living room with the carton of eggs tucked under her arms, ready for battle.

"What the hell are those?" she also slurred.

"What bad bitches wear when they do bad things."

We put on the suits.

Curvaceous. Dark. Menacing.

Riding boots, gloves, and leather jackets.

Faye looped her arm through mine and we set off on our very first payback adventure, no more talk and no more lists.

We headed north to a posh Del Mar Hills home that sat precariously above another precariously positioned house that sat above another. We wound our way up the hill until we stopped in front of a beautiful, softly lit home. The two-story structure had west-facing windows with an unobstructed view of the Pacific. Soon those picturesque windows would have egg slime that would stiffen, and then bake with the next day's sun, making the ocean impossible to see.

"Bombs away."

Faye chucked the first egg. We watched it whiz past a few treetops and sail toward the glass. It fell short of its target and landed on the front walkway.

"Here. You focus on that." I pointed to a beautiful red Ferrari parked in the circle driveway. It was one of his many toys, according to Faye.

"I'll get the windows."

She giggled with delight as her egg oozed down the side of his car.

"Why do you hate him so much?" I asked, more so to keep her riled.

"I shit turds bigger than his dick!" she shouted as she flung another egg. It landed in the middle of the hood and remained there.

"He can go blow himself…" She launched another. It hit the windshield.

"That was well placed."

"…bigger." She snuck in the last word to finish off the sentence.

I shook my head and chuckled. Faye never really told me what happened. I just knew she hated him and that was enough for me.

We threw all twelve eggs. And like a kid out of snow for snowballs, we were sad.

"We could go get more eggs?" she suggested as if it were the most brilliant idea ever.

Faye went into 7Eleven while I revved the engine and blasted rock music. As getaway driver on our caper, I wanted to act the part. I bounced my head around, rockin' out, until I saw Faye running towards the car. She breathlessly jumped into the backseat.

"Get the hell out of here!" she shouted.

I played along and sped off as if we were in hot pursuit and on an important mission to get the Russian spy "chip," or some other thing so important that if we failed, the world would cease to exist.

"I stole the fucking eggs!"

I punched the radio button off, instantly silencing the car.

"What?" I slowed the car and nervously checked for flashing lights.

Faye was in hysterics. She was laughing so hard that she couldn't talk. I chuckled but I was thinking, *great, she gets caught on camera stealing eggs; her angry ex reports the incident; then she gets called in for identification; Faye goes to jail and I follow as her accessory for the felony crimes—destruction of property and theft.*

"I don't know what came over me," she finally admitted.

I drove home for fear of being picked up with the contraband.

Faye and I laid low for a while; no cops showed up with warrants to search my refrigerator. I was relieved, but because of the nature of adrenal rushes, Faye's prodding for us to continue our mission and to have another Gunther and Ava-less weekend, I was actually anxious to target our next victim.

Payback gave me the sense of taking control. I felt powerful in the process, from plotting our plan, right up to the moment of execution.

Our mission that night was to extort an A grade from Faye's professor, with whom she had had previous sexual relations, a classic case of misplaced feelings for an intelligent authority figure. Neither she, nor I, saw any reason for her to stress her brain with trivial details of English literature, going to class, or taking tests because of her short-lived love delusion.

Faye dialed his number and since it was she who had called things off, mainly due to his flaccid man boobs and saddlebags, his egotistical side agreed to meet her; maybe he thought she was coming back for more of his sexiness.

When we arrived at the small neighborhood coffee shop, we ordered, and then positioned ourselves at a table near the door to see who was coming and going, but more so in the event we needed to make a quick escape.

The Professor came in with a huge ear-to-ear smile; happy to see Faye and even happier, I suspected, that she had brought along an attractive friend—judging by the way his beady eyes lingered over my body as he hugged Faye while subtly sweeping his palm over her ass.

*Fucking asshole!*

I couldn't wait to make his mouth frown and distort with disgust. I imagined the contortion and gave him a wickedly sexy smile while moving my long hair behind my ear, followed by licking my lips; movements that would most likely make his pecker stiffen.

Everything had to be purposefully done to make the pain of what we were about to do that much more excruciating.

The waitress brought out three coffees. I wasted no time.

"How would this affair affect your tenure?" I asked as I slowly sipped black coffee for effect, as I never drank coffee.

"Excuse me?" he aggressively questioned.

"How would this affair affect your tenure?" I repeated with indignation and enunciation.

"I don't understand."

*Of course you don't. It came from left field sounding nothing like how's about a threesome?*

"This. This." I quickly flicked my pointed my finger between him and Faye several times as if to say, *please do not mess with me. You know what the hell I mean, doc.*

His face distorted.

*Yes! That look is clearly disgust. He hates me. Bravo!*

He looked away, searching for words that we would not let him use. I gave Faye a slight nod. Faye removed five blank, multiple choice answer sheets called Scantrons from her purse, stacked them on the table, and slowly placed all five fingers on them, and then even more slowly, pushed them across the table.

She stared him square in the face like an evil black widow spider going in to behead her baby-daddy, but his eyes were focused on her appendage that was creeping toward him. She stopped and quickly drew back her hand.

The professor looked at the Scantrons for a few seconds, no doubt weighing his options. He picked them up and tucked them into a pocket located inside of his scholarly tweed sports jacket.

As far as we were concerned, our coffee date had just ended. I held the chair for Faye as she got up.

The Professor suddenly found some courage and was about to explode with emotion as told by his rouge cheeks and furrowed brow. He was on the brink of attack.

I quickly, with the stealth and strength of a pouncing lioness protecting her cub, came within a quarter of an inch from touching his face with my own. I smelled his coffee breath and he mine. My look and stance were telling. He shut his partially opened pie-hole and sat back down.

I walked from the restaurant as if I were the female version Tony Montana and Michael Corleone rolled into one. The bitch, Vannah, was being fed. Each moment in the presence of the bitch Faye strengthened her appetite.

Once in the car, Faye and I exhaled. My heart that was beating so hard calmed down. The slight fear was replaced by an eruption of giddy laughter. Reliving the night by repeating what had just occurred, we fueled the rush by relishing the power and loving the intensity.

Even with all of the extraordinary manipulation feats and payback attacks that I had executed in my past like kneeing Bradford the bully in the balls and forcing him to pay me, stealing all of the right shoes from Paco's closet, thieving from Doctor Wilson's wallet, tit for tat with Gizel and abandoning Alberto, none compared to our missions. This was different. Faye and I were like lifer cellmates, married by circumstance.

It was destroy or be destroyed. I had a partner, a cohort, and a trusted agent on missions to right wrongs and pillage our male counterparts relentlessly, purposefully, and eventually fearlessly.

We drove to our favorite watering hole, The Flame, and ordered shots of tequila.

"Two fuckers down and three to go." We toasted as our glasses clinked.

Faye was elated; she too had found her evil twin.

Meanwhile, Gunther's control had reached new heights. He and I argued daily. Our arguing was frustrating for Gunther but a comical pastime for Faye and me. With her assistant coaching, I would psychologically pound him. I didn't care. Gunther wasn't going anywhere. I had proved it over and over again. It seemed his sickness ran deeper than mine. He was addicted to the sucker punch, in it until the end. It would have to be I who walked away, and even then, he would chase me, dangling money, jewels, trips, or whatever it took to win me back.

During one of our routine squabbles, Faye left the bedroom. She returned smelling slightly of vomit masked with mouthwash. She was getting worse at drinking, unable to hold it like she used to.

I slammed the phone down while Gunther was in mid-sentence; tired of his accusations.

"Vannah, forget the penny-ante bullshit. The plan that you need to be formulating should include a house from his ass. I hate to state the obvious, but you ain't getting any younger, missy."

Again, Faye was right. I was a couple of months away from my twenty-ninth birthday. Next year, I'd be old, out of my twenties with nothing but a couple of hundred thousand dollars to show for it. I needed assets. But Faye's favorite book was entitled, *Men Are Pigs and Deserve to Die*, by Sonya Steinem. I never read it, but figured the title said it all.

Yes, we *hated* men but relied heavily on them no less. I didn't want to plot revenge on a man who paid my bills. I didn't want to threaten, extort, blackmail, or murder Gunther. Faye had Gunther in her sights; I did what I could to prolong any discussion of tactical maneuvering on Operation Fuck Gunther Up.

"Look we've been systematically making our way through your bucket list of assholes. Don't you think I have one too?" I said.

It was another planned distraction. I wasn't expecting her to take me too seriously.

"Man, let's get started on it." She didn't laugh or joke.

*Alright!*

Part of me wanted to produce people like the boy at the gym who keyed my car after I denied him a date, or the lady down the hall who routinely dropped trash in front of my door on her way to the garbage shoot because her man had a staring problem. But another part of me wanted to produce the real guilty fuckers. I wanted to feel the cleansing of "get even pay back" like Faye felt, especially with the people who had caused me real detriment, people like Marquetta.

Faye coughed. She had trouble catching her breath. I got up to get her water. While I was up the phone rang. It was Tristan. I took it.

When I got back, Faye was sound asleep.


Real estate markets across the nation were booming, and Gunther and I were renting. It was Business 101, and we were being left behind. I was putting tons of pressure on Gunther to buy (me) a house. He hated my selfishness and simply wanted me to desire to live with him, even though, he would never have wanted to live with me, or probably could not, because his primary life was in San Francisco.

I was forced to play his psychological mind game.

"Please let's get a house together. You know we could make

it work. I'll find a house that can accommodate the fact that you would still need your privacy…Please?"

He didn't promise, but at least he was temporarily satisfied with my nicely painted, false fairy-tale.

Within days, I found a house big enough for him to have his own (maid's quarters) separate entrance, living area, kitchen, and bathroom. The house was magnificent and only cost 1.6 million. I even went so far as to get an agent friend to draw up papers. I forced Gunther to tour it a few times. The last trip to my dream home was a disaster.

"We'll take it!" I said in front of Gunther and the agent.

Gunther stomped off toward the car. I joined him and out of desperation added a phrase.

"C'mon, don't tell me no; tell me yes."

The pressure and manipulation had taken its toll. He threw a silent tantrum. His refusal to speak to me was the first time Gunther broke.

While Gunther was pouting, I worked out regularly and funneled my energy into fixing myself—at least superficially.

I made appointments for two new procedures: Brite Smile—had my teeth whitened and with my orthodontist—Invisalign to straighten my slightly crooked teeth.

Still no call from Gunther.

I was also amongst the first to try the new procedure of laser eye surgery. I had spent my entire life nearly blind. To wake up with 20/20 vision was unbelievable. My vision was so good, I was seeing through things. I thought that was my reciprocity for being a student of Coke-bottle eyewear and hard contacts during my impressionable years. I could see why people with money remained polished; procedures were addictive.

Still no call from Gunther.

Microdermabrasion. False eyelashes. Hair extensions.

A personal trainer working me out, six days a week.

No word from Gunther.

Yoga.

Maybe Gunther had had enough.

As I was focusing on my physical appearances, Faye was scarce. We talked on the phone occasionally, but school and work kept her away and our conversations really brief.

During one of our talks, I mentioned her cough that hadn't gone away. She said she was taking something and joked about how irritating it was to her perfected craft of dick sucking.

It had been months since our last caper. I asked what we should do about that. I was ready for more adventure.

Faye had moved through her list without me. She took care of two more schmucks; one she fixed by calling the cops on him after she had seen him and his new girlfriend sip down two bottles of wine. She waited until he had pulled out of the restaurant and frantically called 911 to report that he had nearly sideswiped her. She passed the drunks on her way home. Her ex was in cuffs. The car was being towed. The second was her former boss, who fired her without cause. Well, the cause was he wanted her and she treated him like a leper.

"Girl, I'd rather eat off my own hand than go on a date with him."

That made me laugh. But as she continued, I realized that I was sad.

"He ran the Boy Scouts of America in San Diego and was a chronic user of pot. He almost always had a joint on or near him. I called the regional office posing as a concerned parent who wanted to remain anonymous; I reported that the scumbag had offered another woman's son marijuana. They'll at least have to investigate."

After she finished spewing the details of her solo performance, she noticed my silence.

"You there?"

"Yep."

I was shocked that our partnership had ended. Faye no longer needed me.

"The last person on my list is Gunther, Vannah, but we'll plot that when you're ready. I wanted to clear my list to get started right away on yours."

I took no notice that Gunther, a man she did not know, was on her list. I was elated that Faye wanted to get started; I didn't care with what. I didn't want to lose my criminal companion. I would create a list that would keep us busy for years on payback shit! But first, I had to update her with my Gunther news.

"Girl, I took your advice. I've been pressuring Gunther for a house. We went looking and I found just the one but he kinda snapped. I haven't heard from him in months."

"Months? Did you call him and apologize?"

"No. For what?"

"For something! Just call and invite him to lunch."

"I have never done that."

"Well, you never had to. Don't fuck this up by being stubborn, Vannah."

It was a Wednesday night when I called Gunther. He was out of town but was due to return on Friday. He asked if I would like to have dinner at our favorite place, Mille Fleur, to kick off the weekend.

"Only if you accept my apology," I said.

"I need to apologize to you, Vannah. You need what women your age have, a husband, a nice car, a home. Let's talk on Friday."

I hung up the phone. Like the card in the bouquet of flowers, I didn't know what to make of it.

No sooner than I hung up, my phone rang.

"Hello?"

"Hey."

"Hey! Wow."

My heart fluttered.

"I miss you."

"Man. I miss you too."

"Well?"

"Well."

"Are you single?"

"Yep," I lied.

"Can I see you?"

"Yep."

"I'll make plans."

"The sooner the better."

"Okay, baby. I'll call you later."

"Bye, Tristan."

Ava came in as I was getting off the phone with Tristan. I could tell she had something on her mind.

"How's school?"

"Mom, do you think Jonathon is cute?"

"Heck yeah!"

Ava smiled. She had buttered me up for the real reason she was in my room; she told me about a project that was due in two days. She needed supplies. I gave her a lecture on not waiting until the last minute to do important things while I got ready to take her to the art store.

Faye was waiting for me when we got back. Ava loved Faye. Faye became her mentor, giving advice that was clearly meant for her later years.

"Don't ever let a man call you a bitch. Bash his head in with whatever you can find. If you let him do it once, he'll do it again, and soon, 'Stupid Bitch' will be your name," Faye said purposefully loud to make Ava giggle at her use of a swear word in my presence.

"All men are dogs," Faye whispered, not so inaudibly.

"Nothing matters if your butt isn't smart. Go do your homework," I added.

Ava said her good-byes, accompanied by a hug, and then went to the office to start her project.

"You look great, Vannah."

"You too. You look like you lost some weight."

"Just finally getting over that bronchitis."

We spent the night drinking, laughing and putting the finishing touches on Ava's project. Faye whipped up dinner. After Ava went to bed, Faye and I sat on the couch polishing of a bottle of wine.

"Did you make your list?" she asked.

"Yeah. It was difficult."

"Let's see it."

The truth was I hadn't really been as interested in paying back the people on my list as I was in the camaraderie that Faye and I shared in executing the revenge. The elation of payback was secondary to spending time with her.

I pulled out a notebook and handed it over. She studied it intensely.

"Okay. We'll start here." She pointed at Marquetta. "I'll need a last name and her age."

"My mom probably has that information," I answered.

"Matter of fact, I'll need the last names of these three assholes and Sarah."

"Why?"

"Well, unless you know where they are, we will need to hire a private investigator. I know someone. He's good. Vannah, are you sure that's it?"

"Yeah."

I knew she was expecting Gunther to be on the list. But I still didn't know why he should be.

Suddenly, Faye took my hand and led me to my bedroom.

We stopped at the edge of the bed. A strange feeling came over me. I was excited that Faye and I were standing in close proximity to what could potentially turn into something worth getting excited about. But we had taken this route dozens of times and had just hopped up in my king size bed to watch foreign flicks.

Faye, still holding my hand, maneuvered behind me. She gently moved my hair to one side and kissed the back of my neck. This wasn't a show, like outside of The Flame. This was real.

# seventeen

I was perfectly still, unsure of what to do next. Faye kissed the same spot.

I turned around. The look in her eyes made all inhibitions leave the room. She was so beautiful. Her genuine affection and concern for me, like no other person in the world, made me trust and love her equally and unconditionally. We shared secret truths. She had the key to my vault and I to hers.

We stood eye to eye for what felt like forever. I wasn't nervous. I was frozen. My imagination had played out a whole scene of possibilities, but we just stood.

I could smell her subtle sweetness. I imagined the first kiss and became instantly moist between my legs. Her hand was still holding mine.

Almost drawn together by an outside force, our lips met. We kissed, slowly at first, tasting each other's mouth and tongue. Her lips were full and soft. She closed her eyes, and I watched her enjoy the sensual moment. We avoided the bed until the time was right. We knew what to do to make the moment perfect, almost as if we shared the same brain.

Faye took time to light candles and put on a light jazz CD. I locked the door, went to the bathroom, and turned on the shower. I dimmed the bathroom light, then undressed and stepped into the steamy, warm water. I thought about my promising call with Gunther, reuniting with Tristan, and making love to Faye.

The candlelight caused Faye's perfectly shaped silhouette to flicker against the bathroom wall. I was turned on when she slunk into the shower, joining me under the tepid waters. She was the seductress. She lathered up a washcloth and slid it over my shoulders. We kissed. She let her sudsy hands move to my stomach. We kissed more. But as we both started effortlessly moving our hands around the other's wet, slippery bodies, we wanted more. Kissing was not enough.

We made the flight from the shower to my satiny, billowy bed.

Her lips made their way from my breast to my naval. She looked up at me and smiled. Her left hand toyed with my nipple and I quietly let out a sigh as the fingertips on her other hand prepared my vagina for her tongue. Her eyes fixated on mine as she slowly moved along my body to her own fingers and made the switch, causing me to moan excitedly in anticipation of what my best friend and now lover was about to do. We broke eye contact. My head fell back and my eyes closed.

Her mouth devoured the whole area, making my legs quiver and my body temperature rise.

Faye and I made love for two hours, stopping only to drink wine and to change the music.

When I woke up Faye was gone. I missed her already.

It was Friday; Gunther and I had dinner plans. Vannah was on a mission! I would do it for Faye. I would get the house, the Mercedes S class, the whole shebang. Gunther would have to pay! Faye was right. I was worth way more than for what I had settled.

As I prepared for my date with Gunther, I gave myself the pimp talk of the year.

*You're aging with nothing to show for your role as that rich motherfucker's woman. Either you are going to be a dumb ass or you are going to get what you deserve. Which will it be?*

The stakes were being raised. I felt good as I prepped for our date. My spiffed up looks that Gunther hadn't yet seen added to my excitement. I was hot!

Gunther picked me up in a brand new silver Mercedes S class.

"Wow. This is nice."

Gunther handed me the keys.

"Happy Birthday," he added.

I stared at the beautiful piece of machinery in complete awe. It was the exact car of my dreams. I was too shocked to move.

"Wow. I don't know what to say. It's amazing. You're amazing. Thank you."

He opened the driver's side door. Instead of turning to get in, I hugged Gunther. He smiled; all was forgiven.

I slid onto the soft leather seats and breathed in the smell of a brand new car.

*Focus, Vannah. This is just a fucking car.*

I drove to Mille Fleur feeling like a new woman. Gunther couldn't take his eyes off of me. His piqued interest gave me confidence.

Once to the restaurant, we were shown to our usual table. Gunther and I ordered, ate, drank, and talked. About mid-way through dessert, my self-assurance made me force out a sentence.

"I want a house." I watched his face as I continued. "The car is amazing. Thank you. But Ava and I are tired of renting. There are beautiful homes everywhere and we live in a complex. That new car is worth more than everything in my house."

Gunther was remarkably open. We discussed house options and future plans. He wanted to make sure that I had no intention of going anywhere.

Shelter, for the third time in my life, had been the ploy to make me stay kept: Alberto, Don, and now Gunther. There were strings attached, always; this would be no different.

"Vannah, I love you. I want you to be happy."

Although what I was about to say was a huge lie, I knew it had to be said. He was anticipating something great. He had led me to this point and I knew that I could not let him down. There was too much to lose.

His eyes focused on my mouth.

*Say it, Vannah!*

My perfectly aligned white teeth under crimson colored lips, mesmerized Gunther. He leaned in a bit closer. He would not miss it.

"I am happy. A new car, a new house, you back in my life, what's not to be happy about?"

His look told me there was more that I needed to say. Gunther, the master of puppetry, was dictating my moves and my words once again, or was it the reverse? The manipulation was exhilarating and perverse. I leaned in as well.

"I love you too, Gunther."

He exhaled. He had waited a long time to hear those words.

*Yes. I am the puppeteer!*

No different from the cat and mouse game played years ago. We sat back in our chairs, both satisfied with the outcome.

*Faye will be proud.*

The very next day, Gunther and I went to a new development in a beautiful part of Carmel Valley. The barren hilly horizon that once had fields of wild brush, weeds, and flowers now were carved out plots of leveled land for the numerous developers who had staked their claim.

We drove up the quiet, newly paved road. I thought back to the ride I took with Alberto to his home, and the ride to the ocean front condo in Miami, sitting shotgun next to men whom I did not, and could not, love. How was this ride any different?

The mix of pure excitement, pride on a job well done, and self-disappointment came across as indifference, even sadness. My conflicting range of internalized emotions evened out to a look on my face that made Gunther ask, "Is everything okay?"

"I'm just so elated about this new start. I kind of want to cry."

The crafty lie worked for us both; if I did cry, the real reason would never be discovered.

We spent two hours touring the model homes. Gunther put down a deposit on a new construction home that I had picked out.

I had a beautiful and loving daughter, a girlfriend with whom I could share my life, an endless supply of money, a hot car, and an extraordinary home set on a fabulous canyon. What else was there? Why wasn't I happy?

Happiness played a very miniscule role throughout my life. I was beginning to wonder why.

Tristan called my cell while Gunther and I were at the bank signing the purchase agreement papers. I let it go to voicemail. In two years, Gunther would quitclaim the property into my name. Gunther wrote a very large check toward the purchase of my million-dollar home.

*Just two short years and this property will be mine.*

Faye came by my apartment to celebrate with me. She wasn't surprised.

"I told you!" She started to cough. It turned to more coughing.

I went to get her water.

"Thanks." She took the water and drank it down with two pills, her medicine. "Well, we're going to have to get busy."

"I know! All those rooms to decorate!"

"Yes, that too. But here." She pulled out a bright yellow file folder and handed it to me just as my phone rang. I looked at the screen.

"It's Tristan. I haven't been taking his calls."

"Why not?"

I ignored the question. I knew as well as she did that he would complicate everything. I would eventually have to tell him to fuck off, but I wasn't quite ready for that conversation. A part of me felt like to let him go would be letting something very important slip away. Plus, wasn't Faye my girlfriend?

I opened the file to see an 8x12 picture of Marquetta. I stared at the photo. She looked exactly the same, just older. The funny shaped birthmark under her eye, a scar on her lip, even her hair was pulled back into the same tight single ponytail that sat too high on her head. I took a breath and turned to the next page. Two plane tickets to Colorado.

"That's where she lives. She's expecting us. We leave tomorrow."

"I meet with the flooring and window people tomorrow."

"So cancel."

"What about Ava?"

"I called the sitter for you," she said—knowing that was my next concern.

I stayed silent.

"Look, we are doing this. Every mo-fo on that list, Vannah."

"Okay. Okay."

I closed the file.

Faye and I watched *La Femme Nikita*. I think she purposefully picked this one out. It had all of the elements of heroically executed revenges. Its purpose was to get me motivated. Faye fell asleep before it ended.

I wanted to ask her about us. What were we? What would we eventually be? We hadn't so much as kissed since crossing into a sexual relationship. I loved her and wanted to discuss this pressing matter.

I tried to wake her but she slept too heavily. I covered her and went to bed. Perhaps leaving things where they were was better.

The next morning, I dropped Ava at her best friend's house. I circled back home, packed a few things in my large travel purse and was ready go. Faye still hadn't gotten up. I sat next to her on the couch. She looked even more beautiful without make-up.

"Wake up, Faye. We gotta get going."

Slowly Faye began to come alive.

"Man, you were knocked out," I said.

"School and this job. I am exhausted. And, I have a ton of homework."

"Are you bailing on me?"

"You can do it."

"Do what? That wasn't the deal."

"Stop being a wimp, Vannah. Go tell that woman how you feel about her ass! I'm going back to sleep."

I took my bag, the file, and left her on the couch, slamming the door behind me.

*How dare she bail. This was supposed to be our shit.*

I drove to a local strip mall and parked. I looked around to see what I could go buy. Shopping eased my worries and made me feel good about life. Pampering had the same effect; I spotted a nail salon.

As my feet soaked, I contemplated my situation. I left the salon with brightly polished toenails, still undecided on whether or not to go it alone. I sat in my new Mercedes and put it in drive. I was heading to the airport.

My cell phone rang. It was Tristan. I let it go to voicemail, yet again.


I pulled the rental car up to 1120 Coral Street, a chipped lime green apartment complex with the front glass missing from the door. I stepped through the frame and made my way past two young boys sitting on the inside staircase that lead to the second floor.

I stopped at her apartment.

*I wish Faye were here.*

I tried to give myself a pep talk, but it was weak. My heart pattered harder. I paced the worn carpet, studying the years of built up grime and graffiti that covered the hallway's wall and thought, *why hasn't the landlord painted?* One fresh coat would do wonders.

Standing a bit more confident in front of 2C, I finally knocked. I puffed my chest out and put on my game face. I thought about the Professor, and Gunther when he pulled the rent check away from me. I thought about Paco and how I kicked him with all my might in his balls. This was a maniacal sociopath who caused me great anguish.

*Fuck her!*

The door opened.

"Hi. Come on in. I was expecting you."

"I'm not sure what or who you were expecting, but I'm sure it's not me."

I closed the door, barricading us in the same space and time.

Her studio apartment could be seen in its entirety from where I stood. The whole place was in shambles; junk in every nook and cranny; dirty dishes, dirty clothes, dirty everything. There was no place for me to sit, even if I had been offered a chair or even if I wanted to.

At only forty-eight, Marquetta, in the middle of the day, wore a nightgown that looked like it hadn't been off her body or washed in ages. She was withered and old, way beyond her years—signs of a hard life. She toted an oxygen tank on wheels, barely making it to a tattered, orange chair to plop her ass down.

"Aren't you…"

I didn't know or care what story Faye had invented.

"…No. I'm Savannah Lovely. You babysat me when I was about five a few times. Well. I should say you molested me."

Marquetta got flustered. She moved in her chair, guiltily. I spotted the bright yellow packaging that could only be Juicy Fruit on a flimsy, rusted, fold-up TV dinner table.

"I see you still chew the only gum I loathe because it was what I remember most about you molesting me. The smell of your breath. Do you remember?"

I canvassed her space, looking at years of dust on aged and worthless stuff, valueless probably even to her. It was just trash being stored because she was too lazy or ill to remove it.

"You covered my Winnie the Pooh lamp with your scarf and licked my pussy. No? Do you remember shoving my fingers into your pussy? C'mon. That's gotta ring a bell."

"I was only..."

"Only what? Only a sick pedophile who got away with it? No. That's not what you were because here I am, and you're not going to get away with it. Are you?

"I...I..."

"That was rhetorical."

I felt my anger evolving. She was trying to explain or come up with an excuse. I wanted to bang her head in with her air tank. My peripheral vision caught a roach moving, in the way that roaches move, across a plate that had remnants of food.

"I'm so sorry."

Her eyes suddenly watered with redness as if she had been cutting onions. She awkwardly fell to my knees, wrapping her flabby, yet skinny arms around my legs.

I stepped back abruptly, making her upper body fall to the ground. Her tubes got entangled because of her own discomfited movement and popped from their rightful place.

She wept onto the filthy, stained carpet.

"I'm so, so, so sorry. I remember that night. I've had that night in my head for thirty years. I am sorry. I was lonely and very mistreated. I had no right to take that out on nobody and especially not no little girl." She was overcome by her own sobs. "I was so ugly. My heart was ugly and rotten from what had been done to me."

She couldn't catch her breath. I looked down at her until I felt an old familiar lump start to form in my throat. I quickly looked to the ceiling to stop the emotions.

*You will not cry over this bitch, Vannah!*

Marquetta began talking between small bouts of air.

"I ha-ted you be-cause you had a nice fa-m-ily and you were so beau-ti-ful. Ba-by, I paid for my mis-take with my life for what I done did to you. I never forgave myself. And I be try-ing every day to make right with the Lord."

I looked around the room and suddenly her belief in God came into focus; the dusty plastic brown cross that hung crookedly above the window; the worn red bible sitting aside the pack of Juicy Fruit; the shellacked placard of the famous Footprints poem on the wall next to me.

No pep talk could stop my tears.

I helped Marquetta to her chair and returned the oxygen tubes to her nose.

She sat quietly except for the forced sucking of air. The tears were still dropping from her scarlet colored eyes.

I kneeled, cupping my hand over hers.

"I forgive you."

I got up and walked out.

The power that I had lost to Marquetta all those years ago, when she held me down and took it, was regained by the use of those three words. Freedom was immediately granted, for both of us.

As I left her dilapidated home, with hall walls that would never get a fresh start, I felt sorry for her and proud of myself, no longer malevolent toward my abuser. Vindication came with three measly words.

On the way back to the airport, I called Faye to share my experience. She didn't answer.

I got home and called Faye. Still no answer.

I picked up Ava, walked into my house, fixed dinner, and called Faye. No answer.

Typically, I didn't worry, but something was different. I felt it.

Days, then weeks, passed. I busied myself with the chores of motherhood and new house projects. I happily flittered between quizzing Ava for her spelling bee and choosing countertops and window coverings; between shopping for end of the school year teacher gifts and things to make our cookie cutter California track home uniquely ours.

Ava and I had a mansion compared to our apartment. It was four thousand square feet of orgasmic space waiting to be sculpted by loving and gifted hands.

I carefully chose the beautiful wood, slate, and tile that prettified my floors, the "I ain't afraid of color" wall paints, and stunningly beautiful carpeting. I decorated with pricey, modern furniture and unique wall art. Fire on Ice, beautiful tempered glass pieces, replaced the old-school logs in the inside fireplaces and outdoor fire pit. I had a huge to-die-for kitchen, Viking appliances (with two ovens), rich granite countertops and a full-length backsplash, custom lighting fixtures, and jazzy handles adorning the cabinetry. My kitchen opened out onto a big, barren California lot. Ava requested a pool and a Jacuzzi.

*Okay, baby!*

I had the means and the time to see the projects through. I didn't dally.

On a few occasions, I tried unsuccessfully to catch Faye at home. Her house was always vacant.

*Where the hell is she?*

# eighteen

Gunther was away. I hadn't so much as thought about him since we bought my house. He put one hundred and twenty-five thousand dollars into my account and left me to it. I had been seeing less of Gunther, and he had stopped trailing me, mainly because I had become predictable. Faye had been the only one leaving messages and coming over. I'm sure he had much better things to do than watch me. After all, his company was expanding at a healthy rate, as were many businesses, including real estate.

My house, after only a few months, had gained over one hundred thousand dollars in equity. But, in order to be able to even qualify for the quitclaim, there were specific things that I needed to do, such as pay the mortgage from my account, expand all my credit limits on my credit cards, and maintain healthy checking and saving accounts. The only thing I worried about was provable income.


My mother called and asked if, instead of me putting Ava on the plane to Minnesota, could she come visit and then fly back with her. I wanted to say, *no*. A mother who spent her workdays sheltering homeless women and children had no business being a witness to her daughter's questionable life choices. But I said, *sure*.

Even though she and I never spoke about the specifics of my life, I knew that she knew that I had comfortably fallen into a mutually beneficial relationship with someone who was not even worth an introduction. What I shielded from her was my standard of living. How would I pick her up in my shiny, eighty thousand dollar Mercedes Benz? How could I show her an exclusive community of newly built, ostentatious homes and point to the biggest on the end with the twenty-foot palm trees and say, *that one is mine?* The more pressing question was how could I cloak my life and give my dear mother an impression of normalcy? Should I rent a car? Swear to silence a six-year-old from mentioning our pending move? Pretend to leave for work every day during her visit?

I had always protected my mother from hard truths. I took the nastiness of my life and burdened no one. I had sucked it up. Bad things happened, and I dealt with it all. My mother doled out heartache and I didn't confront her. I doled out heartache to her and apologized, promising myself to never do it again. I refused to tell my mom about what I did or who I did; Alberto, Don, and Gunther were secrets, kept by me. I learned long ago that when people knew your secrets, they become weighed down. I could not weigh down my own mother.

I called Faye. I needed to talk about the anxiety that I was feeling regarding my mother as well as she and I. I wanted to talk about Marquetta. I needed advice on a number of subjects.

Her cell phone was disconnected. Whatever was happening in her life, she did not feel the need to weigh me down. I resented her for it. We were more than friends and less than lovers; caught in the middle, we were nothing.

I would purchase my mother's plane ticket. Ava and I would pick her up in a mid-sized rental car on the last day of school. We'd continue south to Rosarito, Mexico, and stay at La Paloma for three days. After, we'd drive back and be tourists around San Diego, hitting all the hot spots—the San Diego Wild Animal Park and Zoo and Sea World. I would pack a summer's worth of clothes for Ava, write my mom a check, and send them on their way. I'd still have two weeks to pack up my apartment and move into the house. That was the plan. It did not include a conversation about my lifestyle, Gunther, or my job.

Ava's classmates had a party in the park after school on the last day. I had just enough time to drop off donuts and rush to the airport to pick up my mother. My mom was waiting on the curb when I pulled up only a few minutes late. I helped hoist her luggage into the Corolla's small trunk.

After the formalities of doting were out of the way:

"Where's the new car I've been hearing about?"

"New car?"

"Don't play with me, Savannah. You know I know. My grandbaby can't keep secrets."

*She must get that from her father.*

"It's at the shop for maintenance; a recall on a part that they have to order," I lied.

It's one thing to know about the luxury vehicle and altogether something different to see it, and something amazingly life changing to actually sit in it. I didn't want to change her life.

"Well, what's this I hear about a new house?"

*Shoot! I didn't get to Ava fast enough.*

"Well, we have some time. You want to go see it?"

As we drove, my mother talked about Mikey and his latest girlfriend, Annabel, and her three bad kids. She was not Annabel's biggest fan and hoped that Mikey would move on soon. She shared a funny story about a homeless woman who was Internet dating instead of searching for employment or housing. Our positions were worlds apart. She believed the woman to be shameless, lacking important prioritizing and life management skills. I believed her to be savvy, creative, and resourceful. However, I did not share that sentiment with my mother.

We wound our way through the Carmel Valley hills to my laid stone driveway. I put the car in park. I could tell by the look on my mom's face that the Gunther conversation would be next.

Her unconcealed wonderment and awe even for the little things, like the Calla lily bush and built-in sprinkler system, made me wish I had the forethought to threaten my blabber-mouthed child if she told a soul about our good fate.

Entering the house elicited the same reaction, as would sitting in an S class Mercedes. My mother gasped; her life was changed.

"Oh, Savannah. This is beautiful. My goodness, it looks like a castle."

Indeed. The foyer, with its vaulted 20-foot ceilings sustaining a modern chandelier, was wrapped in a stunning mahogany circular staircase that went from one side of the room to the other, begging for a royal highness to traipse down with an entourage, saying *hear ye, hear ye.*

As she meticulously headed up the stairs to check out my new digs, I went on to a side porch and answered my ringing cell phone.

"Hello."

"Hey. What's up, Vannah? I've been calling for months. Last I heard was the sooner the better. If you changed your mind…"

"No, I didn't change my mind, Tristan. I want to… no, I need to see you. Just been crazy around here."

"Vannah, you know I'm not for the drama. If dude's around, I'm not trying to be around. Period."

"Naw. It's not that. I've been getting myself together. Working. I sold a few homes, bought a new house for myself. Spending time with Ava."

I hated the lies and was probably going to hell just for mentioning Ava in the spiel of heinousness that flowed from my mouth, but there was no way to tell him the truth and no way that I was going to rid myself of Gunther prior to the house being in my name. Lying was the only way I thought that I could have Tristan back.

"So what's up? Are you too busy?"

"No. Come on Monday. Stay for as long as you want."

"You sure? 'Cause last time…"

"I'm sure, baby. I miss you so much."

That wasn't a lie. I did miss Tristan. I missed his hugs.

I heard my mom scream. It was either because of the pool that overlooked the floral-laden canyon or my enormous clothes closet with a shoe shelf that would hold hundreds of my favorite designer's finest.

Sunday, I was preparing for Tristan's arrival. I was moving all of the essential things from my apartment to the house; things like toiletries, cleaning supplies, valuable knick-knacks, and some boxes of clothes and my beloved shoes. I had large boxes scattered around the apartment for stuff that I would be donating, which was pretty much everything. I had shopped for new pots and pans, dishes, kitchen accessories, linen, and towels for all four bathrooms. I realized what a luxury it was to live in our apartment while I was taking time to prepare the house.

Gunther, who would randomly pop down from San Francisco or from other parts of the world, surprised me with a dinner invitation for Wednesday evening. Tristan was going to be in town staying with me at the house. Gunther didn't have to know that the house was inhabitable. But where would I tell Tristan that I was going?

I picked up Tristan and we went straight to the house, up the stairs, down the hall, and fell on to the huge Cali king bed that illuminated a soft orange glow from the underneath the platform when activated by weight. I knew Tristan was impressed with my car, my house, and its décor, but we were long overdue for a full night of raunchy sex; full of moans, groans, and sex talk leaving no room for conversation on miles per gallon or artwork.

At two in the morning after having had sex twice, I was being sequestered for another round. My body responded before my brain had even fully known what was going on. Tristan had always had a way of doing that. We quietly made love again before falling into a deep sleep.

The next morning, I started preparing Tristan for my pending absence, telling him that I was invited to a bachelorette party. He looked at me quizzically. I looked away as not to show signs of untruths.

"Who's getting married?"

I hadn't thought much about my lie and surely not an answer to that random question. I busied myself with the breakfast dishes.

"Faye. I shouldn't be out too long. It's her third marriage. The thrill is long gone." The lies kept coming.

"Cool."

I had the feeling that I was not believable. I also had the feeling that the slippery slope of morality that I had already been plodding up was just made impossibly slick with my vomit of easily expelled lies. Tristan and I were right back where we had left off, with me juggling him and Gunther, except this time Tristan was left in the dark.

Wednesday rolled around all too quickly. Gunther and I met at a nearby steakhouse. Again, I found myself going about the evening on autopilot. My mind was at my house on the hill where my well-endowed prince awaited my return. It was difficult to be in the moment. Twice, Gunther had to repeat a simple question.

"Well?"

"Well…I'm sorry. My head is somewhere else. It feels like an eternity since I've seen you, what, almost three months? How are things?"

"Business is extraordinary."

The hostess brought a box out just as our server set the appetizers down. I nonchalantly scanned the room, hoping that Tristan wasn't the sender of a goodbye bomb. I read the attached card. A check made out to me for ten thousand dollars fell out. Gifts from Gunther.

I smiled more from relief that my two-timing hadn't been discovered.

The professional wrapping reeked of money. I daintily opened it, placing the ribbon and the paper neatly on the seat beside me. I recognized the Rolex box. Inside was a beautiful two-toned diamond-face watch. I held out my hands for him to hold.

"Thank you. It's beautiful."

"There's more," he smiled and continued.

"I won't be around so much as before. European business has been booming and I'm needed there much more..."

A perfect gift! I wanted to jump for joy. Instead, I looked saddened by the news, milking his guilt. His gift wasn't that. He continued.

"...But, I'll set up auto deposits into your account so that you're at least financially okay. Maybe you should consider going back to school, Vannah." He added.

I was so elated by the news of my freedom that I did not respond verbally to his last comment.

*Nope. I'm a smart one, Gunther ol' boy. A smart one, indeed.*

Without Gunther around, I could develop my relationship with Tristan! I could get the house in my name and move on with my life.

I followed Gunther to his apartment. We performed just as we had done for years, except this time he tried to put his penis inside of me. I wiggled away and we finished up with him self-pleasing.

*He is definitely sleeping with someone else.*

After leaving Gunther's, instead of going to my apartment like so many times before, after a night out on the town, I headed to my million dollar house. I had come a long way, baby.

The next day, Gunther called me at 8 in the morning to bid farewell. He didn't know when he would see me next. I made him promise to call often.

Tristan helped me with the last remaining boxes; I could finally abandon my old apartment. It was a surprisingly sad goodbye. As I strolled through the empty space for the last time, memories of Ava streaking through the halls and Faye whipping up meals came to life. "Don't tell me no, tell me yes" echoed, while a vivid mirage of Faye peeking from the kitchen to lovingly gaze at me played out.

*Faye.*

As much as I tried to forget her, I couldn't. I thought about her constantly, wondering why she left so abruptly. Maybe the crossing into unfamiliar territory spooked her. We were not lesbians; at least, I didn't think that I was. I just loved and trusted her. Maybe even too much; I trusted her with my heart. Perhaps she sensed that vulnerability in me and took flight because of it. Maybe, the fact that I was too scared to plot against the hand that was feeding me caused her to abandon me. In any event, I missed Faye. I said a prayer to God.

"Please, bring her back."

God answered my prayer. Several weeks later, long after Tristan had returned to his hometown of Atlanta, Faye appeared on my doorstep with luggage in hand.

It was the first month of summer, a hot and gorgeous day. I was just about to run some errands when I opened the garage door; a taxicab was parked in my driveway. I walked to the front and saw Faye.

A huge grin engrossed my face. I think that she was relieved by the positive reception, and because of my smile, smiled back.

"I thought you'd be mad. So, I had the taxi wait," she said.

I signaled to the driver that it was okay to leave.

"Hello, Faye."

I moved in to take her bag. She stopped me and planted a kiss on my lips. We hugged for a few moments before I shook her free and resumed the migration indoors. We had lots to talk about, like:

"Where the hell have you been?"

"How's Ava?"

"She's good, bouncing between her grandma, uncle, and father in Minnesota. Not like you care."

Guilt was my new weapon of choice.

"Girl, don't try and guilt trip me. If I didn't care, I wouldn't have asked." She paused. "How are you?"

I stared at her. She was different, rested and healthy, with a funky new haircut.

"You look great."

I intentionally avoided her question.

I had no idea how I was. A surge of mixed emotions arose. I was pissed. I was hurt. I was...

"C'mon use your words; pissed, hurt?"

*Damn it. She is good.*

"...Perplexed. Why did you disappear and why did you suddenly reappear?"

"I am going to need a tour of this fabulous pad and a bottle of something ridiculously delicious. Oooh girl, I have just the meal in mind for dinner."

Faye had already made herself completely at home.

My dear Faye had returned.

After the tour, after unpacking, after a trip to the grocery store, and after one of the best meals that I had ever tasted in my entire life, I asked her again.

"So? Why did you leave? Where'd you go and what made you return?"

Faye went up to the guest room where she had her things. She came back to the living room with a briefcase. She showed me pictures.

"This was my mother when I was five."

"This is her as of last week." She showed me a picture of a dead woman poised inside of a casket.

"You could have told me."

"Told you that I was going to kill my mother?"

I froze.

"You killed her?"

"Well, not on purpose. But yes, I believe I pushed her over the edge. She was in a convalescent home, bed ridden, drooling, in and out of coherency. If I ever get like that, promise me you'll put a pillow over my head until I die."

"I promise."

"Shit. I'd do it for you." She was serious.

"Anyways, every time I went to the stupid home during the allotted visiting hours, she was asleep or on her meds. This went on for weeks! I finally got the nerve and bribed a young, college boy attendant to give me something that would keep her ass awake and alert. I fucked him in a closet and he gave me some crushed up No-Doz and a can of Red Bull. I came out on top on that one."

I couldn't believe Faye thought that this was funny.

"Anyhow, it worked. She was wide-awake and 'unusually spry' as the nurse said when she saw me the next day. As soon as the routine checkup was finished, I locked the door and grilled my mother on the whereabouts of my child. It took the bitch five minutes, but she knew exactly where she was. Some things you remember when your nipples are being squeezed hard enough to make you cry."

She paused. I could tell she was unsure if I could handle her next statement, but we were friends, no holds barred.

"I was thinking about bashing her head in. But then she went into a cardiac arrest. I guess my visit was long overdue. She would have died, even if I had rushed for help instead of taking my time. Vannah, you just don't know what a glorious thing it was for me to watch that bitch actually die."

Faye looked at me. I mustered up a concerned, understanding smile.

"As you saw, I stayed for the funeral, just so I could get that photo and slip an evil amulet into her casket so that her soul will be cursed for all of eternity."

I guessed that forgiveness wasn't an option for Faye.

"Did you meet your baby?"

"No. Not yet. I'm going back. I saw her, though, at the funeral. She's beautiful."

"Why not then?"

"She seemed to like the old hag. It wasn't the right time. And I think that I'm a grandmother, and really, I can't deal with that right now."

We sat still for a few moments.

"You could have told me."

"Yeah. Well, you'll see that there are things that you will have to deal with on your own."

Faye pulled out a bright yellow folder and handed it to me. I knew it was for me and about me. Talking about her time was finished.

I opened it. It was complete documentation on three men who I barley recognized anymore. As I slowly sifted through the pages, I learned that, in one way or another, they had suffered terrible fates. Johnny "JoJo" Jordan died from a gunshot wound to the head. Phillip Dunning (the winner) was serving a life sentence in a Federal penitentiary for the kidnap and murder of a young girl. The third rapist was paralyzed in the late nineties from an auto accident.

"Wow. I guess God took care of them."

"What? Two of the bastards are still alive. The quadriplegic can't feel his pecker, but I bet he can feel needles piercing through his eyeballs, and ol' boy locked up can get fucked in every orifice, if we just pull a few strings…compliments from the girl he raped and didn't kill, i.e., you, Vannah."

"No. No, Faye!"

I shut the folder.

"Look. I get it. I just don't have that much hate in my heart. I believe that they are where they are because of bad karma, whether from what they did to me or other evil things they did. I believe that I have karma too, Faye. Egging a house is one thing…"

"Girl, now is your chance to seek revenge," said Faye.

She pulled out another folder and opened it. It contained a photo of Sarah, my father's lover during his marriage to my mother. She was old and fat, no longer the belle of the ball.

Faye flipped open another; it contained an update on the whereabouts of my uncle who had abandoned his children (my cousins) years ago to live in the country, preaching to a small yet dedicated congregation.

"C'mon, where shall we start?"

Faye was convincing, but there was no way I was sticking needles in anyone's eyes.

"I'll start by using three words on the first line of every letter I write."

"Letter?"

"Yes. You, too. You're gonna write one to your daughter."

Faye and I wrote for two days. We poured our hearts onto empty pages, filling them with a soulful voice of heartache crafted for each recipient. I detailed the rape, the days that followed, the pregnancy, and the abortion. I wrote to Sarah that 'witnessing such acts and having to keep them secret from my mother set me up for a lifetime of repeating the same ill behaviors of both cheating and harboring secrets.'

As I forgave, Faye begged forgiveness, both just as healing as the other. I sealed the last envelope with the salty tear that had streamed down my face. Once again, vindicated by three little words.

Faye and I spent a week enjoying each other's friendship, and then, one day, I came home from a hair appointment to find her gone, not weighing me down with the details of her whereabouts. At least this time, I knew that she'd be back.

I booked a flight to Atlanta to visit my handsome football player, who didn't know where he'd wind up that season, as he was a free agent. After a few amazing days, I left him to go spend time with my old friends, Mary, who had relocated to New York, and Dawn, who had returned to Chicago. It was a fabulous summer. But I was ready for Ava to come back. I missed her.

Ava was having a blast. She spent the majority of her time with her father who was being stellar in his daddy duties. I sat patiently on the phone, smiling as Ava (not skipping one detail) described their fun filled days. Ava loved her dad and summer was made extra special because of his love for her.

# nineteen

Both the relationship with Gunther and Tristan also became heavily reliant on communication via the phone. I kept each happy with sentences of half-truths and, more often than not, outright lies. I became very good at painting pictures of their exact dream girl. I convinced Gunther that I was content (although I missed him) and satisfied with being a stay-at-home soccer mom, when Ava didn't even play soccer. I convinced Tristan that I was a workaholic, building my empire in the area of real estate. The truth was I was counting down the months until I could transfer the house into my name and abandon Gunther forever.

Conversation after conversation of lies brought Tristan and I closer. My obvious infatuation for him started to disillusion me. I began thinking about normalcy—a family, marriage, and children. The feelings were mutual. He had his Mrs. Money Right. Soon, he was ending every phone call with an "I love you, Vannah."

Tristan got the word that he had been traded to the Cardinals. I was actually relived. San Diego was too close for comfort, as Gunther would still occasionally pop in. Arizona was much closer than visiting him in Atlanta, but equally as complicated because finding time away during the school year would be difficult.

Tristan had been suspiciously distant and, on a few occasions, I couldn't reach him at night. When he finally called, he would convincingly blame the rigorous two-a-day practices and the need to sleep without interruption, thus the reason he turned off his phone.

To put my mind at ease, Tristan sent me a plane ticket. I went to Phoenix early Friday for the weekend. Upon arrival, as usual, we made love prior to any exchange of substantive words. For some reason, as soon as Tristan left for practice that afternoon, I searched his room for any signs of a woman.

Oh my, how the tables had turned. I was scouring, like Alberto, through Tristan's personal belongings looking for evidence of betrayal. Ironically, like Alberto, I found huge, pink panties. It was the first indication that the love of my life had been cheating.

I was upset that I had stooped so low, but even more distraught that my snooping revealed a nightmare. I paced his hotel room until he came back from practice, my anger bubbling to a rapid boil with each step.

Tristan came through the door, just as sexy and handsome as ever. The boiling anger was in that instant doused with iced water. I didn't have words. I just pointed to the panties that I had placed on the nightstand.

Tristan told me a story about how the item came to find its way into his bag. I listened.

"I had that luggage in storage for years and just took it out. They're probably my sister's or mama's drawers."

I had it in my mind to believe him. Either it was the truth or he lied to keep me or possibly from hurting me with the real truth. Not unlike my lying by omission that cloaked our three-way relationship with Gunther.

I flushed the panties down the toilet and said no more about it.

*Why did I have a need to search his stuff?* I was insecure; that was why.

*Why did I listen and believe his story?* I was in love; that was why.

That was a very dangerous combination.

On my way back to San Diego, I was again tussling with thoughts about the panties; even though I convinced myself of his innocence, everything in me was screaming to dump him.

But, I couldn't do it; I was in love with Tristan. At least, I believed that I was, even as I questioned whether or not I was truly capable of the emotion (as it pertained to men). For years, I had plotted against them, deeming them to be the lesser-evolved species, fallible, weak, and easily manipulated.

Sex and lust, I could do, but not romantic love—not love as I had come to understand it such as the love I felt for Ava, meaning the kind of love that would make you kill yourself because the one you loved had perished. Or the kind of unwavering, devoted love that would make you risk your chance at never-ending ecstasy and travel to the pits of hell to rescue your doomed lover from their evitable fate of spending an eternity in the fiery darkness (like Anabella Sciorra and Robin Williams' characters in *What Dreams May Come*).

*That* was the kind of love I had visualized, not the superficial twenty-first-century BS that had replaced it. I could say I was successful and that I had loved—Antonio, Aaron, even Tristan. Still, I never gave any of them one hundred percent true devotion. It wasn't in me. I cheated, gave up, failed to commit, and now I was choosing to lie in a relationship that could amount to true love.

A lifetime of living a double life is institutionalizing.

How would I squeeze love into that scenario?

*Unless I could change.*

How would I negate the argument that money was my first love? My heart sought love, but could my lifestyle accommodate it? Could I and would I make the necessary adjustments? Or was I immutable? Was Tristan laudable? Was I even worthy of love? My ambivalence on the subject kept me awake.

*God, please help me to figure out this crap.*

I needed answers…

I tossed and turned. None came. Alone, I grappled with

whether or not to enlighten Tristan on the details of Gunther and my money obsessions. I played the "what-if" game and called Tristan at four in the morning.

"Baby, *what if* some man wanted to give me a million dollars to sleep with him?" I casually asked.

"I'd call you a ho and bounce."

"*What if* I split it with you fifty/fifty?"

"I'd take the money, call you a ho, and leave."

*Well, if I were offered a million dollars, I'd call you stupid and not give you a dime.*

Tristan was a judgmental, narrow-minded man. He was not street. He was nothing like Ava's father, Aaron, who would have praised me for having such a tight hustle.

My decision was made.

If love were going to prevail, there'd be nothing that I could do to stop it. Never mind honesty and disclosure. I would let nature take its course.

*Do not tell Tristan!*

Time would tell if my decision was right or wretchedly erroneous. I said good night to the love of my life and fell into a restful slumber.

Ava returned tanned and ready for the challenges of second grade.

# twenty

Almost a year had breezed by. I spent it loving Tristan and taking Gunther's money. I only talked to Faye a few times, but our conversations lasted for hours. Our updates were thorough. She had moved in with her daughter, who resided in South Carolina. She loved being a full-time grandmother and that was coming from someone who deplored children. I told her all about Tristan and how close we had become. She was surprised that I had seen Gunther at all when I mentioned that we went away three times, always internationally, always full of gifts, shopping, and fine dining.

"Aren't you in love with Tristan?" she had asked.

We went back and forth. Her argument hinged on autonomy. She explained that Tristan needed full disclosure, so that he loved the same person he believed himself to love. I knew that it was much more complicated than that. I also knew Tristan. Plus, she did not take into consideration how I had lived my life; I was kept. What she was asking was implausible, especially just months from the house transfer. Faye concluded, by arguing that in order for complete happiness to occur, I had to stop living a fucking lie. She told me to cut Gunther off and tell Tristan the truth about my life. I hung up on her.

Gunther and I talked all the time. Our phone relationship made us stronger than we had ever been. I realized that he was a very kind and generous man who had grown to love me regardless of my flaws. He was actually interesting and ironically revealed a sense of humor. The fact that I rarely saw him and saw large amounts of cash, in excess of twenty thousand, deposited every first day of each month, made me appreciate, even like, Gunther. Gunther had found the exact dollar amount to tame and quiet me, making me kind and committed (at least in words).

Gunther ended each conversation with the same words as Tristan—"I love you, Vannah."

I successfully juggled my two men. Living my dual life was remarkably easy.


Gunther and I met in Vegas for my birthday. We had a great time traipsing around our old stomping grounds. I was maturing and Gunther was overly chivalrous. We fell into a comfort zone. Being kept had become an easy job, a far cry from the formulating years.

During another overly priced meal, I asked about his availability to conclude the quitclaim. He fumbled with his words. I knew then that things could get sticky regarding the transfer of my house. Large amounts of equity might cause me to take flight. Gunther couldn't hand over the key to unlocking my freedom. It was his only mechanism of control. After many years, he had me where he needed me to be. Would I stay put, fight, or walk away? It was a question that raced through both of our minds. The game of emotional and financial tug-o-war continuing as it always had.

Out of curiosity and exploration of my options, I asked Tristan about living together.

Tristan didn't seem at all interested in that arrangement, which raised my suspicions.

"Baby, I'm not in a position to take care of you the way I want to just yet. One more year ballin' out and I'm good," he said.

His words pacified me. His ego wanted him to be in a better place before we began our eternal bliss under the same roof. He wanted to be the breadwinner. I let the subject go and tried to keep things, as they were, long distance.

When I did see Tristan, we'd devour each other so passionately that a casual affair was impossible. Together, we laughed and joked. He was caring and kind. We hung out with his friends on the team and did things hand in hand/arm in arm. I was emotionally and physically addicted. However, he was a totally different person when he was at home and we were apart. The little gut check was nagging me—something wasn't quite right.

Tristan probably had another love interest, but my own closet was full of skeletons, double standards, lies, and Gunther rubbish of course hung neatly on wooden hangers. I wasn't ready to expose Tristan's waywardness, and I wasn't ready to admit my own. In actuality, I was buying time. I had to figure my own life out before kicking the only man who excited me to the point of snooping to the proverbial curb.

*What good will it do to reveal such a silly detail as a dual life just yet?*


Ava and Aaron had talked daily. They were as close by phone as they had been together. Although Aaron had a stint of doing better, it came as no surprise when he disappeared.

He hadn't returned Ava's calls in weeks. Her concern for her dad's well-being was taxing. I made the decision to tell Ava the truth about her father.

During the previous years, I had made it effortless for Aaron to appear to be a good dad. I went as far as to give him money for her birthday and Christmas presents. He didn't pay child support, ever. I even lied to her and told her that he had called to say he loved her when he hadn't. To say I bent over backward would be an understatement; I was an acrobatic gymnast. Protecting her from that day was my only goal. But he had developed into a selfish, careless deadbeat. Everyone who loved him had grown weary of his ways—especially me.

Ava came into my room. I tried to cover the fact that I

had been crying. She immediately panicked when she saw my wet eyes. I rarely cried in front of her, so my crying meant something terrible had happened.

Sugarcoating was not my style, so I just said it.

"Your father hasn't called you because he has been using drugs. No one has heard from him. Right now, we're hoping he's not dead."

I realized that I should have left that last part out.

Her eyes got big and teary. She couldn't talk. I quickly added a disclaimer.

"He's fine, baby. Just self-centered."

Her mind couldn't wrap itself around the possibility that he might very well be rotting on a crack house floor (where I conceived her in my nightmares years ago).

When she asked which drug he used, I sighed.

"Crack cocaine."

My daughter's blood-curdling scream hurt my heart. She believed crack to be the worst of the worst. It was an ugly, humiliating drug, and she refused to believe that her father could be its victim. Her hurt-filled wails made my tears flow easily from their sockets.

"No! No... not my daddy..."

I held her tight and rocked her for hours.

I whispered softly, "It's gonna be okay, Angel."

I explained his addiction, truthfully.

"He's been an addict your whole life, even before I met him."

More tears.

"And as addiction sometimes goes, he's getting progressively worse. You have to prepare for tough times. He needs help."

She cried herself to sleep, spending the night in my arms.

We knew that we were all we had. It had been that way

her whole life, but my daily presence, over-the-top concerns for her general well-being, and that particular turn of events solidified the fact.

Aaron had worsened to the point of lamp-less, penniless bleakness. His disappearance lasted for a month. When he surfaced, he claimed to be ready for treatment.

Voluntarily, he went to a rehabilitation center in Arkansas. The time for a cure seemed laughably short for someone who had been an addict for twenty years. But we were supportive and held out hope that he would come out in thirty days fixed, or at least somewhat reminiscent of the Aaron that we once knew. After all, he was the one who wanted change.

Both Ava and I wrote long letters disgorging all the usual rhetoric that someone who cares tells a druggy in rehab.

# twenty-one

My heart was impaired from suspicions of dishonesty from the love of my life, a house that I loved that may never truly be mine, and my sick baby daddy. I pulled out the bright yellow folder and the names of the corresponding culprits: Tristan, Gunther, and Aaron.

The number I found, during the search through Tristan's belongings, was the number to an ex-girlfriend who had been dumped prior to his NFL career. She had never gotten over him and was like a weed that returns seasonally to annoy. It was our second conversation and I had had enough of her ignorant whining.

"Give me the goods! Even if it implicates you as a deceitful, green-eyed woman who's trying to win her ex back by seducing him, even though you are fully aware of the fact that he has a girlfriend. I'd respect you more."

I'm not sure that she understood any of those words, so I shortened things up.

"Is he doing you or not?"

As it turned out, he wasn't sleeping with his ex, as hard as it was for her to finally tell me. I hadn't found enough reason to incriminate him, so she added, "It is rumored that he is living with a woman named Wendy."

*Damn.*

She got me with the hand grenade that she so badly wanted to use.

Rumor, my ass. My heart, that had sped up and thumped nervously, knew it to be true.

The lack of phone calls during the late evening hours when

he was home during the off-season proved it. So did his lack of a home! He never invited me to his hometown anymore, only wherever he was playing. He claimed it was because his roommate was a weed-smoking slob, and he didn't want me to see a place where he just "laid his head" for a few months. When I insisted on meeting his family, he became edgy. Also, he got extremely nervous when I came anywhere near his cell phone. He might as well have duct-taped the device to his inner thigh.

Of course he was living with a girl, and his ex knew quite certainly what her name was. She even had the chick's number.

Like with Aaron, Alberto and Gizel, Don, and Gunther, I had conditioned myself to take abuse for the sake of seeing where it might go. Would he fight for me like them or give me up? I hung up with his ex and dialed the number of his other girlfriend.

My chest tightened. The answering machine kicked in. Her voice was older, not ditsy but bordering. I left a message. Later that night, she called back. She was sultry and matter-of-fact. She confirmed that they were living together.

My heart froze. It shattered into a billion pieces. The moment of realization is the worst feeling in the world, though my gut checks had warned me long ago. My insides ached. I wanted to curl up into a ball and cry myself a river. How could he deceive me?

As I was emotionally crumbling, she took on the attitude of a smug winner of the grand prize: Tristan. She was surly and uncaring toward me. I didn't understand it. I was not at fault. I had discovered that he was involved with us both and was bringing it to her attention—why was I suddenly her enemy and the one to blame?

She made a quip about him dealing with me because I had money. Her diffidence made me ill. I wanted to jump through the phone and backslap her until her cheek bled. How dare she know things about me? How dare she facilitate his dual life? She was purposefully involved in our three-way affair, whereas I was an unknowing victim of his secret lie. Strangely, she motivated me to fight for *my* man.

Dating a football player, living the fast life of money and cars, eating at nice restaurants, and shopping at Neiman Marcus made it easy for her to accept the role as his chick on the side.

Then it really hit me. She was no different than myself. Everything that I had convinced myself that I was not, I was, namely, money hungry and selfish. I was wrapping my head around that and then—swoosh—another wave of thoughts came.

*Can it be that my feelings of reciprocated love are so far off base, and I am just being used, as she claimed?*

I thought back to all the trips that I paid for to see him and the thoughtful and expensive gifts. He did have security in knowing that I could take care of myself and that I wasn't after his baller money.

I was confused trying to decipher the plethora of pieces of information that shot through my thoughts.

Were we in love?

How could he possibly love a stupid bitch that had lain dormant as he did what he pleased?

Did he not see she was there for money and could care less about him?

Was this the man whom I thought to be so special?

Was this a love of wanton cruelty?

Of course, he could love me *and* shack up with the doormat.

I had lied and deceived him our whole relationship.

I loved him and was the stupid bitch of a rich businessman.

Were our violations so different? Hers and mine? His and mine?

Why in the world was I surprised by this nasty little turn of events?

It could have just as easily been him making the call to Gunther and uncovering deceitful lies about the love of his life.

I was never honest about anything pertaining to how I actually made my fortune.

Tristan was with a hypocritical shape-shifter.

Should I fault him for being what I was?

My profligate life had come home to roost.

I was confused and in no mind-set to make sound decisions, but I decided that Wendy's short, snappy sentences and overly confident attitude were to blame for turning me into a rancorous maniac. I hated Wendy for not crying, or at least co-plotting his demise with me, her twin. Instead, she wanted me to hand him over so that she could spend the next—however long—making him pay for her broken heart by guilt giving and promises of a brighter, more faithful future.

Well, that was exactly what I wanted to do! My twin had to go.

The Savannah/Gizel exploits would pale in comparison to what I was prepared to engage in with Wendy. The gloves were off.

"Let's three-way call Tristan." I took charge.

She was obviously too passive for such aggressive moves. If left to her, she probably would not have mentioned our conversation to him at all and went along with taking his doled out treats. His phone rang.

"Hello."

*God, I love his voice.*

"Hey, baby."

"Hey."

"Do you love me?" I held back tears.

"Yep. I love you."

"Who's Wendy?"

Silence.

"Some girl I used to fuck."

"Used to or *do*?"

"Used to, why?"

I swear I heard his heartbeat quicken.

"I talked to your ex; she gave me Wendy's number."

*Shoot. I ratted on my snitch.*

What happened next was uncontrollable. I burst into heavy sobs. Tears poured freely from my eyes, real tears from heartache. He claimed he didn't love or even like her and that he was only living with her out of convenience.

"Bullshit! What convenience is that? Convenient sex?"

He begged me to listen to him and pleaded with me not to do anything rash until we could talk face-to-face. I told him that it was over. He was free to give all of his love and affection to one woman. She deserved that.

"I love you, not her. She's a stripper who don't mean shit to me."

Wendy remained silent, even through that last comment. That was the moment she lost all of my respect. To let him call her someone who doesn't mean shit is to be a Stupid Bitch; take advice from the handbook of Faye.

"Wendy? Are you still on the line?"

Tristan hung up, and so did I. I sobbed into my pillow.

*My heart, oh my heart.*

Tristan probably called Wendy and professed his love and then spent the rest of the evening trying to reach me.

Ring.

Ring.

Answer? For what, I did not know. His cowardice was repulsive and I didn't want to hear any fake confessions. An atmosphere of distrust had pervaded our relationship. He was a very sad and confused man. I didn't care. To think I had been prepared to fight for him.

I had made up my mind to accept defeat, cry for exactly six

days, and take a trip to somewhere, anywhere. But then, Wendy called.

She rubbed in the fact that he was on his way back "home."

I was spent. She was getting on my nerves.

The message he left said that they had had a huge argument and he was not on his way to eat dinner and watch the evening news but to gather some things. He would stay in a hotel, leaving her time to get her stuff and vacate his condo.

Faye phoned, as if my personal crisis had reverberated throughout the universe and she was the only decipherer and translator of the SOS. Faye, equipped with the knowledge had from her pursuing and obtaining a degree in psychology, peeled off layers to reveal psychological dysfunction that started as a child. I listened, but her timing was off. I was angry and defensive. I needed a shoulder to cry on, not another phone conversation of words that were meant for my brain and not my heart.

Faye called every day pushing her therapeutic agenda. Her persistence melted my armor. It was the first time that I had displayed any kind of emotion other than hatred regarding men. She heard my pain. I was surprised by my own honesty about my feelings. I loved Tristan, truly. It was also the first time in my life that I had loved this deeply. But transparency in love was stopped cold by my adopted unyielding hypocrisy and duplicitous ways. I knew Faye was right.

I mulled the whole relationship to pieces as Tristan called fifty times a day. I let it ring. I had won. He wanted me and dumped Wendy, but still, I was empty. I didn't trust him and couldn't forgive him that easily. I had to be stern. My heart hurt. I was dizzy from crying and expelling so much emotion in one day. I needed to sleep.

Ava was an unfortunate witness to my depression. I slept and drank heavily for two days, before cleaning up the residual mess.

Meanwhile, Aaron had disappeared for the longest stint ever.

Ava was distressed. No matter what her grandmother or I did to ease her pain, we knew that the only thing she wanted she would never get. She wanted her daddy back—the dad who used to laugh and act silly and take her fishing and to concerts; the dad who never missed an important day or holiday; the loving father who put his daughter on a pedestal. No, that daddy was gone.

He preferred the taste of a crack pipe, running around in the same clothes for days on end, and spending his days with people who could never share his passion for his own daughter. She knew it and cried herself to sleep every night. I knew it and hated him for it. She eventually quit calling his phone. Then, she stopped inquiring about him. Finally, she couldn't even bring herself to shed tears. What were we collectively doing to our little girl?

It was just days before Thanksgiving and we had no word from Aaron.

Gunther was preparing for a trip to the United States and an escape with me to the Hawaiian Islands, leaving just after Christmas. And since Tristan was a lying, cheating asshole, I was able to plan the whole vacation guilt free.

I avoided conversation with Faye. She was eerily reminding me of a higher, moralistic conscious.

Christmas was rough. Ava held out hope that her dad would show up at my mother's house. It *was* the most festive time of the year; surely, he wouldn't miss it.

Ava bought him a new shirt and tie. She wrapped it and put it under the beautiful tree. Ava woke up on Christmas morning, early as usual, but didn't rush to wake us; instead, she went and sat by the window. She fell back asleep on the floor under the sill; she was waiting for her father. When I saw her, I felt the sorrow that a mother feels for a daughter who is in deep pain. I made her get up before my mother woke up. The scene would have killed her.

"Ava, I promise that wherever he is, he is thinking of you."

"Why won't he just come home?"

"He is far too embarrassed for that," I said, hoping she knew what I meant. "Please stop looking for him. He's not going to come."

That made her cry.

"What if—"

"Ava, he's just ashamed; that's all. I need you to make this easier not harder for your grandmother by being strong. Can you do that?"

She wiped away her tears and took a deep breath.

"Yeah, I can do that."

"I'm sorry, Angel. The truth hurts," I said.

She wasn't up for my lesson in "bad things happen." I kissed her and went to retrieve a small box shaped like an iPod.

She went to wake up her grandma.

The three of us had a decent Christmas. We gave Ava everything she asked for and oodles of other contrition gifts that she hadn't.

Later that same day, Ava had shed her sadness and had adjusted to the festivities without her father. I was a blubbery mood killer. I went to my old childhood room—turned office— to sulk. I secretly wished I had my old AM radio. I could use some Steely Dan.

My brain was riddled with thoughts of Tristan's trickery. I had the feeling that Wendy wasn't out of his life. Wendy was definitely the type to take a backseat, rather than get kicked out of the car.

If the AM radio were alive, it'd probably be blasting the Gambler's Song ..."You got to know when to hold 'em..."

Through all of the messages, I gathered that Tristan wanted to move on and forget that Wendy ever existed, but my gut was aching and he didn't do enough to calm the nerves or erase the mistrust. He used his words, just as I had, and like mine, they had a plethora of meaning; none could be trusted.

"...Know when to fold 'em..."

I knew I needed to call Wendy. I picked up the office phone and dialed her number from memory.

My suspicions were on point. She was a backseater. Even though she knew he was with me, she was indulging him. He vehemently argued that she was lying.

*Merry friggin' Christmas.*

"...Know when to walk away..."

"Let's get Wendy on a three-way," I insisted.

Wendy knew and said things that she could only have known if he had been with her, like the description of a sweater I had sent to him for Christmas.

The rest of the holidays were a blur.

Aaron was depressing our daughter, and Tristan was depressing me.

*Thanks, Kenny Rogers.*

"...Know when to run..."

Another vacation was in order.

Ava and I could get over our respective oppressors. We just needed the proper distractions. Ava's grandmother would take her to Belize. I would go to Hawaii with Gunther.


I returned to San Diego to prepare for my trip. As I was repacking, removing the warm wool sweaters and long underwear and replacing them with bikinis and miniskirts, my phone rang. It was Tristan. My heart fluttered nervously when I answered. But my words cut like shards of glass.

"I have nothing to say. You won't ever change. Your energy is best spent with a dimwit like Wendy. She is the perfect shag carpeting for you to lay your ass on."

He was very convincing in his emotional outburst.

"Wendy was what it was. She's a flexible-ass stripper that liked to fuck. She was easy. I didn't take her anywhere, hold hands with her, or kiss her! She was a convenient fuck with a nice body. Period. She's fucking with you. Every time you call, she knows what to say

278

to get you riled up. She hopes that you'll leave me. She hates me 'cause I chose you. I almost got arrested because I tore up my own house after she called and told you all that bullshit."

I was a glutton for punishment. After all my years of lying and manipulation, of course, his speech had a familiar ring. I wanted so badly to believe him that I did.

Tristan and I were not opposites; we were synonymous. He and I were perfect for each other. I could not let him go. I wanted to take on the project of "changing" him; at the same time, I could also work on a transmutation of myself. I knew what I was dealing with; he was my mirror image. It is very difficult to explain the psychology of such a counterintuitive, self-destructive act but ultimately, I knew that his infraction paled in comparison to the sins I committed and would continue to commit.

Wendy was a desperate, do-anything whore, who would not go away because she was addicted to the good life and Tristan was a thrill-seeking, two-timing baller with a huge penchant for sex. I was a spoiled, well aware of the facts, guiltless liar who refused to leave her soul mate in the lap of a foul stripper who would further derange *my* man's soul. I concluded that Tristan needed me just as badly as I needed him. With his future in my molding hands, we would one day be completely and honestly in love.

*Just not right now.*

We both had more deceit and pain to dole out before the construction of a fresh start could occur.

After his explanation, I simply hung up the phone.

Tristan would be excited and eager to please me when I called in one week. I missed him dearly, but my lesson in humility was for the greater good. If I gave in, he would act out worse later. I had to nip his cheating ways in the bud and deal with my own sickening double standards.

I was pushing back. Tristan had to suffer, suffer, suffer. Plus, I had a week of Gunther to deal with. I needed to concentrate on how I would get my house. I pulled out the bright yellow folder and drew a red X through Tristan's name; Resolved. One down, two to go.


Happy New Year!

Gunther and I brought the New Year in drunk. I didn't remember much.

Hawaii was a chore. Gunther and I spent time touring Maui by helicopter and car, sucked through pineapples at luaus, ate at five-star restaurants, drank until we couldn't walk, and sat around and talked about people who were singing show tunes at the dull, lobby piano bar. Mainly, we lazed around the popular Waikiki hotel pool and soaked up the rays while reading Vince Flynn novels.

I called often to check on Ava's sanity. She was still living it up in Belize. She wasn't thinking about her dad. I couldn't get Tristan out of my head.

Gunther seemed a bit distracted too. Under the influence, I asked about his other girlfriend, the one I thought him to be sticking his penis into. He lied. I could tell by the way his eyes darted away from mine. I didn't care either way. I just wanted him to know that I knew, and more important, feel badly.

"Have you thought anymore about the quitclaim?"

He stuttered; his eyes darted, again.

"Uh…uh…"

"Look, Gunther, that was the deal nearly three years ago now! Either you will give me my house or I will walk away! It's not fair and you know it."

It was an ultimatum that I hadn't fully thought through. I hoped that he didn't allow the latter. He agreed to talk in depth about it when we returned to San Diego.

I felt our years together coming to an end.

# twenty-two

After returning from Hawaii, a cab dropped me off at my house and as soon as I entered, I picked up the ringing house phone. It was Tristan.

"Where have you been?"

"Hawaii. Why?"

"I'm coming to see you."

"Fine."

Gunther disappeared. I hadn't heard from him since our trip. I figured he decided to let me walk away. Nearly six hundred thousand was at stake, an expensive payment for a woman who was simply his side dish.

Tristan did come to visit.

Through the blur of saltwater, I could see him studying my face. He ignored the flesh that was falling off in sheets from a chemical peel that I voluntarily elected to perform in hopes of beautifying even more. He pulled me to his broad chest. I maintained my closed, hardened stance.

"I'm sorry, baby. You deserve better, but no one will ever love you like I do. I'm not perfect, but I love you and won't live without you as my woman."

He had been practicing.

His kisses melted into my heart and pierced my soul. His touch made me shudder. His perfect navigation of my body sent waves of emotion up and down my spine.

Eager to have me naked, he ripped my silk nighty and dropped his jeans. We made love on the stairs leading to the bedroom. He looked into my eyes, held my chin, not letting me look away, and repeated, "I love you," until I came. He carried me (still inside) to the bedroom where we made love for hours. I cried the entire time. He wiped every tear away with soft stokes of his strong hands.

Afterward, we were spent, physically and emotionally drained.

We were also starving.

I didn't care that my crispy, flakey face shouldn't have left the confines of my home, if he didn't. We sat quietly over Ruth Chris' half-eaten steak and stuffed chicken. It was the perfect backdrop for a confession story of Gunther. But I could not do it. Tristan was full of his own regret. What would be gained from the truth? The truth would only hurt.

Tristan tried very hard to make up for all the pain he caused. My heart was still wounded, and I questioned my trust in him. Only time would tell if Tristan was trustworthy. I, on the other hand, *knew* that I was not.

My hypocrisy was at an all-time high. I justified the difference between Tristan and me by rationalizing to myself that Gunther was a job and my spending time with him had nothing to do with desires, sex, or love. It was a job—a *secret* job. Only after Tristan proved that he was capable of being trusted would I make the necessary adjustments, ridding myself of my covert employment.

As an alternative to confessing my sins to Tristan, I persecuted him for his deceit and betrayal. He could never be unfaithful again, if I remained his girlfriend. If there were ever any reason to believe that Wendy or anyone else was milling around, I would cut him off and never speak to him again.

My acting skills kicked in and I was vindicated. He would spend his energy trying to make things right. He was remorseful, sentimental, and loving, and I was the same old, sad ass. I detested myself.

I so badly longed to be a better person, but I had become dependent on Gunther's handouts. Money was my vice. I was an addict and Gunther my ever-present dealer.

I didn't know how to get a job and support myself. My

résumé was pathetic. How could I write that I had been a sinecurist for the past thirteen years? My mind set was lazy because I was privileged. How could *I* be a subordinate? It had been so long, that I couldn't even fathom a measly hour lunch.

My house was a burden, and my expenditures were far too high. I was spending more time and money traveling with Tristan. I was going to see him more often because of my insecurities. I was tending Ava's wounds (made by her father's drug use) and my guilt (from paying so much attention to Tristan) with Band-Aids called expensive gifts and exquisite vacations. The bottom line was that I was spending more than the amount Gunther was dishing out.

In desperate, quick come-up attempts to sustain my lifestyle, my hustle became less than perfect. Pummeled by the stock market crash, I lost more than I care to remember.

I didn't whine about my financial fate. I knew from years of gambling in Vegas that you couldn't and wouldn't always win. Expenditures and losses were just a part of the game. Actually, loss, pain, and negative experiences were what made me wiser, more determined, and more resilient. So does heartache in love.

To love wholeheartedly was all I wanted, yet I was bogged down by so many self-inflicted financial constraints. How would I even begin to rearrange my priorities? How did I get so lost that I couldn't leave my oppressor? How did I manage to turn into Gizel?

Tristan deserved more from me. He was at least trying to change. I should have been execrated and left to burn in hell. Tristan had done everything that I had asked and more. He was available and good to my daughter and me. I felt his incontestable faithfulness. I was at peace with my decision to stay with him after his affair.

Then four words shot through my vertebrae and out the top of my head causing a lingering feeling of horrid unworthiness.

"Will you marry me?"

I hung up the phone without giving him an answer. I needed time to think.


"Me and my girlfriend; all I need in this life of sin is me and my girlfriend. Down to ride 'til the bloody end, me and my girlfriend." I blasted my favorite artist and former pen pal, as I went to gather up Gunther. He hadn't walked away. He had actually arranged things so that the transfer could be done without penalty or hardship. He was giving me my house.

I turned to easy listening just before Gunther got into the car. Ironically, Glenn Frey bellowed the lyrics: "Are you gonna stay with the one who loves you? Or are you goin' back to the one you love? Someone's gonna cry when they know they've lost you; someone's gonna thank the stars above."

After we took care of the final paperwork, Gunther asked me to join him on an around-the-world trip. I'm sure he had hoped I'd bite like a rabid dog. I simply said no. I had no desire to be within spitting distance of Gunther.

All the years of desperate maneuvers to make me love him had failed miserably. I couldn't love Gunther and *never*, under any circumstances, would. I recognized the symptoms of an addicted man and felt sorry for him.

I wanted a shot at love, so I swept my past and Gunther under the carpet and prayed that Tristan wouldn't trip on the monstrous bulge.

*God, forgive me.*

*Forgive the selfish hypocrisy that I portrayed so casually throughout my entire life. I am sorry. I am so, so sorry to all the victims of my grandiose and heartless drills.*

Gunther left town. I had my house paid for outright; I was responsible for only taxes, insurance and maintenance. Gunther would still fork over the same amount—twenty grand a month. This should have been a thrilling time for me, but it wasn't. A part of me didn't care.

That house, and every house that I had ever had been given, came to represent a type of jail. I was self-confined inside of it. After all the energy expelled trying to make my house something else/something beautiful; trying to own it; trying to make it make me happy, the realization came. I needed to walk away.


I called Faye to apologize for my childish behaviors. Her raspy, weak voice instantly made me concerned.

"It's all good, girlfriend, but I'm dying and you have very little time to take advantage of my great big ol' brain." She tried to laugh. Her daughter took the phone. I quizzed her. Her responses set my body in motion.

I began frantically packing, making arrangements for Ava, booking a flight, and throwing things into a bag.

Why hadn't I seen the signs?

The trip to South Carolina was arduous. I wanted to blink and be there. Faye was dying. Somewhere in my subconscious had I known all along? Her constant coughing, loss of weight, sleep deprivation, sudden disappearances, her short haircut, and, the most obvious, her fucking bucket list. God, what kind of selfish, self-centered person was I? My best friend was dying and I hadn't put any of the pieces together.

I arrived at her daughter's home, not knowing what to expect. I was frightened. For the first time in my life, I realized how unimportant things are. I would have given anything for Faye to be okay.

I took a deep breath and knocked on the door. Faye's daughter answered. It was clear that she had been crying. After a brief introduction and update on Faye's condition, Bonita lead me through her modest home to a room that smelled like a sick person had been held up for months.

Faye looked very bad. Her hair was thin and straggly. Her skin was gray, pale, and damp. When I went to hold her hand, I was stopped by shock at the amount of weight that she had lost. I bit the inside of my lip and could taste a small amount of blood.

*Stop it! Crying will not be helpful.*

"Why didn't you tell me?"

"Girl, there are some things that you have to go through on your own."

A tear fell from my eye without my awareness.

"But not death, Faye. Not death."

"This thing has been at me for a minute. I will die eventually, but not today. So don't think you can make off with my Manolo's."

"How much time do...?"

"Six months maybe."

At that moment, I knew exactly what I should do.

"Come live with me."


Bonita, her ten year old daughter Cynthia, and Faye moved to San Diego. Faye resumed her treatments under the expert care of the Scripps Cancer Center with the top oncologist. Faye's optimism was contagious. But her disease was terminal. The passing of time was not her friend.

Faye and I spent the days appreciating the little things that life had to offer like a walk on the beach, a road trip to Disneyworld with Ava and her granddaughter, cooking, eating, and watching foreign films.

One day, Faye and I strolled the Carmel Valley neighborhood, taking in the things that I had driven by hundreds of times and had not noticed, like a beautiful orange tree teeming with happy bees and a recreational center where neighborhood kids congregated on the far side, away from view. Just as we got back to the house, I asked Faye if she could change anything about her life what would it be.

"I would have met you sooner and I would have allowed our friendship to go deeper."

"It can't get deeper than this," I said with all sincerity.

"Yeah. But I should have told you. I just didn't want my circumstances to change your life."

"My life desperately needed changing."

"Needs."

"Needed."

"Needs, Vannah! Dammit! I haven't hounded you about it, but dumping Gunther, getting the house, that's one thing and if I'm totally honest, it wasn't just 'cause he felt compelled to give it to you."

"What do you mean?"

"I mean it was me all along. I made the motherfucker stay away and give you twenty grand a month. I made him pay off the fucking house by threatening to expose his double life to his wife and to his kids, Vannah. He may hate my guts and even want to kill me, but as you know, I don't give a shit. I'm dying. Fuck it."

I couldn't believe what I was hearing. Was I that removed from the things that were going on around me?

Faye again made the trip to the guest room to retrieve a thick, bright yellow folder. Once again, I found myself flipping through a thorough investigative report, partially from a hired professional and partially written by her hand. I learned that Gunther had a wife and three children all about my age. He also was a member of a private club that practiced masochism. He had another girlfriend acquired around the time he started disappearing; her name was Faye.

I couldn't believe what I was reading. Faye had started manipulating Gunther shortly after I told her about him. My intuition had been correct; there was someone with whom Gunther had been copulating, I was just surprised to learn that it was my best friend.

Faye went rogue to execute Operation Fuck Gunther Up. I sat there reading the explicit details and thinking, *this is one badass bitch.*

Faye waited for my reaction.

During my lifetime, I had never met anyone like Faye. She was devious and even more caring. Faye saw what I could not see and did what I simply could not do. She didn't do it for herself; she had done it for me. I didn't give a rat's ass about Gunther, I wanted his handouts; she doubled what he had been giving me and saw to it that it was consistent. I wanted a car and a house; she made it so. I wanted freedom; she was constantly preaching on how to obtain it. I needed love and Faye was there for that too. I loved Faye and she loved me just the same.

There were no words. I held out my arms for a hug.


Tristan hadn't heard from me much in the thirty days that had passed since his proposal. My best friend and her set of circumstances had taken precedent. He was understanding and patient.

When I finally saw him, I brought up the subject of marriage; he appeared nervous. Sweat beaded up around his hairline. He couldn't look me in the eyes. He nearly sprinted for the door, hands plugging his ears, wailing like a three-year-old. My very astute observation: Tristan didn't really want to marry me. It was okay, because I didn't want to marry him either. The proposal was a tactic, like Aaron's so many years earlier. I felt it.

He would string the engagement out for*ever*. Tristan just wanted me to know how far he was willing to go for us.

With Tristan in love, I knew that I could arrange my moral compass to point toward good and away from evil. His love and adoration was all that I required. I wouldn't mention marriage until I was free from the worry of causing more pain by relapsing into old familiar ways. I had already made a huge stride by vowing that Gunther would not be privy to my time or body. I felt as if I were on the right path.

Tristan did propose that we live together. I was elated. It would be perfect. Ava and I could live with Tristan, and I'd leave Faye to spend quality time with her family in the house on the hill.

I made an agreement with Faye that she and her family could live there. Whenever I decided to sell the house, I'd split the proceeds between her daughter and mine—the only two truly deserving benefactors from this whole debacle.

Tristan retired from professional football but wasn't perplexed like other athletes who leave the game before they are truly ready. He was already on track for his next career: coaching. He had a few job offers; one was at UCLA.

Ava, Tristan, and I sat down like a family to discuss the options.

*Los Angeles, here we come.*

The move would be easy. Ava and I only had to bring clothes.

Together, the three of us found a lovely home just a few blocks from the tranquility of the deep, blue sea and the bustle of the Santa Monica Promenade. I was in love and in heaven.

We left San Diego. I was starting over! This time not with some man who hoped to take advantage of me, but with a man who I truly loved. I felt a shift that emerged from the depths of my soul; it was the rebirth of "Savannah."

I had my fill of scheming. I just wanted to find my passion and amount to something substantial, become someone of substance whom Ava could be proud. Tristan needed me to love him wholly without distance and distraction. I wanted peace and serenity for us all.

I was doing well in treatment, staying clear of Gunther, but I was still receiving the deposits.

Gunther was unaware that I had moved and was now residing with the love of my life. My rebirth was a stillbirth, and I had faked the recovery process. Although not outright lying, I was omitting the truth with both Gunther and Tristan, and it was definitely counterproductive to rehab. What was wrong with me? I reasoned that the lack of money was the root of evil and not the money itself.

Tristan believed that he was with a self-sustaining woman. He was proud of who I had portrayed myself to be; the real me was the type of woman he hated the most. I was so caught up in the web of deceit that I started having anxiety attacks. How much longer could I fake it? Even though Gunther and I were no longer healthy for one another, if we ever were, I allowed the deposits to keep showing up. I did and said nothing about it. I wanted to sever ties with Gunther, but the money that was coming in was just too damned easy.

Gunther left several messages on my phone stressing the urgent need for a conversation. I waited until Tristan was away and called him back.

"Hello."

"Hello, Vannah. I really miss you."

I kept silent. No more lies.

"I'm calling because I'd like to see you."

The request made my stomach turn.

"I don't think that that's a good idea, Gunther."

I felt the strength.

290

*You can do it!*

"Matter of fact, Gunther, you can stop the automatic payments. You have no responsibility to me. I don't want your money."

"But I love you, Vannah."

"I'm sorry, Gunther, but I never did and never will love you. I'm truly sorry. But I have to move on with my life. Please don't call me anymore."

"I knew I shouldn't have given you the house!"

"It's not about the house. I actually gave that to Faye."

"Faye! That bitch!"

"Yes, that bitch. What this is about is control and I'm taking mine back. Take care, Gunther."

With that, I hung up the phone.

After years of servitude, I was free. I no longer had to be anxious about Gunther calling and Tristan asking questions, lying and wondering whether or not either of them believed me. I no longer had to intercept the mail to hide my bank statements, or worry about plotting conversations with Gunther when Tristan was away. I was free to stomp the bulging carpet into eternal submission, concealing my past.

I found the yellow folder and crossed out Gunther's name. I made an X through Aaron's name; he alone had to wrestle with what he was doing to the relationship between himself and Ava. I threw the bright yellow folder in the trash. No one was on the hit list.

Faye called and asked how things went with Gunther.

"I'm free. I am free at last, Faye! I never thought I could live without the financial safety net. But I did it, Faye. You were right. It feels good. No more puppet strings!"

"That's just the beginning. You have to tell Tristan about Gunther." She was weak. Her once forceful voice was barely eking out her side of the conversation.

291

"Well, not really. I can just move forward in honesty. No more disgorged lies. What Tristan doesn't know won't hurt him, right?"

"No. What he doesn't know hurts you and your healing process. He has to know and forgive you. You have to tell him, Savannah."

"When did you start calling me Savannah?"

"Just now. That's your name and that's who you are. Vannah needs to die; I'm smothering her with a pillow. That's what friends do for each other."

Faye had brought it up for the third time. She wanted me to kill her. She could no longer take the pain and the deterioration of the person she was. I could not do it. I loved her.

"If you loved me, you would." It was as if she was reading my mind.

She was wrong.

Her hacking cough turned into an unending event that probably led the hospice staff and nurses to her side. The phone went dead. I packed a suitcase full of clothes.

My mother would come to stay with Ava and Tristan's brother was in town. They would be happy to be rid of me for a few days. I got in my car and drove well over the speed limits down to San Diego to spend the remainder of my best friend's life by her side.

I rushed to the hospital. It was too late. The last conversation with my dear friend would be our final one. Although it was after visiting hours, the kind nurses took pity on me and allowed me to sit in her room; they knew death was near. Faye had already been put on life support. She was unconscious and hooked up to machines that kept track of all her weak vitals.

She looked peaceful.

I held her frail hand and wept until she was gone.

# twenty-three

Faye had requested not to have a funeral, a memorial service, or even to alert anyone of her passing. She just wanted me to read a letter to her daughter and granddaughter and give them her ashes to scatter wherever they saw fit. It read:

*To the better part of me:*

*It took a lifetime to gather the nerve to find you and even then it was prompted by a diagnosis of inevitable death. For that I have deep regret. With the grace, love, and guiding hand of a higher being, I was able to face my fear. I was truly blessed to live out the remainder of my life with the love of my life who was graciously born from my womb. I love you and my dear, sweet grandbaby (who better amount to something great). I will always be with you both.*

# twenty-four

Tristan and I were learning how to share space (without murderous tendencies) and be a real, full-time couple. It was not easy. The thrill of having a live-in partner was long gone.

The little things became huge argumentative points, such as his inability to replace the empty toilet paper when it ran out after his use, the fact that he left his shoes in the middle of the bedroom floor, or my not wearing sexy garb to bed. But we got through the turmoil. I'd kick his shoes, aiming at his head; he'd write cute notes on the cardboard tissue tube; and I wore the lingerie.

We settled into a comfortable routine of hard work and play. We relished the convenience of the area; everything was within walking distance. We took walks together and became best friends.

Ava was well adjusted and popular. *Socialite* was a befitting title. I was a very content mother, satisfied with her persona.

Aaron started treatment. He had yet to rebuild the relationship that he had destroyed with his daughter, but he worked on it every day. He sobered up and took it one day at a time.

I was repenting daily by being everything that Tristan could ever want in a woman. Deep inside, I knew that the lies needed to be forgiven. My pain couldn't go away until I purged and the pile under the carpet was thoroughly dissected and removed from its hiding place. Then and only then would I be truly free.

One night after drinking a half-bottle of wine, I stared for thirty minutes into the mirror.

What kind of person was I? Savannah or Vannah?

Had I changed?

Was Faye right in that I should tell Tristan the truth about

Gunther? Or should I just let it go and pray that his love would carry him through the pain if he ever found out I was conjoined with the root of all evil, greed, and deceit?

I pondered the situation but no easy answer was to be had.

I tried to run away from my thoughts. My mother and I took Ava to Holden Village, the remote mountain community where I lived my first year in high school. Ava needed a break from ostentation and materialism, brawling babes, and boys. She needed to be enveloped in a place that cradled your spirit and hushed your worries. I too needed healing. My spirit was tired.

The quiet, calm open space and endless hours of self-reflection were intoxicating. The mountains sang lullabies as I took afternoon naps in their arms.

The daily hikes, fresh mountain air, nourishing food, and time without business and noise did us both a world of good. Like with all of our escapes, we headed back to reality to start anew.

I reached a conclusion: I had to keep my secrets cleverly concealed. I was sick of myself, but I took solace in the fact that keeping the secret was less hurtful to all parties involved than telling the truth. The need to purge was replaced with the "don't let the right hand know what the left hand had done" theology, and the résumé of my life would be shredded. Faye was gone; her advice died with her.

The years of being kept had its horrible residual effects. The anxiety attacks did not go away. I was waking up in cold sweats because of nightmares having to do with being found out. My self-loathing ran deep. I did not like who I had become. I was ashamed of my past. I had no accomplishments. I was scared of chasing my own dreams and what I might amount to. Tristan was with a confused and lost shell of woman.

I called my mother. I wanted to go home for a few days. Maybe a trip away would result in better answers than what came of our trip to the mountains.

Going home brought me pleasure. I loved my family. My mother and Mikey made me proud. Yet, I was experiencing pangs of jealousy and regret. I wondered, "Who would I have become if I had never met Alberto, Don, or Gunther?" Would I have developed into a more confident and self-reliant woman? Could I have sustained myself? Or was life as a 'kept' woman always in the cards for me? Maybe I'd have been more inclined to pursue higher education, perhaps become an attorney like Mikey. Or maybe, I would have followed in my mother's footsteps as a philanthropist. Had I stayed and lived amongst my family, could I have been that selfless young woman who diligently road the horse of morality around town passionately contributing to society? Maybe I would have joined my mother in her crusade to abolish human suffering through social justice.

Suddenly, I felt like Ebenezer Scrooge looking at the ghosts of Savannah's past. I had to stop this. What had passed had passed; what was done was done. I came back to make today the first day of the rest of my life. Alberto, Don, and Gunther may have had a hand in creating me in the yesterdays, but today forward is mine…mine and Ava's.

This walk down memory lane got me thinking about my cousin Joy. So while at home, I took the opportunity to put a childhood memory to rest. I had never outright asked anyone in my family whether they believe my uncle to have molested his middle daughter, Joy.

I rang the doorbell. While I waited for someone to answer, I noticed that the wooden stairs were never replaced; they were still in disrepair, still threatening splinters.

My oldest cousin Tammy answered. She was as surprised to see me, as I was she. She had not aged well. Her once athletically sculpted body was hunched over, and her energetic spirit was forlorn. I actually had to focus on her smile and the intonation of her voice to confirm that it was indeed she.

"Wow! What a great surprise. Come on in."

We headed to the area of the house that was off limits as children; where the furniture had always been preserved in clear plastic and where the carpet in high traffic areas was protected from the nine kids via plastic runners. It was refurnished with a comfortable sofa, void of protective covering.

I didn't want to spend hours hashing over our lives to date. I had come seeking an answer to a question that haunted me.

"I know this may sound crazy, but did your father molest Joy?"

My cousin looked at me with deep concern.

"Absolutely not. I hated my father and even filed claims against his pastoral income for child support of the younger kids after he left. If I had one inkling of foul play when it came to my sister, I would have killed him, Savannah! You must trust me on this." She took a long pause.

"Can I ask why you bring this up after all this time?"

"The months I stayed here as a kid, he took Joy into his bedroom. She came out a different person and never recovered... mentally," I said.

"He took us all into his room, Savannah. He washed us under the 'holy' shower. He sat up all night making us read scripture by candlelight because the power had been shut off. Crazy bastard couldn't keep a job."

My cousin paused again before asking.

"Would you like something to drink?"

"No, thank you," I said. She continued.

"Savannah, my father kept us home every Friday from school because he thought Friday to be an evil day for children. Where others looked forward to the day, we dreaded it because starting at 5:00 AM we were reading bible verses out loud. We did that until lunch. After lunch, we wrote bible verses until dinner. My father was a completely certifiable lunatic. Yes, he was a weirdo...

almost for certain mentally ill, but he was definitely not capable of incest." She shook her head as she repeated the word no. She truly did not believe that to be the case. She continued.

"He almost had a breakdown once when he thought he had wronged God by attending a family social function on his holy rollin' sacred Sunday. Incest or even recreational sex would have sent his mind into an irrevocable tailspin of confession and purging, confession and purging until God granted him serenity... most likely taking five years or more according to his insane punishment timeline."

"Then what about Joy?" I asked.

"Well, in my opinion, Joy was born touched and without medical attention, because my father didn't believe in it, she just slowly worsened. There were days when she was fine and then the very next day she would be completely off her rocker. Once, I listened for thirty minutes or more to an in-depth conversation that she was having with herself."

As Tammy continued her defensive and explanatory line of chatter, I thought back. Had I misread things? Had my own "secretive closed doors" experiences caused me to imagine that sexual abuse and other horrors were occurring behind *all* closed doors? First there was Marquetta, a parasitic babysitter, who shut us away from the world so that she could privately torment me, and then there was my own mother who locked us out as she attempted to take her own life. And of course, when I did find the courage to open one of those doors, I opened it only to discover my father and Sarah. Very bad things happened behind closed doors, even into my adolescence and adult life.

Did my child's mind place Joy in that room where danger and bad things seemingly always dwelled? Had I imagined that Joy was being held behind that door being subjected to horrendous pain, secrets, and evil?

I recalled the walk in the woods and Joy staring into the

trickling waters with an empty gaze. Had she started drifting from reality? Were the sexually illicit stories cries of desperation from a young teen trying to hold on to her sanity? Could this all have been the onset of something far less sinister, such as Schizophrenia? My God.

As I stood to leave, I had the assured feeling that my uncle had not molested my cousin.

"Savannah, they also did an autopsy. Joy had died a virgin."

Instantly, sadness overwhelmed me, and my nose began to run. I turned and walked out. I had no idea that my favorite cousin had passed away.

The thirty-minute drive back to my mother's house gave me the time I needed to think. I said a prayer out loud for Joy's soul. I asked her to forgive me for disappearing from her life.

I turned to MPR (Minnesota Public Radio) and caught the tail end of a story about a boy who had lost his entire family in a plane crash. I cried the majority of the way home; I was an emotional wreck.

The next days, I asked myself over and over: Who was I, and what did I want? I knew it was a cliché for me because I had been asking those same questions all of my life. I cried for days, believing that I had lived a meaningless, shallow existence whose root had been firmly planted in cold hard cash.

Being home around a solid and simple family made me realize that I needed to turn my priorities around. My life had sprung up in captivity and was growing under fake light, forced air, and a timed sprinkler system. I wanted freedom. I wanted to flourish like a wild flower, bask in the sun's rays, breathe in fresh air and plant my roots in untainted soils.

A nagging inner feeling was tugging at my soul. I had to confess my sins to Tristan regarding Gunther. The bulge would not just disappear.

Tristan had assumed I had told the truth regarding

Gunther's absence in my life. Tristan had trusted me. He believed me to be the self-made, independent lady that I portrayed myself to be. I, with reckless abandonment betrayed his trust. I had decided to tell Tristan the truth.

After I returned home, from the first step inside the doorway, I knew something was gravely wrong. CNN was not blaring the latest on the presidential race and farm tools hung in the balance, waiting to behead me by Tristan's sheer will. A cold breeze momentarily stopped me before I slowly shut the door.

The house's mood lights were off. Tristan was sitting on the sofa in near darkness. I could feel his negative presence radiating through the frosty air.

Thoughts raced through my head: *He answered Gunther's call. He saw pictures from Hawaii…* I tried to lighten the mood.

"What's up? Why's it so spooky dark in here?"

He turned on a lamp. The worst-case scenario had manifested. A letter addressed to Tristan was opened and sitting on the table. Faye had written him, disclosing every detail of my relationship with Gunther.

Reality hit Tristan like a wrecking ball. I had been a gold-digging, dependent mistress for the better part of my life. The armory of truth diced his heart into a billion pieces. I knew I had no words to heal it. His pain became my pain. The only salve would be my heartfelt remorse and time.

His eyes were red, his feelings crushed. I couldn't say a thing. I just sat with him. He was expecting something, anything. I had nothing. He was hurt, and my deceptive actions were the cause. What would my spoken words, historically all lies, do but add insult to the injury? I sat quietly, hoping that he could see an upside. He didn't.

He picked up his car keys and walked out.

"I'm so sorry," I whispered.

As he left, I closed my eyes and played the "if/then" game

with tightly crossed fingers. *If* he turned around... I opened my eyes... *then* we'd be okay. He did not look back.

Perhaps, I subconsciously wanted Tristan to know the truth; perhaps, my loving and trusted friend Faye who had guided me to freedom in so many other areas was doing it again.

Yes. Faye was right even in death. Tristan needed to know about everything.

Maybe his unconditional love and affection was what I was searching for all along. If he knew my past, would he still love me?

I so badly needed that answer to be yes. I was full of cowardice. I took the easy way out and swept it all away; with every infraction, the broom and carpet got bigger and my guilt and self-reproach more burdensome.

I believed in the law of attraction. I believed that I was in charge of my destiny. I could create my world the way that would make me happy. I used the distinctive power wrongly. I lied. My disillusioned and complicated webs of deceit spun lie after heinous lie until my world was altered, even beyond my own recognition. Nothing was real, not even what I perpetrated as love. Love, as it should be, doesn't include dishonesty and justification of that dishonesty. My cynical hypocrisy would cost me the man I loved.

My heart ached; my life was a mystery. I was a skanky human being who deserved her unknown fate. Bad things were happening at my own hand, and I was not even in control.

I could have easily retracted to a dark and dank place, sought comfort in alcohol, and remained detached like my cousin Joy, but unlike Joy, I didn't succumb to the looming depression and despair.

I rushed out the door and caught Tristan before he had gotten too far. I so badly wanted to be exonerated. The words flew from my mouth, backed with feeling, tears, and a deep fear that that was not going to be enough. I pleaded for my life.

"I am sorry that I never told you about Gunther, baby. It's not something that I am proud of. I hated being so secretive. It ate me up inside. I just wanted you to love me and not judge me."

I held his chin and wouldn't let him look away.

"I always knew that I loved you. Always. From the moment I saw you. Please don't let this destroy what we've built. Please don't let me go because of my past. Please forgive me. Please forgive me. Please fight for me. Fight for me. Fight for me."

His eyes watered, but before a teardrop fell he turned and walked away. And just like that, he was gone.

It was over.

I was left with three words pounding in my head and falling from my lips. "Fight for me …"

# twenty-five

For the first time since high school, I remained without one or more male counterparts.

Initially, I felt lonely and lost. Tristan was the reason I changed, but now he was gone. My old life could resume with just one call or one night out in Beverly Hills, but my spirit was altered. Going back was no longer an option.

If the American people (with the country's wicked past) could vote a Black man into the highest office, then darn it, change can happen; hope reigns contagious.

I quit drinking altogether. It was an ignored, worsening habit that needed to be addressed. Abstinence was the only answer. I even started using my full birth name, Savannah, again. I learned to appreciate solitude. There was no one to witness the grand transformation. I celebrated in silence, rejoicing in the new me. Loving myself wholly became my focus.

Yet still, the self-analysis persisted.

My mind delved into its own depths and emerged with questions regarding morals, character, strength, and personal goals. I had a clear mind and wanted answers. It was time to redress my duplicitous life.

I lived in captivity. I was handcuffed by my own will to my own irony. I remained that way even when I was handed the key that could set me free. I carried the key around until I was forced to use it. When I finally had the courage to try the key, before turning it, I had to ask: *is this the right one? What will I do once freed? How will I survive? Am I really missing that much more of what the world has to offer?*

After a slight turn, I heard the click of release from the first cuff, still I refused to break away. I justified my wayward behaviors. Then, my hand was held as I unlocked the remaining steel trap. The cuffs lingered just a few moments, but finally I was shook free by a freethinking spirit from the afterlife and forward thinking dear friend.

My spirit, which had been so bright and hungry, was quiet and starved. I paid a high price and lost. I was a hypocritical, money-hungry fraud who had lost a great love. I beat myself up thoroughly for months. But the feelings of negativity and hatred I harbored only hurt my spiritual and mental growth. So I set about the task of forgiving.

My father and I had an actual conversation (with words and whole sentences and even paragraphs) after decades of silence. He began with a simple sentence, words so rare that I could remember the few times that he said them.

"I love you."

It broke the frozen tundra that had compiled between us over the years—three simple yet tremendously mighty words. My father recalled his abusive childhood; his father (a drunk) would beat him until he could not walk, swallow, see, or pee. He ran away at age fifteen, never to return, and was loathed by his eight siblings, who then bore the abuse that had previously only been his. He told of the ills of serving his hateful country in the prime of his life as an inglorious medic who killed mercilessly and watched friends die under his limited medicinal hands.

He spoke of falling deeply in love with my mother through letters that he wrote and received while in Vietnam, and then of how the aftermath of war and the reality of life, marriage, and children were altogether different.

He admitted to having a voice only via alcohol; he had no words to say exactly what he was feeling, unless under its spellbinding hold.

He spoke of parental regret, terrible mistakes, and a life of mostly sadness. He said it with very few words, not as an excuse, but as an apology for his effect on our lives. He'd been thinking of a conversation with me, but it never would have left his cerebral cortex. He was a shame-filled man who so badly wanted the love of his children, but who could never find the way or words of expression. Tears absolutely welled, but like Tristan, my father wouldn't show weakness. He was off the phone before they fell.

We were liberated from our mistakes and years of regret. I would never be closer to or more proud of my dad than at that moment. I wrote my father a forgiveness letter and sealed it with a promise of better relations.

The load had finally lightened.

That night, I got down on my knees. With nearly a lifetime of suppressed, inappropriately directed prayers, I prayed.

I forgave Aaron, Alberto, Don, Tristan, and Gunther.

I prayed Ava would understand and forgive me for choosing such a life. I also prayed that she was smart enough not to choose it for herself.

Prayer set me free. A tranquil feeling of pure grace touched my soul. My heart was jumping for joy from the power of prayer and forgiveness.

It took some time, but I even forgave myself.

# twenty-six

I took Ava out to dinner to discuss our life plan. I felt a need to start fresh, maybe where both our lives had started, but my primary concern was how she felt about it.

"Ma, you're my heart. I never doubted for one second in my lifetime that you wouldn't do anything or die for me. I am your biggest fan, forever. Wherever we go, as long as I'm with you, I'm home."

I excused myself from the table. Trying to hold back the unstoppable onset of tears, I dashed to the restroom and cried uncontrollably into a stranger's arms.

# twenty-seven

*Where did all the time go?*

My fortieth birthday came without fanfare—no diamond necklaces or expensive watches; trips to Miami, Vegas or abroad; or new cars. I did receive a package from Faye, just as I had every year since her death; it contained a four-page letter and a bright green folder inside the heading read: Forty is a great age to start living and loving. Her name was crossed out. I knew it would be the last letter that I would receive from my beloved deceased best friend.

No departures or returns. No begging someone to stay or watching them leave. No wanting someone to leave or needing anyone to come. I spent the gorgeous spring day with my nearly eighteen-year-old daughter, doing nothing more than just being.

We strolled arm in arm through a bustling lunchtime crowd in downtown Minneapolis.

"If you could trade your life in for someone else's, would you?" Ava asked.

I studied the faces of the passersby and turned to my daughter. I planted a soft, ruby track of mommy love across her forehead and answered honestly.

"Nope."

"Me neither," she said.

It was the best birthday ever.

# twenty-eight

## THE BEGINNING

# epilogue

*"It is never too late to be what you might have been."*
—*George Eliot*

# *kept* Study Questions

1. Describe positive and negative character traits of Savannah.

2. Describe, in detail, what beauty means to you.

3. Do beautiful women have transactional advantages over "Plain Jane's?"

4. Under what circumstance is it acceptable to use beauty and/ or the promise of sex to manipulate someone into providing something you value?

5. How was Savannah's or Gizel's life as a kept woman different from that of a stay at home mother who is miserable in her marriage?

6. How do improper sexual experiences at a young age later affect Savannah's attitudes toward sex and men?

7. What are the psycho-emotional costs of trading sexual favors for money and/or "security"?

8. How did security of shelter play a role in Savannah's decisions?

9. Do you believe one should have sex exploitations without love? If so, what are some of the short-term and long-term consequences of that mind-set?

10. What should and what can be done to adults who prey on the sexual innocence of children and/or young adults?

11. Do you believe Alberto, Don or Gunther to be "bad guys" in general as they dealt with Savannah?

12. Why do you think the author chose a George Eliot quote? What does the quote mean?

13. The author makes correlations throughout the book between coming and leaving/staying and going, find one or more such instance/s and dissect its/their relevance.

14. Cite times during which music was influential in Savannah's life.
A. How did music affect her viewpoint?
B. Do you have a genre of music/artist/song that has influenced your life?

15. Did you ever have times in your life during which you felt numb?

16. Savannah references usages of alcohol. How did alcohol affect Savannah's life?

17. Without Faye do you believe Savannah would have reached the same conclusion?

18. Where did Savannah always return throughout her life? Why?

19. Is it morally wrong to exercise revenge? Explain.

20. Which was paramount in Savannah's life: greed or love?

21. Do you feel like Savannah had a life of fortune or depravity? Explain.

22. A. What lessons do children draw from parents who trade sex for money or security? B. How do you presume Savannah's life choices to have affected Ava?

23. What lessons did Faye learn from Savannah?

24. Would facing death alter your behaviors? If so, how?

25. Do you believe Tristan should have walked away?

26. What would you have done differently than Savannah at any point in the story?

27. Whose life story would you like to expand upon? Ava Aaron Faye Savannah Gunther

28. Where, in your fictionalized ending, is Savannah and what is she doing with her new life?

Extra Credit: Analyze one or more of the following - the significance of water, the cover, the author's name, the analogy of puppetry, the significance of the number 13, New Year's Eve, or Savannah's birthday.

# Other Quotes by George Eliot

*The strongest principal of growth lies in human choice.*

*What greater thing there is for two human souls than to feel that they are joined... to strengthen each other... to be one with each other in silent unspeakable memories?*

*One must be poor to know the luxury of giving.*

# About the Author

The author navigates her prose through many genres, including scriptwriting. She spends much of her time volunteering for a nonprofit organization geared towards helping homeless families. The author resides in the big, bad world with her daughter, family, and friends. This is her first novel.